Sports Illustrated

HOCKEY'S GREATEST

HOC

GREA

KEY'S
TEST

Wayne Gretzky

NO.
2
MOST
ENTERTAINING

PHOTOGRAPH BY PAUL KENNEDY

BOBBY ORR

CONTENTS

BILL SYKEN *Editor* / STEVEN HOFFMAN *Creative Director*

CRISTINA SCALET *Photo Editor* / KEVIN KERR *Copy Editor* / JOSH DENKIN *Designer*

STEFANIE KAUFMAN *Project Manager*

SPLITTING HAIRS

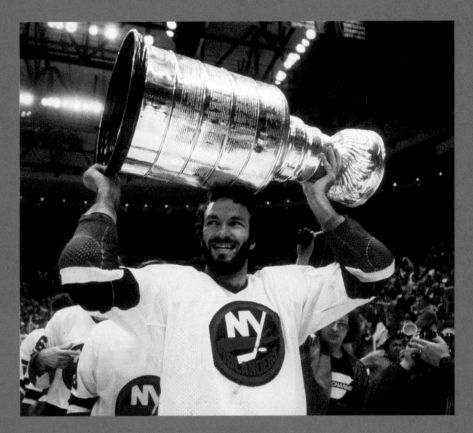

WHETHER THE TOPIC
IS TOP DEFENSEMAN
OR BEST BEARDS, THE
CALLS ON THE ALLTIME
GREATS TEND TO BE
VERY CLOSE SHAVES

BY MICHAEL FARBER

THIS COLLECTION STARTS WITH AN APOLOGY: THERE IS A GLARING OMISSION in HOCKEY'S GREATEST one entirely unrelated to the estimable Red Kelly's not being among the Top 10 defensemen. (Outrage!) While 23 topics have been included, everything from rivalries to rightwingers, inexcusably there is no list of the best playoff beards. If you were going to compile a ranking of the leading hockey playoff traditions—a topic which, like an inept doctor trying to stitch up Rocket Richard, also missed the cut—the beard probably would be no lower than No. 3, behind postseries handshakes and players' names being engraved on the Stanley Cup. Of course depending on your level of fondness for Gordie Howe—and who doesn't adore Mr. Hockey?—you might bump up the Detroit octopus toss, a rite of spring that began with the Cusimano brothers, fishmongers Peter and Jerry, in 1952. In that case HOCKEY'S GREATEST could really claim to cover the waterfront. (For an extended discussion of this fascinating topic, SI soon will offer a cephalopodcast.)

The Islanders' Ken Morrow had the first playoff beard, but was his the best?

In deference to our abiding fascination with the follicle, however, this book does have a Top 10 list of hockey hair. The 1980s phrase "hockey hair" remains culturally relevant, although it could be argued the playoff beard would have been a more compelling topic considering sports like baseball and even clean-cut golf have begun aping hockey in their postseasons. If you have not thumbed ahead, presently you will learn that on the Best Hockey Hair list Jaromir Jagr, who would be serenaded by Aerosmith's "Dude Looks Like a Lady" in the Flyers' arena whenever his Penguins visited, an homage to No. 68's distinctive mullet with its cascading locks, nipped No. 2 Guy Lafleur, sometimes referred to as Le Démon Blond in Montreal because of the lank flaxen hair that would flow behind him as The Flower hurtled down the right wing. You can debate the order. After all, this is America, where everyone is entitled to an opinion, however uninformed, a great country founded on the principles of life, liberty and the hirsute of happiness.

The point: These Top 10 lists split a lot of hairs.

N THE FALL OF 1966, I WAS A SOPHOMORE IN high school, living in Providence. An hour to the north, a rookie, Bobby Orr, was living large with the Bruins. On a Saturday morning in November, I took a bus to Boston, made my way over to the rickety arena atop North Station and bought an upper balcony Rangers-Bruins ticket from a scalper. (There were only six teams then, and no one yet considered them particularly original.) I paid double face value—five bucks. For the next two and a half hours I watched, mouth agape, as Orr controlled the game, buckling every swash, swerving past defenders, starting and sometimes finishing a rush. At some point during that game, a 3–3 tie, I concluded Orr was the best player in the history of hockey. I did not make that summary, and maybe prescient, judgment because Orr was or would be the best—you can make that argument even though the staggering heft of Wayne Gretzky's otherworldly statistics could give you a hernia—but because I was 15. That is truly the golden age of sports. The best thing that has ever happened, or could ever happen, on the ice or playing field—the greatest players, the top games—occur when you are maybe 12 or 13 or 15. The games and the people who play them likely will never mean quite as much to you again.

THE CONCEPT OF WHAT CONSTITUTES GREATNESS, WHETHER IN DEFENSEMAN, OLYMPICS OR EVEN HAIR, IS FILTERED THROUGH THE MEMBRANE OF PERSONAL EXPERIENCE, VIEWED CHIMERICALLY THROUGH THE LENS OF OUR LIVES.

The concept of what constitutes greatness, whether in defensemen, Olympics or even hair, is filtered through the membrane of personal experience, viewed chimerically through the lens of our lives.

This soft-focus approach to Top 10 lists is perhaps even truer of hockey than other sports. Hockey came late to the analytic revolution. Fancy stats such as Corsi and offensive zone starts are in their relative infancy. (The sport, like the 2014–15 Toronto Maple Leafs, often seems to be playing catchup.) The NHL was formed in 1917, and any comparisons between the net artistry of George Hainsworth (94 shutouts in 465 games in the '20s and '30s) and Dominik Hasek's wizardry in the late '90s before the full effects of what I christened the Dead Puck Era seem specious. Unlike baseball, there is no widely accepted statistical road grader such as, say, WAR (Wins Above Replacement value) that can level the playing field and meld eras—World War II when many able-bodied Canadian players were in the military, Original 6, Curved Stick, Expansion and Dead Puck—into a comprehensible whole.

The tardiness in embracing decimal points that could have made the lists in HOCKEY'S GREATEST indisputably authoritative (and less fun) might be simple indolence. Or maybe it has something to do with the inherent nature of the sport, free-flowing and amoebic, played on a one-inch thick slippery sheet by

Gordie Howe made our Top 10s, but Red Kelly just missed.

men and women whose blades are typically .155 of an inch thick.

Typically hockey is referred to as a game of mistakes. I think of it as a game of oops. In hockey, shifts happen.

THERE IS ANOTHER ELEMENT THAT distinguishes the Top 10 lists in HOCKEY'S GREATEST from those of BASEBALL'S GREATEST, BASKETBALL'S GREATEST and FOOTBALL'S GREATEST, the other books in this SI series. Hockey is unabashedly international. Of course baseball also has a distinctive foreign accent—the impact of the Latino player in the past half century has been titanic—and basketball trails only soccer as a universal game. The difference, however, is a player who toiled only in baseball's Caribbean leagues or tore up European basketball without putting his Air Jordans on an NBA court would not come anywhere

near our lists; if you are not here in those sports, you basically are nowhere. Despite an innate conservatism—some old-time hockey men would consider partaking of an After Eight mint at 7:30 positively radical—the sport accepts that greatness has occurred regularly outside the confines of the NHL's 200-by-85 foot rink. The attitude is reflected in these lists, which include a coach and a goalie,who, during their active careers, never were directly involved with the NHL.

Consider Vladislav Tretiak, the Russian goalie who checks in, to borrow from the late list-maker Casey Kasem, at No. 8 among this book's Top 10 goalies. In 1972, as a 20-year-old, he dazzled in the eight-game Summit Series against Canada. Three years later he backstopped the Central Red Army, outshot 38–13, to a 3–3 tie against the Canadiens at the Montreal Forum, a game many consider the best in history. (The famous 1975 New Year's Eve match is No. 3 in this book's 10 Best Games.) Tretiak was drafted by Montreal, in 1983, but retired a year later in part because he was not allowed to leave the Soviet Union.

The European migration, which started in earnest in 1973 when Swedish players Börje Salming, who plausibly could have made HOCKEY'S GREATEST's Top 10 defenseman list, and Inge Hammarström joined Toronto. The Europeans, reflected in these pages in Jagr, Alex Ovechkin, Teemu Selanne and others, contributed so much to the NHL, including, cynics say, soccer-style diving. To blame Europeans as the source of the diving scourge is to give short shrift to antecedents such as Newsy Lalonde, who was a Hall of Famer but did not crack this book's Top 10 centers list. The Jan. 15, 1912 edition of the *Calgary Daily Herald* reported future Hall of Fame center Russell Bowie "sent hundreds of players to the side by faking an injury. He had a great trick of playing the rubber to the boards and if his check blocked the puck, he would clap his hand to his head or side and drop to one knee. The referee would instantly stop the game and under the impression Bowie had been short-ended, chase the other fellow to the penalty box. Aside from his tricks, he had 'the goods.'"

The goods. Maybe it could rank 10th on the Top 10 list of hockey expressions behind: 1) biscuit in the basket; 2) top cheese; 3) five hole; 4) sin bin; 5) Chiclets; 6) twig; 7) bar down; 8) flamingo; and 9) chucking knuckles.

So...PLAYOFF BEARDS. THE tradition began with the 1980 Islanders, and it would be nice to give defenseman Ken Morrow pride of place on a best-of list. Unfortunately, he would trail at least two other defensemen, Raymond Bourque, who had glorious russet-colored strands woven throughout his lush growth, and Scott Niedermayer, whose black Cup beard in 2007 had distinguished streaks of gray, giving him a Cruella De Vil look.

The wild card here is "Cowboy" Bill Flett, who won a Stanley Cup with the 1974 Flyers. His was the lunatic fringe. But he sported his astonishing beard all the time, not merely in the playoffs, which might lead to another controversy—why didn't Cowboy make the list of Top 10 nicknames?

Anyway, I give it to Flett. By a whisker. ∎

HOW WE RANKED THEM

These Top 10 lists bring together the expert opinions of seven writers and editors whose knowledge of the game runs deep

FOR THIS BOOK SI WRITERS AND EDITORS WERE polled before the 2014–15 season and asked to submit Top 10 lists for 16 categories. Votes were tallied with 10 points awarded for a first-place vote, nine points for a second-place vote and so on. Voters were also asked to justify their choices, and those comments appear with each Top 10 selection. In most cases, if one panelist had a player ranked higher than his colleagues, he was asked to speak on that player's behalf.

It was left to voters to decide whether to include players from international leagues or to limit their selections to the NHL. Most had at least one international player or coach on their ballots, but not all did. In general panelists were not directed toward any set of players or limited by any preset criterion. They were simply given categories and left to chose names from the entire history of hockey. Panelists were also given the opportunity to create one list on their own, choosing the topic as well as the population of the Top 10. Those personal lists close out the book.

THE PANELISTS

MARK BEECH *SI Senior Editor*

BRIAN CAZENEUVE *former SI Staff Writer*

MICHAEL FARBER *SI Special Contributor*

KOSTYA KENNEDY *SI Special Contributor*

SARAK KWAK *SI Writer-Reporter*

PIERRE McGUIRE *SI Special Contributor*

E.M. SWIFT *former SI Senior Writer*

BOBBY HULL

NO.
1

LEFT WING

PHOTOGRAPH BY LEE BALTERMAN

NO.
9
FRANCHISE

PHOTOGRAPH BY FRED VUICH

ISLANDERS-
RANGERS

NO.

7

RIVALRY

Sports Illustrated

HOC
GREA

TERRY SAWCHUK

NO.

3

GOALTENDER

PHOTOGRAPH BY EVAN PESKIN

KEY'S
TEST

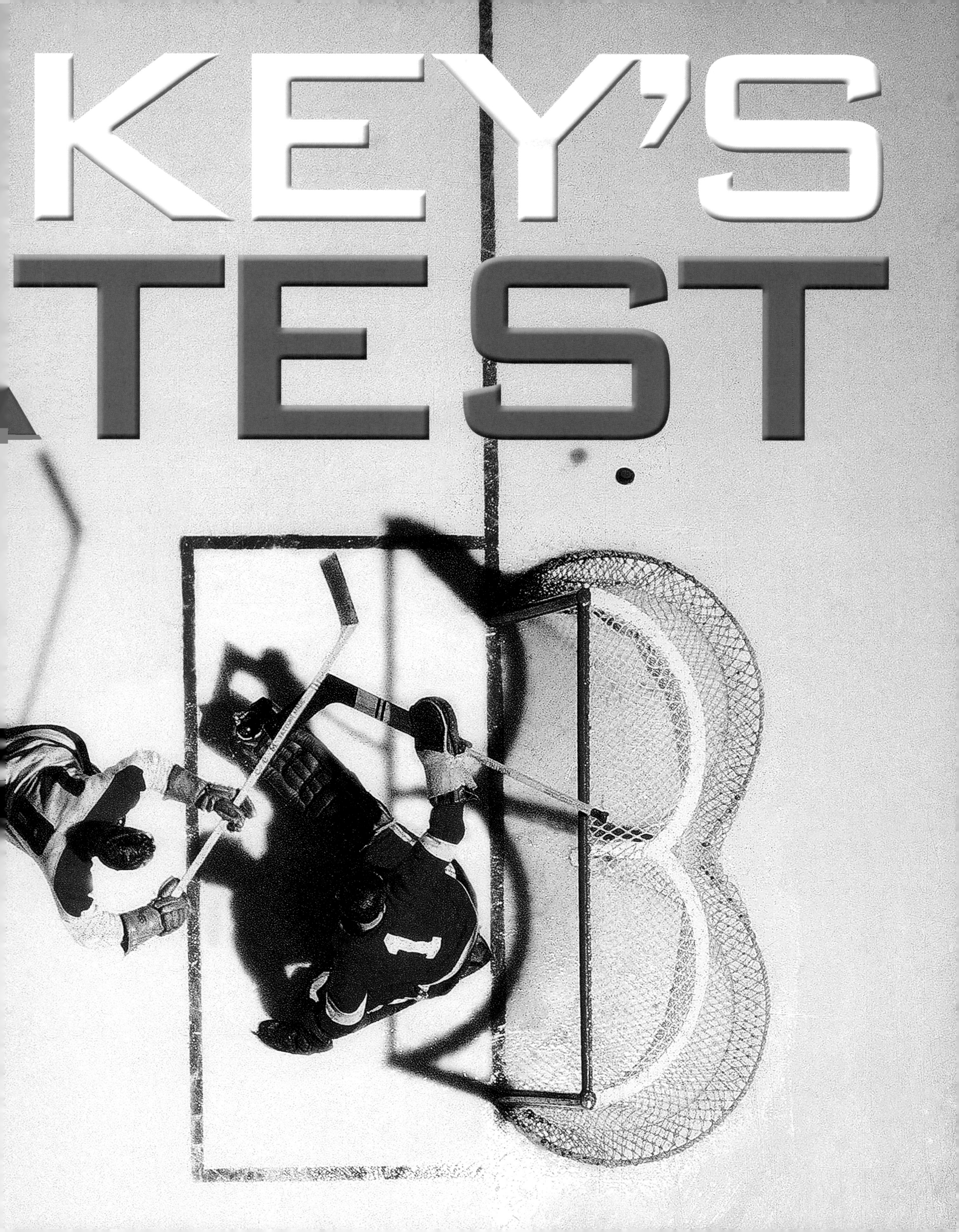

THE 10

BEST CENTERS

FOR NINE SEASONS IN EDMONTON, TWO OF OUR TOP 10 CENTERS PLAYED ON THE SAME TEAM. WAYNE GRETZKY AND MARK MESSIER HAD, AS YOU MIGHT EXPECT, TREMENDOUS SUCCESS, GIVEN THAT THEY RANK 1-2 ON THE ALLTIME SCORING LIST. THEY WON FOUR STANLEY CUPS PLAYING TOGETHER WITH THE OILERS, BEFORE GRETZKY MOVED ON TO LOS ANGELES.

IN 1996 THE TWO TEAMED AGAIN WITH THE RANGERS. WRITING ABOUT THE REUNION FOR SI, E.M. SWIFT CALLED THE TWO MEN HOCKEY'S VERSION OF RUTH AND GEHRIG, AND SAID THAT "THOSE WHO WORRY THAT GRETZKY WILL HAVE DIFFICULTY ADJUSTING TO PLAYING ON A TEAM THAT, FOR THE FIRST TIME IN HIS CAREER, IS NOT HIS TEAM DON'T UNDERSTAND HIS RELATIONSHIP WITH MESSIER. GRETZKY MAY HAVE BEEN CAPTAIN IN EDMONTON, BUT MESSIER LED IN THE LOCKER ROOM."

MESSIER HAD EVEN GREATER STANDING IN NEW YORK, HAVING LED THE RANGERS TO A LONG-AWAITED TITLE IN 1994, AND GRETZKY UNDERSTOOD THAT, DESPITE HIS CELEBRITY THAT CAME WITH BEING HOCKEY'S GREAT ONE, THE RANGERS WERE HIS FRIEND'S TEAM. "AND THAT'S HOW IT SHOULD BE," GRETZKY SAID. IT WAS MESSIER WHO WORE THE CAPTAIN'S C THAT SEASON. BUT IN THE WIDE WORLD OF HOCKEY, AND IN OUR CENTER'S RANKINGS, IT IS STILL GRETZKY WHO STANDS ABOVE THE REST.

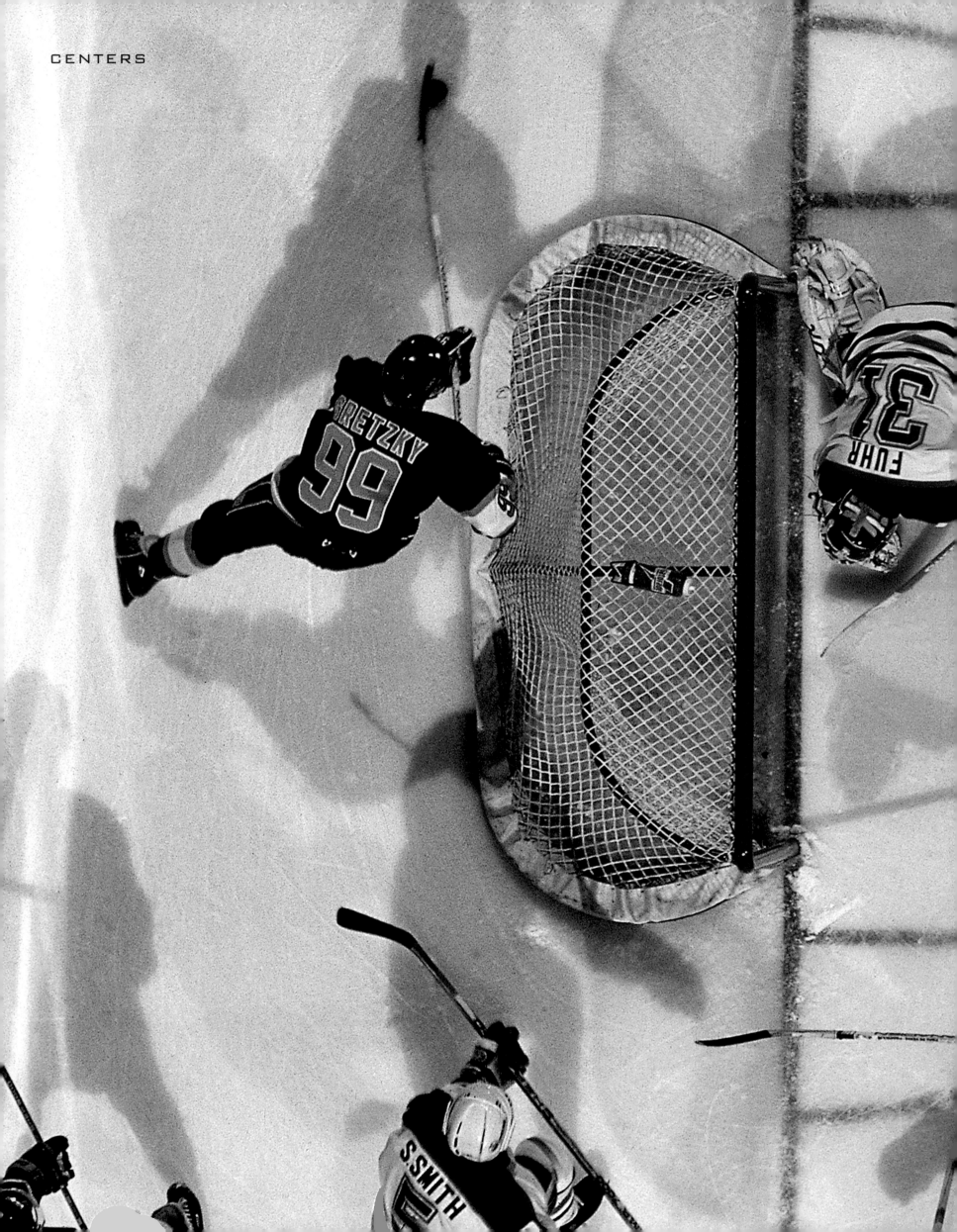

WAYNE GRETZKY

OILERS 1978–1988
KINGS 1988–1996
BLUES 1996
RANGERS 1996–1999

" Gretzky viewed the game through a different prism, one that seemed to bend space and stop time. Not only could he anticipate the play, he could also peer several seconds into the future. If the puck and other players on the ice were not exactly where Gretzky foresaw—well, they probably should have been. " —MICHAEL FARBER

▸ NHL'S ALLTIME LEADING
SCORER
▸ NINE-TIME HART TROPHY
WINNER

WALTER HAD his son on the backyard rink before Wayne was three years old. He began teaching him fundamentals when Wayne was four. The backyard rink wasn't just for yuks. Walter would throw a puck into the corner and tell Wayne to get it. After Wayne had chased several pucks around the boards, Walter would say, "Watch me." He'd throw it and skate to a spot where he could intercept the puck as it caromed around the boards. "I always told him, 'Skate to where the puck's going to be, not to where it has been,'" says Walter. "I've never believed that it's an instinctive thing that one kid anticipates better than another."

—E.M. Swift, SI, October 12, 1981

Gretzky has eight of the NHL's top 10 scoring seasons.

PHOTOGRAPH BY DAVID E. KLUTHO

2

MARIO LEMIEUX

PENGUINS 1984–1994,
1995–1997, 2000–2004,
2005–2006

" A big man (6' 4") with magical hands, Super Mario could use his giant wingspan to play keepaway. It looked so easy critics thought he lacked intensity, until he led his Penguins to their first two Cups, icing Lemieux's legacy as one of the greatest players in history. " —E.M. SWIFT

▸ THREE-TIME HART TROPHY WINNER
▸ LED NHL IN SCORING SIX TIMES

THE COMEBACK tale of Mario Lemieux may or may not have a happy ending, but it certainly had a page-turning Chapter 1. After 18 months away from hockey to deal with a series of medical crises that included Hodgkin's disease, two operations on his chronically sore back, a rare bone infection and a case of anemia, Lemieux has returned to the ice feeling like the $4.5 million that the Penguins are paying him. Lemieux said he was not coming back to be an average player and on opening night in Pittsburgh, he was as good as his word. Stationed at his familiar spot along the left wing boards on the Penguin power play, he assisted on four goals in an 8–3 drubbing of the Maple Leafs. He feels good. He looks good. The four best words in hockey are, Mario is still Mario.

—Michael Farber, SI, October 16, 1995

Lemieux rose from captain to Penguins owner in 1999.

MANY HAPPY RETURNS

Of all the storied careers in hockey, none has had more chapters than that of Mario Lemieux, whose retaking of the ice at age 35 was a boon to the league and to his team

BY MICHAEL FARBER

THE MASSIVE BANNER READING LEMIEUX 66, 1984–1997 that had been suspended from the ceiling of Pittsburgh's Mellon Arena was lowered in a chilling pregame ceremony on Dec. 27, only to be replaced by suspended disbelief the moment the puck was dropped. Mario Lemieux's return to the ice was so astonishing it seemed fictional. "A movie," Hockey Night in Canada announcer Bob Cole kept calling it on the air. "My new nickname for Mario is Batman," said Tom Rooney, the Penguins' chief operating officer. "A suit-wearing executive by day. At night he puts on his cape and plays."

After a sabbatical of 44 months, Lemieux—father, team owner and player again at age 35—stepped into the NHL void, reinvigorating a league of faceless players and system-mad teams. On his first night back he needed only 33 seconds to set up a goal against the Toronto Maple Leafs. Later that evening he scored and then assisted on a third goal. The 17,148 fans and 20 stunned Maple Leafs (who played more like unindicted coconspirators than opponents) witnessed perfection. Lemieux's nearly 21-minute performance was so impeccable, his accomplishment so pure, that it had to be reduced to fit our shrunken frame of reference.

The night begged not for the arch praise of NHL commissioner Gary Bettman, who offered that Lemieux's comeback transcended sport, or for the exuberance of a local radio commentator, who proclaimed it Pittsburgh's greatest sporting moment, but something smaller, some symbolic shortcut to capturing the essence of the most important regular-season game in years. The standing ovations (numerous) were too raucous, the television ratings (a record locally, double ESPN's usual numbers in the U.S., playoff-sized in Canada) were too obvious, the tributes (universal) were too fulsome—at least compared to the homage Lemieux received the following day. Next to his stall at the Penguins' suburban practice rink was a splendid wooden box with WELCOME BACK carved on the top and several bottles of red wine inside bearing Lemieux labels, a gift from a local wine merchant. There. Vintage Lemieux.

The return was simply déjà vu Lemieux, who always has accepted his excellence with a Gallic shrug. A convergence of considerations—an age that dictated a comeback now or never; the long-term health of Lemieux's investment in the Penguins; his own health; his only son's wish to see his father play; his affinity for the Pittsburgh players; a brooding Jaromir Jagr; a chance at another Stanley Cup; the NHL's welcome, though sometimes stuttering, crackdown on slashing and hockey's other dark arts; the threat of his records being surpassed by mere hockey mortals—triggered a decision that touched off spasms of excitement throughout a league that barely bothered to wave goodbye the first time.

His number 66 wasn't lowered—with Mario's four-year-old, Austin, eyes wide, mouth agape, at the rink's edge—so Lemieux could be a ceremonial player. He had come back from injury and illness earlier in his career, and he had the hubris to think that in the eight weeks after he began working out on Nov. 1 he could sweat out three-plus years of cigars, fine French reds and golf and perform at a rarefied level. He returned not to be the Mario the Magnificent of a decade ago, a goal-a-game terror who would strip defensemen and sell their parts for scrap, but to be the connect-the-dots forward who, after missing almost two seasons because of back operations and Hodgkin's disease treatments, returned to win two more scoring titles. His game now, as then, is a comfortable 160 feet. At the Dec. 12 press conference confirming his comeback, he teared up while relating how Austin, who weighed two pounds, five ounces at birth and spent the first 71 days of his life in the hospital, had asked to see his father play. After the morning skate on the day of the game against Toronto, Mario said that Austin was requesting a hat trick. He even wore a microphone for TV during the game and gave NHL Productions total access in the dressing room. (This comeback truly was a movie.)

Lemieux's transformation into the face of the game is as startling a before-and-after as any cheesy weight-loss photos in the back of a fitness magazine. Judging by the beefed-up schedule of Penguins games on ESPN2 and the ticket-buying surge for his first three road games, in Washington, Boston and on Long Island, hockey couldn't be happier.

"Mario is the bright color of the game," Detroit Red Wings center Igor Larionov says. "People want to see a Monet, a Rembrandt at work. Whenever he's on the ice, he's capable of producing a masterpiece or at least the unpredictable or unexpected. It's art, hockey performed at its highest skill level. If people are appreciating him more now, it's like an artist who gains the proper recognition only after he passes away. But he lives again."

Lemieux's first two games were the easy part. There are going to be matches not played under the yellow caution flag, nights when his skill and confidence won't carry him. "A couple of weeks ago he could get on a plane and play golf for three or four days," says Guy Carbonneau, a Montreal coach. "He can't do that now. I don't know how his mind is going to work when he goes through a tough time, like a slump or if his back hurts again or if he gets injured. I just hope he came back for the right reason. If he did, then the mind can overcome anything."

The right reason is a four-year-old wearing a mushroom haircut and a number 66 sweater who stuck his head into the dressing room after his father's first game and said, "I saw you. I saw you." ∎

3

JEAN BÉLIVEAU

" Béliveau was of the most dominant centers ever. When I think of him I think of grace and dignity, both for how he carried himself off the ice and how he played the game. He's one of the great champions in NHL history. " —PIERRE MCGUIRE

▸ TWO-TIME HART TROPHY WINNER
▸ 10 STANLEY CUP TITLES

ZAP GOES the puck over the shoulder of Gerry Cheevers, Bruins goaltender. Montreal wins the series; Béliveau, the idol of French Canada, moves a little bit nearer actual sainthood. The best thing about Béliveau is that he is in fact a paragon. Gentlemanly on the ice and off it, a miracle of modesty, a dutiful husband, he has all the old-fashioned virtues.

—*Gary Ronberg, SI, May 5, 1969*

Béliveau led the NHL in goal scoring twice.

PHOTOGRAPH BY JAMES DRAKE

Messier captained two franchises to titles.

PHOTOGRAPH BY DARREN CARROLL

4

MARK MESSIER

OILERS 1979–1991
RANGERS 1991–1997,
2000–2004
THREE OTHER TEAMS

———

" Among the most feared players in history, Messier enjoyed such respect that the NHL's leadership award is named for him. " —BRIAN CAZENEUVE

———

‣ TWO-TIME HART TROPHY WINNER
‣ SIX STANLEY CUP TITLES

"YOU THINK of Patton, you think of MacArthur . . . that's how we feel about Mark," goalie Glenn Healy says. "We sometimes say a guy has all the tools but no toolbox. The game is about having a toolbox, and no one understands that better or helps put things in perspective like Mark. We believe in him, in what he represents."

—*Michael Farber, SI, February 12, 1996* ‣

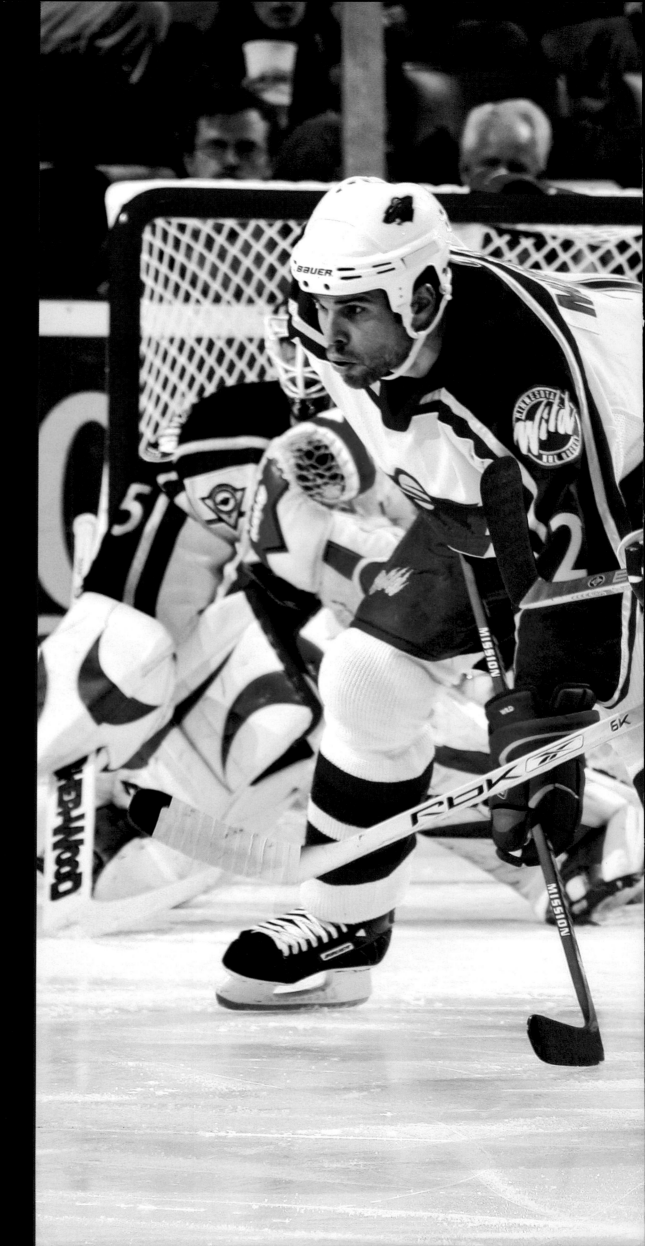

5

STEVE YZERMAN

RED WINGS 1983–2006

"No player evolved more over the course of his career than Detroit's longtime captain. An offensive dynamo in his early years, Yzerman showed no qualms in adapting to become a more complete two-way center." —SARAH KWAK

- ▸ NHL RECORD 19 SEASONS AS TEAM CAPTAIN
- ▸ 1,755 CAREER POINTS

MAKING YZERMAN captain was one of coach Jacques Demers's first moves—and biggest gambles. But Demers had called Yzerman's parents and his coach at Peterborough and knew that Steve responded well to challenges. The team captaincy was just that—a challenge to Yzerman to stop retreating into his Walkman. It worked. The Wings improved by 38 points over the previous season. In the second round of the playoffs, Detroit trailed the Maple Leafs 3–1 in games but eventually won the series. The cover of this season's Red Wings media guide shows Yzerman's celebration after scoring a goal in that series, a picture of unbridled ecstasy. It is the most animated that anyone can remember seeing him. Fortunately, the shy Yzerman deals in a currency NHLers understand better than words—goals.

—Austin Murphy, SI, February 8, 1988

Yzerman played for three Cup winners.

PHOTOGRAPH BY DAVID E. KLUTHO

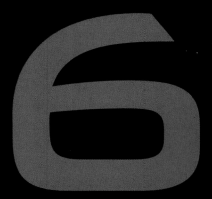

SIDNEY CROSBY

PENGUINS 2005–PRESENT

"With the NHL in need of a superstar after the 2004–05 lockout, Crosby was thrust onto the scene as the face of the league. Preternaturally talented, he is also always improving." —SARAH KWAK

▸ TWO-TIME HART TROPHY WINNER
▸ TWICE LED NHL IN SCORING

CROSBY HAS the turning radius of a Mini Cooper because of a skating technique known as Ten and Two. He has the uncommon ability to skate with his left foot pointing to 10 o'clock and his right skate pointing to 2, a vaguely Chaplinesque position that enhances mobility in tight quarters. Says former NHL player Phil Bourque, the Penguins' radio analyst, "The advantage with Ten and Two is you don't have to stop. You can roll off guys. While most guys glide, Sid's lower-body strength is such that he can actually propel himself, push off when his feet are open. He's almost a freak of nature." After Crosby's behind-the-net romp with Ottawa's Jason Spezza [in the first round of the 2010 playoffs], Penguins GM Ray Shero asked Mario Lemieux, the team's co-owner, "You ever do that with your feet?" Lemieux replied, "Are you kidding me? With my hips? Nowhere close."

—*Michael Farber, SI, May 10, 2010*

The strong-legged Crosby is a great stickhandler.

PHOTOGRAPH BY LOU CAPOZZOLA

7

PHIL ESPOSITO

BLACKHAWKS 1963–1967
BRUINS 1967–1975
RANGERS 1975–1981

❝ The emotional heart of the Big Bad Bruins of the early '70s, Esposito, one GM said, "couldn't skate, couldn't check, and couldn't shoot. All he could do was score." He led the league in goals six seasons in a row. ❞ —E.M. SWIFT

▸ TWO-TIME HART TROPHY WINNER
▸ LED NHL IN SCORING FIVE TIMES

AT HIS center-ice position Phil Esposito is a study in Houdini-like deception. He never seems hurried, and some have erroneously charged him with laziness. A stopwatch shows the fallacy. Where busier skaters will go down the ice in short strokes—*zzzt, zzzt, zzzt*—Esposito will cover the same distance in a single, long-striding *zzzzzzt*. On offense he tends to position himself 10 or 15 feet in front of the goalmouth and fire away with the slingshot ease of a metal center in a pinball hockey game. He has neither the awesome slap shot of a Hull nor the fast feet of an Orr, but he has one of the quickest sticks in hockey. "He gets the puck and fires it into the goal while you're still trying to figure out how he got the puck in the first place," says Bruins teammate Eddie Johnston. "He's so strong that he can fend off the other guy with one arm and skate right around him."

—*Jack Olsen, SI, March 29, 1971*

Esposito's feats include a 76-goal, 76-assist season.

8

STAN
MIKITA

" He could shoot, pass, play defense, and he was lethal on the face-off dot. Mikita was the NHL's best center during Chicago's 1960s heyday. He was an innovator too, pioneering the use of a curved stick blade. " —KOSTYA KENNEDY

▸ TWO-TIME HART TROPHY WINNER
▸ LED NHL IN SCORING FOUR TIMES

PLAYERS AS good and as small as Mikita are obvious targets for the bigger men in the league, and Mikita has a reputation as a "chippy" player. Allan Stanley of Toronto sums him up this way, "If you give Stan a little jab, he reacts immediately. Most players will wait for a chance to retaliate, but Mikita will give it right back to you in the same motion."

—*William Leggett, SI, January 31, 1966*

Mikita matured from ruffian to Lady Byng winner.

PHOTOGRAPH BY TONY TRIOLO

CENTERS

BRYAN TROTTIER

ISLANDERS 1975–1990
PENGUINS 1990–1992, 1993–1994

❝ He was the leading 200-foot player of his era. Playing between Mike Bossy and hard-nosed Clark Gillies, Trottier centered one of the most dominant lines in NHL history. ❞ —MARK BEECH

‣ 1979 HART TROPHY WINNER
‣ SIX STANLEY CUP TITLES

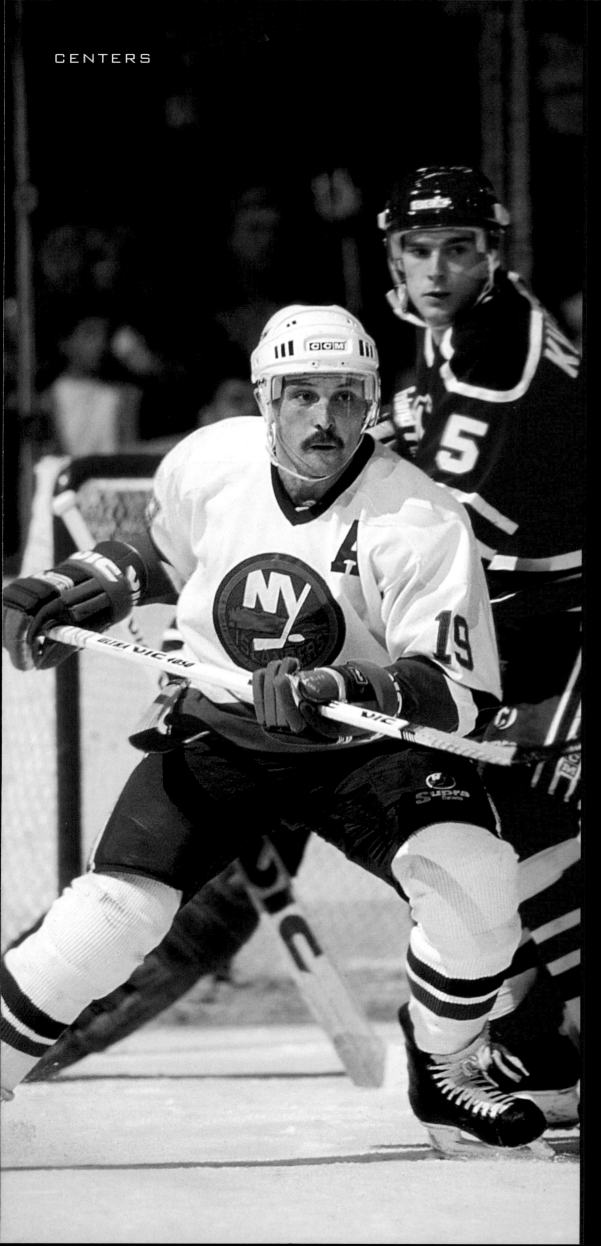

THE ISLANDERS had fourth choice in the 1974 amateur draft. In the first round Bill Torrey took Clark Gillies, and in the second round he picked a center named Bryan Trottier. "I don't think a lot of teams knew about him," says Torrey. "He was only 17, and he played in Swift Current [Saskatchewan], which is off the beaten track. When I went up to see Bryan, the windchill factor was something like minus 83 degrees. I've never been colder in my life, or in a colder rink. Trots didn't do much the first two periods, but in the third period he scored two goals. I decided to stay over another day." Torrey left Trottier in junior hockey the next year, although there was little question Trottier could have made the Islanders at 18. "Everyone fought me on it," says Torrey. "He was certainly as good as the players we had. But I wasn't going to bring a kid that age into New York and put him under the gun."

—E.M. Swift, SI, October 11, 1982

Trottier anchored the dynasty-era Islanders.

PHOTOGRAPH BY BRUCE BENNETT STUDIOS/GETTY IMAGES

10

Morenz was known as the Stratford Streak.

" He was the best player of hockey's first half century. Six weeks after breaking his leg during a game, Morenz died, at age 34. On March 11, 1937, 50,000 mourners streamed by his casket at center ice of the Montreal Forum. " —MICHAEL FARBER

FIFTEEN THOUSAND fans sat in silence. Another 10,000 gathered outside on St. Catherine Street, and thousands more lined the route to the Mount Royal Cemetery, where they laid [Morenz's] body to rest. The service was broadcast over the radio and the chaplain called [him] "the greatest of them all."

—E.M. Swift, SI, June 7, 1993

HOWIE
MORENZ

▸ THREE-TIME HART TROPHY WINNER
▸ FOUR STANLEY CUP TITLES

10

BEST LEFT WINGS

AFTER A HALL OF FAME CAREER AS A RED WINGS PLAYER TED LINDSAY RETURNED TO THE FRANCHISE IN 1977 AS A GENERAL MANAGER. THE TEAM WAS, AT THAT POINT, TERRIBLE AND IN NEED OF A SPARK. AS PETER GAMMONS REPORTED FOR SI, "ALL SUMMER LONG OL' SCARFACE SHOWED UP ON BILLBOARDS AND ON THE COVERS OF SEASON-TICKET SALES COME-ONS, WEARING A SCOWL AND A T-SHIRT THAT READ "AGGRESSIVE HOCKEY IS BACK IN TOWN."

LINDSAY, ONE OF OUR TOP 10 LEFT WINGS, WAS THE IDEAL FIGURE FOR THAT SALES PITCH. AS A PLAYER, TERRIBLE TED WAS THE REASON THE NHL ADOPTED PENALTIES OUTLAWING KNEEING AND ELBOWING. HE WAS ROUGH STUFF. IT'S TRUE OF HIM, AND OF MANY OF THE OTHER PLAYERS IN OUR TOP 10.

BUT ONE OF THESE LEFT WINGS ALSO HAD A CIVILIZING EFFECT ON THE GAME. BRENDAN SHANAHAN, NO SOFTIE OUT ON THE ICE, CONVENED A MEETING OF HOCKEY'S LEADERSHIP DURING THE 2004–05 LOCKOUT AND, AS DETAILED IN THIS SECTION'S STORY EXCERPT, THAT SUMMIT SPURRED MANY CHANGES IN THE GAME, INCLUDING A STRICTER ENFORCEMENT OF THE RULES—THE SORTS OF RULES THAT HAD BEEN ENACTED TO RESTRAIN PLAYERS LIKE LINDSAY. SHANAHAN LATER BECAME HEAD OF THE NHL'S DEPARTMENT OF PLAYER SAFETY AND THE LEAGUE'S CHIEF DISCIPLINARIAN. THANKS TO THIS TOP 10 LEFT WING, CIVILIZED HOCKEY WAS BACK IN TOWN.

1

BOBBY HULL

BLACKHAWKS 1957–1972
JETS 1972–1980
WHALERS 1980

" The Golden Jet and his curved stick were a goalie's worst nightmare. There's no telling how many goals he might have scored had he not abandoned the NHL for the WHA in 1972. " —MARK BEECH

▸ SCORED 610 GOALS IN NHL, 303 IN WHA
▸ TWO-TIME HART TROPHY WINNER

"THE SPORTS College of Canada and Fitness Institute has described Robert Marvin Hull as the "perfect muscular mesomorph." Hull stands 5'10" and weighs 195 pounds. His biceps measures 15½ inches—bigger than that of either Cassius Clay or Floyd Patterson. His skating speed has been timed at 29.2 mph, the fastest in the NHL. Perhaps the most fascinating statistic about Hull reveals that his wrist shot is faster than his slap shot. At 95 mph Hull's slap shot is the fastest in the league, but his wrist shot, that seemingly easy flick he uses when in full flight, has been timed at 105 mph. Goalie Glenn Hall was asked how he feels during the hours of practice when he has to defend against Hull's attacks. "There are days," says Hall, "when you just step aside and leave the door wide-open. It is a simple matter of self-preservation."

—*William Leggett, SI, January 25, 1965*

Hull led his leagues in goals eight times.

2

" Maybe you remember his hair (coiffed and lush) or his incandescent smile, or, most relevantly, the sight of him potting one of his 668 career goals. He was never truly dominant, but perennially one of the league's best. " —KOSTYA KENNEDY

ROBITAILLE HAS what linemate Igor Larionov calls "a smell" for the goal, but to dismiss his success as serendipity and harp on his bear-in-a-circus skating is to miss the point. No one has done more with less than Robitaille, who was drafted 171st in 1984 and has no conspicuous gifts except for soft hands and hockey sense.

—*Michael Farber, SI, April 22, 2002*

LUC
ROBITAILLE

▸ EIGHT-TIME ALL-STAR
▸ 1,394 CAREER POINTS

Lucky Luc scored the most goals (557) in Kings history.

Lindsay (leaping) played with furious energy.

PHOTOGRAPH BY ROY BASH/BETTMANN/CORBIS

3

TED LINDSAY

RED WINGS 1944–1957,
1964–1965
BLACKHAWKS 1957–1960

" Terrible Ted was a 5' 8", 163-pound ball of fury whose impact is still felt today. The NHL introduced elbowing and kneeing penalties in response to his style. He also pioneered the player's union. " —MICHAEL FARBER

▸ 11-TIME ALL-STAR
▸ 1950 ROSS TROPHY WINNER

HIS NICKNAME was Scarface, for the more than 900 stitches that were sewn into his map. The Red Wings have not been the same since Lindsay hung up his skates and Gordie Howe had to go it alone. In fact, since Lindsay's retirement they have made the Stanley Cup playoffs just once in 12 years.

—*Peter Gammons, SI, October 31, 1977*

4

ALEX OVECHKIN

CAPITALS 2005–PRESENT

" He plays with the wild, reckless abandon that characterizes the speedier, stronger postlockout NHL. And he remains one of the most entertaining players in the league, with his penchant for throwing his body around and the wicked one-timer that often precedes his jubilant celebrations. " —SARAH KWAK

‣ THREE-TIME HART TROPHY WINNER
‣ LED NHL IN GOALS FIVE TIMES

ALEXANDER OVECHKIN rifled the puck between the pads of Flames goalie Miikka Kiprusoff, skated toward the boards, threw open his arms, shimmied and offered a share-my-ecstasy embrace to his Capitals teammates. This was sunshine, lollipops and rainbows, a snow day and Christmas morning wrapped into one. The goal was critical—a league-best 10th game-winner gave Washington a 3–2 win to keep its playoff dreams alive— but then every goal seems to tap a wellspring of pleasure in Ovechkin. Does anybody enjoy anything more than Ovechkin enjoys scoring goals? "If there was ever an athlete who you'd pay to see no matter what his team did, he'd be the guy," Blue Jackets coach Ken Hitchcock says. " I think he's the evolution of our game—a young, reckless, skilled player."

—Michael Farber, SI, March 24, 2008

Ovechkin combined great speed and dazzling creativity.

PHOTOGRAPHS BY LOU CAPOZZOLA (LEFT) AND DAMIAN STROHMEYER

5

FRANK MAHOVLICH

Mahovlich won four of his six Stanley Cups in Toronto.

PHOTOGRAPH BY JAMES DRAKE

❝ One of the greatest scorers of his day, the Big M chafed under the iron fist of coach Punch Imlach, who purposefully mispronounced his name to the press. The Big M eventually left Toronto and found his way to Montreal, where he won two more Stanley Cups. ❞ —MARK BEECH

▸ 15-TIME ALL-STAR
▸ 533 CAREER NHL GOALS

MAHOVLICH HAS thrived emotionally in Montreal. "For the first time in his career Frank does not have big pressure on him," says Jean Béliveau. Throughout his career Mahovlich has never satisfied his critics. "Even when I scored 48 goals for the Leafs," Frank said, "they were not happy."

—Mark Mulvoy, SI, November 15, 1971

6

VALERI KHARLAMOV

CSKA MOSCOW AND SOVIET
NATIONAL TEAM, 1967–1981

" Kharlamov was so brilliant during the 1972 Summit Series the only way Canada could stop him was to break his ankle, which Bobby Clarke did with a slash. Small (5' 8"), smart, and startlingly fast, Kharlamov died in a car crash at 33. " —E.M. SWIFT

▸ TWO OLYMPIC GOLD MEDALS
▸ EIGHT WORLD
CHAMPIONSHIP TITLES

KHARLAMOV, EASILY the best player on the ice, scored twice in the second period and the rout was on, all right, but it was going the other way. Although Team Canada narrowed the margin to 4–3 midway through the third period, they did not have enough physical stamina to skate with the Russians the rest of the game, seeming almost helpless as the Soviets added three goals against the beleaguered Ken Dryden. The Russians skated better, shot better, checked better and hit harder than the Canadians; they were whirlwinds, never pausing to let the befuddled All-Stars catch up. A one-on-one rush, say Valeri Kharlamov against Brad Park or Rod Seiling or Don Awrey, instantly became a Kharlamov-in-alone-on-Dryden as Park or Seiling or Awrey melted away.

—Mark Mulvoy, SI, September 11, 1972

Kharlamov had 507 points in 438 Soviet League games. ›

PHOTOGRAPH BY BRUCE BENNETT STUDIOS/GETTY IMAGES

7

BRENDAN SHANAHAN

DEVILS 1987–1991, 2008–2009
BLUES 1991–1995
RED WINGS 1996–2006
TWO OTHER TEAMS

" Smart, skilled and powerful, Shanahan, at 6' 3", 220 pounds, was a game-changing power forward with a swift and heavy wrist shot. He was original—and funny—in the room, and a vital part of three Cup champions with Detroit. " —KOSTYA KENNEDY

▸ 656 CAREER GOALS
▸ EIGHT-TIME ALL-STAR

IF HE is richly textured off the ice— Shanahan is a gregarious 27-year-old with easy charm and workaday concerns who also happens to know Jay Gatsby from Hall of Famer Bill Gadsby—he also can be several things at once on the ice. In 1993–94, while with the Blues, Shanahan tallied a hat trick of versatility by scoring 50 goals, exceeding 100 points and being penalized more than 200 minutes. He has averaged a goal every two games in the '90s while playing like a ruffian. "When Shanahan was in St. Louis, one of the Blues did something and our bench was chirping, 'Who's going to fight your battles for you?' says Chicago assistant Lorne Henning, who then coached the Islanders. "Shanahan skates by and says, 'I will.' Our whole bench shrunk."

—*Michael Farber, SI, November 18, 1996*

The physical Shanahan logged 2,489 penalty minutes.

FROM SPORTS ILLUSTRATED
JANUARY 30, 2006

HE MADE A DIFFERENCE

During a meeting which became known as the Shanahan Summit, players, coaches and league pooh-bahs engineered changes that pushed the game's tempo after a lockout

BY MICHAEL FARBER

COMFORTABLY ENSCONCED in a private dining room in Calgary not long ago, the Detroit Red Wings were watching an NHL game on a giant-screen television when the referee raised his arm to make what struck the Wings as a phantom call. All heads in the room swiveled in the direction of forward Brendan Shanahan, who at that moment might as well have had a whistle in his mouth instead of the taste of dinner. His teammates pointed at him. Then, in chorus, they began to boo. "What?" Shanahan protested. "What?"

A year after organizing a conference of hockey's movers and shakers that laid the groundwork for the most stunning remake of a professional sports league in memory—a rules overhaul that most players embrace but that has some complaining about the increase in penalty calls—what did he expect? That phantom call was on him.

The lockout was an important year for the 37-year-old Shanahan because it afforded him a chance to "glimpse behind the door of life after hockey," even while he was preparing to play again. He put his children to bed every night and spent more quality time with his wife, Catherine, but perhaps the most impactful thing he did during that unscheduled sabbatical was put together a two-day meeting at a Toronto hotel in December 2004. It's now widely known now as the Shanahan Summit, which hints at something more august than 26 guests (players, coaches, general managers, owners, agents, television executives) brainstorming about the NHL. Shanahan deflects credit to commissioner Gary Bettman, NHL director of hockey operations Colin Campbell and former Players Association executive director Bob Goodenow (all of whom supported the meeting), but Shanahan was the one who extended the invitations ("I felt embarrassed calling, like I was a salesman," he says), and he was the one who footed the bill.

At a time when management and labor were barely talking at each other let alone to each other, his conference illuminated the dark season. Based on the consensus reached in Toronto, Shanahan outlined numerous proposed rules changes and took his wish list to Bettman and Goodenow, in separate face-to-face meetings. By the time the NHL returned last fall, the league had instituted sweeping changes that included more vigilant officiating, adding the shootout to break ties, allowing the two-line pass, disallowing line changes for the team that ices the puck, setting limits on the size of goalie equipment and creating a competition committee that has active players on it. The new rules have greatly enlivened the game—and virtually all of them were the product of the Shanahan Summit.

"He put a lot on the line," Detroit forward Kris Draper says. "Shanny stepped up when nothing was going on, not that we don't give him heat about it." If insults are the lingua franca of the dressing room, the Red Wings are among the most loquacious of teams. "Doing a story on the savior? The messiah?" asked captain Steve Yzerman through a tight-lipped grin, as Western Conference–leading Detroit checked into a Denver hotel last Thursday. Like NHL referees in 2005–06, the Wings don't let much go—certainly not a year-end story in Toronto's *Globe and Mail* that named Shanahan the most influential person in Canadian sports, nor his No. 10 spot in *The Hockey News* ranking of people of power and influence in the game.

Well on the back nine of a career that as of this writing had produced 580 goals (including 99 game-winners), 2,329 penalty minutes, three Stanley Cups and an Olympic gold medal, Shanahan shook his head when told he might best be remembered for chairing a conference. "I hear that," he says, "and I think, Dummy!" The men who previously changed hockey—Jacques Plante popularizing the goalie mask, Bobby Orr rushing the puck, Wayne Gretzky dishing from behind the net—did it because of a peculiar on-ice genius, something beyond Shanahan's humbler gifts. "You watch my game and nothing jumps out," he says. "I'm the tortoise in the fable." So he left his indelible mark while wearing a snazzy black suit, not the winged-wheel sweater.

"You sit around with guys after a game, and you hear all these ideas how to make things better," Shanahan says. "Then you wake up the next day, and it's forgotten. I started thinking about [organizing a meeting] after the [November 2004] Hall of Fame induction of Ray Bourque, Paul Coffey and Larry Murphy. I read comments Coffey made [decrying] the state of the game. So I thought maybe we should all talk about it. I called one player and one agent and asked if a meeting like this could ever happen. They both told me no. So I went ahead and tried to do it."

Though Shanahan bridles at the notion that the NHL's revival has mirrored his own—"If this is a rebirth," he says, "when did I die?"—there is undeniably an added zest to his play. After scoring 25 goals in 2003–04, 14 below his average over the previous 10 full seasons, Shanahan was tied for the team lead with 22, making him one of only nine NHL players to score 20 or more goals in each of 17 seasons. "He made the rules; he better be playing better," says Detroit Red Wings goaltender Manny Legace, laughing. "He seems more energized. He's eager to play, eager to practice. He's one of only a couple of guys I've seen who work on their total game in practice. He's always asking me if a goalie comes across [the crease] a certain way, where's the best spot to put the puck. It's impressive the way he thinks about the game." ∎

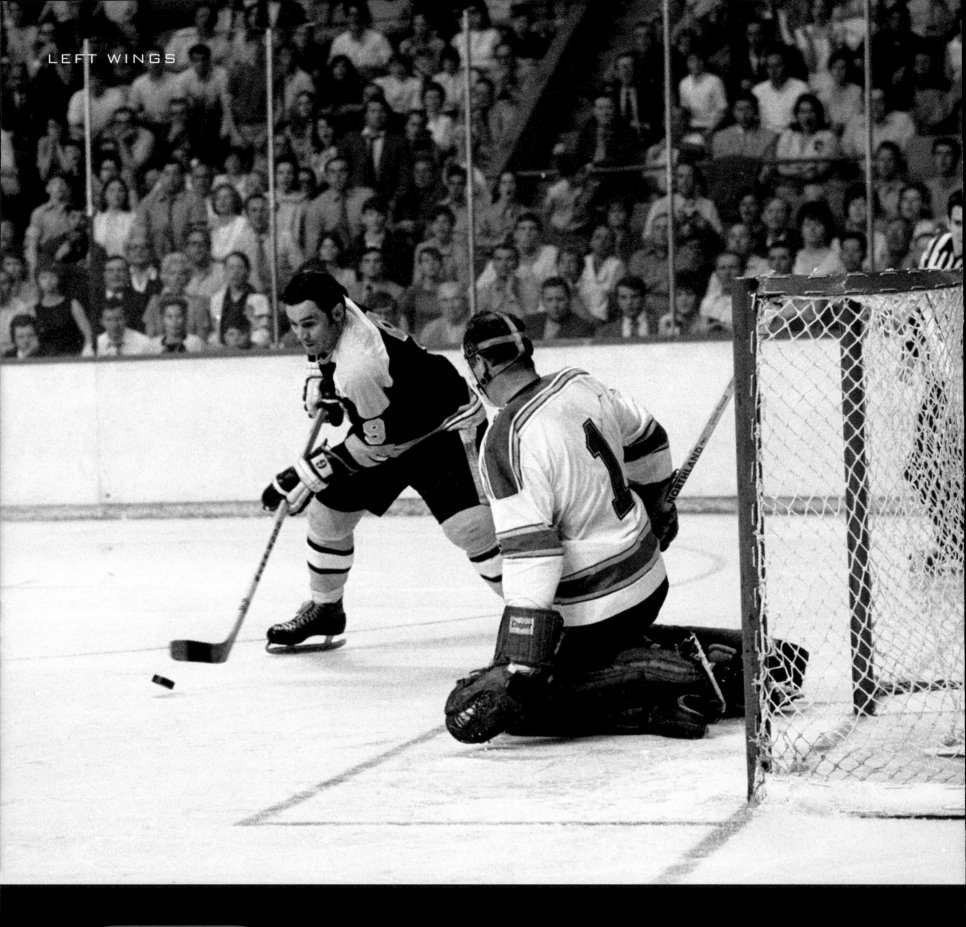

RED WINGS 1955–1957
BRUINS 1957–1978

Bucyk won two Lady Byng Trophies.

PHOTOGRAPH BY DICK RAPHAEL

8

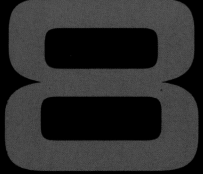

" Well before the proliferation of the power forward, Johnny Bucyk was a dynamic goal scorer and durable master of the hip check who was still respected for gentlemanly play throughout his career. " —BRIAN CAZENEUVE

BUCYK, A notoriously slow starter, has been so hot that he is second only to Bobby Hull in scoring. "There's much less pressure on me this season," says Bucyk. "This is the first year I don't pick up a paper once a week and read that I'm about to be traded."

—Pete Axthelm, SI, December 11, 1967

JOHNNY BUCYK

▸ SEVEN-TIME ALL-STAR
▸ 1,369 CAREER POINTS

9

DICKIE MOORE

CANADIENS 1951–1963
TWO OTHER TEAMS

"Sometimes lost amid the glitter of the Canadiens dynasty of the late 1950s, Moore was a dynamic stickhandler and scorer. He broke Gordie Howe's regular-season record with 96 points in 1958–59, a mark that stood through the pre-expansion era." —MICHAEL FARBER

▸ TWO-TIME ROSS TROPHY WINNER
▸ SIX-TIME ALL-STAR

IT WAS always the blight of some vaudevillian's life to be billed behind Jolson. None of them liked it and few of them profited by it, but somehow they did it. For six years Dickie Moore found himself in a similar position, behind Maurice Richard. He gathered what goals he could get and accepted modestly any applause that was left over.

—*Sports Illustrated, January 4, 1960*

Moore had 608 career points in 719 games.

PHOTOGRAPH BY JOHN G. ZIMMERMAN

10

KEITH TKACHUK

JETS 1991–1996
COYOTES 1996–2001
BLUES 2001–2007, 2007–2010
THRASHERS 2007

" For a large man he had tremendous speed and acceleration, and hand skills too. He was a devastating forechecker, and he knew how to get to the front of the net. " —PIERRE MCGUIRE

▸ FIVE-TIME ALL-STAR
▸ LED NHL WITH 52 GOALS IN 1996–97

HE SPENT last summer's vacation establishing himself as the game's preeminent power forward, helping lead the U.S. to the gold medal in the World Cup. In that tournament he scored five goals in seven games and struck a blow, literally, for countless NHL players. In an early-round game against Canada, Tkachuk squared off with Avalanche winger Claude Lemieux, one of the league's most despised players. In the ensuing fracas, Tkachuk broke Lemieux's nose. Says Phoenix winger Jim McKenzie, "There were a lot of toothless smiles around the league." For such an adept pugilist, Tkachuk has surprisingly soft hands. He is exceptionally strong, and he's tough to knock off the puck, a trait center Bob Corkum attributes to Tkachuk's "low center of gravity." Center Craig Janney elaborates: "He's got a big ass."

—Austin Murphy, SI, March 3, 1997

The 6' 2", 235-pound Tkachuk knew how to use his size.

10

THE

Best Right Wings

IN MARCH 1960 SPORTS ILLUSTRATED ASKED NHL PLAYERS AND COACHES: WHO HAS THE BEST SHOT IN HOCKEY? MOST RESPONDENTS, RATHER THAN SETTLE ON ONE PLAYER, SPIT OUT SEVERAL POSSIBILITIES, AND NAMES INCLUDED ANDY BATHGATE, JEAN BÉLIVEAU, BRONCO HORVATH, BOBBY HULL, AND BOOM BOOM GEOFFRION. THOUGH MAURICE RICHARD WAS PLAYING IN HIS LAST SEASON, HE RECEIVED A DECISIVE NOD FROM RANGERS GOALIE GUMP WORSLEY: "WHEN IT COMES TO SPEED AND ACCURACY, THE OLD MAN, ROCKET RICHARD, STILL IS AS TOUGH AS ANYBODY. HE CAN CATCH THOSE CORNERS BLINDFOLDED."

THE NAME THAT DREW UNQUALIFIED ENDORSEMENT WAS GORDIE HOWE. "HE TAKES ONE LOOK, SEEMS TO KNOW WHERE THE GOALIE IS GOING TO MOVE AND LETS GO," SAID TORONTO GOALIE JOHNNY BOWER. DETROIT GOALIE TERRY SAWCHUK AGREED. "DURING MY SEASONS IN BOSTON, GORDIE GAVE ME THE MOST TROUBLE OF ANY PLAYER," SAWCHUK SAID. "EVEN NOW I'M STILL AMAZED AT HOWE'S SHOT—NOT JUST THE SPEED OF IT BUT ALSO THE FORCE."

MORE THAN A HALF CENTURY LATER, THAT FORCE STILL RESONATES THROUGH OUR LIST OF TOP RIGHT WINGS. HOWE WAS VOTED TO THE TOP SPOT BY EVERY PANELIST, WITH ROCKET RICHARD A NEAR UNANIMOUS SECOND. SO MUCH HAS CHANGED ABOUT HOCKEY, BUT THESE THINGS REMAIN THE SAME.

1

GORDIE HOWE

RED WINGS 1946–1971
AEROS 1973–1977
WHALERS 1977–1980

" Howe, the only NHLer to play in five different decades—he retired at 52—was nicknamed "Power" because of his strength. Tough, ambidextrous and a little dirty, a "Gordie Howe hat trick" was a goal, assist and fight in the same game." —E.M. SWIFT

▸ SIX HART TROPHIES
▸ SCORED 801 GOALS IN NHL, 174 IN WHA

THERE ARE MEN who point to the success of a 51-year-old grandfather as proof of the sorry state of hockey today, but for those who love the sport, it is an affirmation of the game's subtleties that a man who has lost his youth and speed and recklessness can still succeed with strength and savvy and guile. Time does not diminish instinct. Nor, surprisingly, does it necessarily erode strength. Howe is still tremendously strong, which is less of a surprise to his doctors than to the kids he plays against. Dr. Bob Bailey was the Michigan physician who gave Howe the go-ahead to come out of retirement the first time, at age 45, to play in Houston with his two sons. "What I found really incredible was his pulse rate, which was around 48," says Bailey. "That's almost the heart of a dolphin."

—E.M. Swift, SI, January 21, 1980

Howe led the NHL in scoring six times.

PHOTOGRAPHS BY AP (LEFT) AND TONY TRIOLO

CANADIENS 1942–1960

Richard played on eight Stanley Cup winners.

PHOTOGRAPH BY BETTMANN/CORBIS

"The NHL's goal-scoring trophy is named for the Rocket, who was a cultural icon to French Canadians. Enraged by a suspension given to him in 1955, Montreal fans rioted during the next game, leading to more than 30 injuries and 60 arrests." —BRIAN CAZENEUVE

THE ROCKET, known for his flair for sensational single-game performances, had the highest percentage of games in which he scored more than one goal. In fact, if you had to pick one man to play one important game, you would undoubtedly choose Richard."

—Pete Axthelm, SI, February 12, 1968

▸ RECORDED NHL'S FIRST 50-GOAL SEASON
▸ LED NHL IN GOALS FIVE TIMES

MAURICE RICHARD

3
GUY LAFLEUR

" Golden hair streaming, he punctuated his rushes with a slap shot that was as hard as it was accurate. The Flower was both the leader of the Flying Frenchmen and the personification of the Canadiens' last dynasty. " —MARK BEECH

▸ LED NHL IN SCORING THREE TIMES
▸ 560 CAREER GOALS

LAFLEUR HAD a clear shot on the goaltender, who suddenly seemed uncertain. "He has all the shots and he always uses the right one," murmured Al Millar of the Sabres. This time it was the wrist shot. Flash. The red light was on. Lafleur had scored again, and the people in the Coliseum started their sing-along: "Il est en or," they chanted. *It is gold.*

—Mark Mulvoy, SI, March 1, 1971

Lafleur had six consecutive 50-goal seasons.
PHOTOGRAPH BY MANNY MILLAN

4

JAROMIR JAGR

PENGUINS 1990–2001
SEVEN OTHER TEAMS
THROUGH 2015

" He had the hands of a surgeon and the brains of a Mensa member, but the best part of Jagr's anatomy was his derrière. He could stick out that rump and protect the puck for chunks of time, studying options before spinning free to make a play. When he had the puck in the corner, booty called. " —MICHAEL FARBER

▸ LED NHL IN SCORING
FIVE TIMES
▸ 722 CAREER GOALS

ZIMNI (WINTER) STADIUM, Kladno. A large, nearly toothless woman is making her way down the aisle, eyeing Jagr, her helpless prey. He sees her coming but cannot, or will not, escape.
"This is my idol," the old woman, speaking Czech, says. "I cried when he went to America. I could not have liked him more if I had given birth to him. Why? Because he's tough and fearless." Czechoslovakia's revolution of 1989 enabled Jagr to fulfill his lifelong dream of playing in the NHL without having to defect. When the Penguins made Jagr their first draft choice in June 1990 it was the first time a Czechoslovakian player had attended the NHL draft with his government's blessings. As a result, Jagr can return to his family in the summertime, to the farmhouse near Kladno where he grew up.

—E.M. Swift, SI, October 12, 1992

Jagr has 1,802 career points.

5

MIKE BOSSY

ISLANDERS 1977–1987

"A finesse player with just two major penalties in his career, Bossy averaged nearly 1.5 points per game in every one of his 10 NHL seasons. He reached the magical mark of 50 goals in 50 games in 1981 and became the only player to score four game-winning goals in the same series, against Boston in 1983." —BRIAN CAZENEUVE

> SEVEN-TIME ALL-STAR
> THREE-TIME LADY BYNG
TROPHY WINNER

BOSSY IS a sinewy man with an angular face and sunken eyes, and he is a no-frills trip on or off the ice. He scores economically, beating goaltenders with what seems to be almost casual disdain. He speaks softly, yet makes his points. He is one of the most outspoken opponents of violence in hockey and has publicly stated that he will never drop his gloves to fight. He's a devoted family man who has said he will retire at the age of 30 if he feels that hockey takes too much away from life with his wife, Lucie, and 16-month-old daughter, Josiane. And Bossy keeps a low profile away from the rink, avoiding crowds and publicity. "He's really just a straight guy who's among the best who ever lived at what he does," says teammate Glenn Resch.

—Larry Brooks, SI, January 19, 1981

Back pain ended Bossy's career prematurely.

PHOTOGRAPH BY ANTHONY NESTE

The speedy Selanne was known as the Finnish Flash.

PHOTOGRAPH BY JEFF GROSS/GETTY IMAGES

6

TEEMU SELANNE

DUCKS 1996–2001, 2005–2014
THREE OTHER TEAMS

"Selanne was of the most consistent players ever in the NHL. He was an offensive force, a tremendous skater, and one of the great ambassadors for the game." —PIERRE MCGUIRE

▸ 684 CAREER GOALS
▸ LED NHL IN GOALS THREE TIMES

HE DONATES most of his endorsement earnings to [his children's foundation]. When he scores a hat trick, he collects the caps the fans toss onto the ice and ships them to Finnish orphanages. "Athletes are so lucky, and it doesn't take so much for us to do these things," Selanne says.

—Johnette Howard, SI, January 27, 1997

7

BRETT HULL

Hull became a team executive after he left the ice.

" Hull is the greatest sniper ever listed at right wing, and late in his 19-year run he began playing defense too—a big reason he won Cups in Dallas and Detroit. " —KOSTYA KENNEDY

▸ 741 CAREER GOALS
▸ SCORED 86 GOALS IN 1990-91

AN AMERICAN playing in an American city, he has helped sell the game in the States. He is a pure goal scorer, a home run hitter in a league starved for such glamour boys. Hull is a major reason why the Blues franchise, which has spent more time on the ropes than Rocky Balboa, is now profitable.

—*Austin Murphy, SI, March 18, 1991*

SHOOTING FROM THE LIP

Brett Hull talked as sharply as he played, and when he left St. Louis to head to Dallas, he brought the wisecracks with him, saying he couldn't do it any other way

BY JOHNETTE HOWARD

E'S A SURE FIRST-BALLOT Hall of Famer and the NHL's biggest crank. Brett Hull, the Dallas Stars' new wing, admits that his celebrated mouth is as big as Texas, and he acknowledges that by last July, when he had reached the bitter end of his 10-year career with the St. Louis Blues, "I was portrayed as some sort of monster, a coach killer, a guy who shoots from the hip."

Were those descriptions correct?

"Well," Hull says with a smirk, "I am a pain in the ass. I give other guys crap. I'm a yapper. They say they want the truth, and then they say, 'How can he say that?' I think, Well, it's the truth, isn't it? So what's the big deal?"

He's sitting on a bench in the Dallas locker room as he talks, and by the way he folds his hands in his lap like a schoolboy there's no reason to suspect that Hull is telling you anything but the truth. Still, he knows that some of those words he so freely tosses out are verbal hand grenades and that on occasion he has lobbed one into his team's bunker. "That's why I came to Dallas a few weeks before training camp, just to skate with the guys, become a familiar face," Hull says. "I bet a lot of guys here have heard stories about me and were wondering, What the hell kind of guy is he? What kind of tornado is coming in? Ask them."

"Was I worried?" says Dallas captain Derian Hatcher when pressed about Hull's reputation. "Well. . . . " Long pause. "Yeah."

Many of Hull's salvos are delivered with a swaggering, almost roguish air. He never settles for a tepid word when a caustic one comes to mind. To him, something isn't just disappointing, it's stupid, ridiculous, pathetic. People who make him unhappy aren't irritating, they're morons, idiots, jerks. When Wayne Gretzky played 31 games with the Blues at the end of the 1995–96 season, he told Hull, "You say all the things I wish I could say."

"What the hell, I never plan it," Hull says. "I'm an emotional guy."

Says Hull's wife, Allison, "It's not just to teammates. Some days he'll look at me and say, 'God, that's an ugly dress.' "

Ugly might be an appropriate word to describe Hull's relationship with Iron Mike Keenan, who was the Blues' coach from July 1994 until December '96. During an October '95 game Hull barked at Blues goalie Grant Fuhr because Fuhr had given away the puck, then after the match Hull and Keenan got into a heated argument over Hull's comments. That prompted Keenan to strip Hull of his captaincy, telling reporters, "It's nothing personal." Hull retorted, "The hell it's not."

During a practice about a month later, Fuhr made a similarly careless pass, and an unrepentant Hull yelled, "Hey, Fuhr, that's the same play that cost me my C!"

In St. Louis, Hull was an eight-time All-Star, a three-time NHL goal-scoring champion and the 1990–91 league MVP. Like Gretzky, he's not particularly swift, but he's extremely smart on the ice. He excels at anticipating the action and making creative passes. When he gets the puck in shooting position, Hull snaps off one of the quickest, hardest one-timers in the game. "He's the absolute best I've seen doing that," says Mike Modano, Hull's new center.

Hull has made a few impolitic remarks—he says Dallas plays the same "robot hockey" St. Louis did and insists he could "play until I'm 50" and "win the Selke [the best defensive forward award], no problem" if he didn't have to worry about creating magic with the puck. But even when Hull grouses, it's usually concerning things he cares about deeply: playing winning hockey and scoring artistic goals. He often alludes to the support he gets from Allison, whom he married last winter after a 14-year relationship and the arrival of their first two children.

Asked if Hull's proposal was romantic, Allison laughs and says, "Nope. We were at the kitchen table. Christmas Eve. Brett had Jude bring the ring to me, which was sweet. Then we had about three weeks to plan the wedding. So I bought my dress off the rack—it really was beautiful. We flew to Las Vegas on a Thursday, got married on Friday and flew back on Saturday. As I was walking through the lobby of the hotel in my wedding gown, these strangers were screaming, "Don't do it!" We were married in this place in Vegas called Cupid's Chapel. It's owned by this bookie we knew from Minnesota. When they played the wedding march, there was this loud *etccccchhh* because someone scratched the record. And the minister, oh, the minister, was he a piece of work!

"He began the ceremony by saying, 'I trust you two know each other.' When it was over, a friend made the sign of the cross. The minister hurried to her and said, 'Thank you for that. I thought I was alone with God here today.' I was laughing throughout the ceremony, and Brett, if you can believe it, got mad at me. He said, 'Allison, you're making a mockery of our wedding!' "

Hull isn't fooling around when it comes to Dallas's Cup chances, either. He certainly didn't tiptoe into town thinking, Just don't screw everything up. To the contrary, he says, "I want people to look at us and say, 'This team had a great year, and Brett was right in the middle of that.' "

Asked if one of his other goals this season is to avoid a scolding from NHL commissioner Gary Bettman, Hull can't help himself. A smile begins to play at the corners of his mouth, and he laughs. Brett Hull? Make a promise to shut up? "I can't," he says. "I mean, I couldn't, you know. I would never say that." ■

OILERS 1980–1990
KINGS 1991–1996
THREE OTHER TEAMS

Kurri twice led the NHL in goals per game.

PHOTOGRAPH BY BRUCE BENNETT/GETTY IMAGES

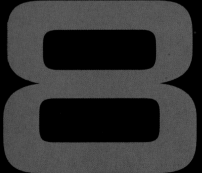

8

JARI KURRI

" Kurri was Wayne Gretzky's righthand man. One of the top defensive forwards of his day, he was also a great sniper and playmaker. Master of the one-timer, he played on five Cup winners in Edmonton. " —E.M. SWIFT

▸ LED NHL IN GOALS, 1985–86
▸ EIGHT-TIME ALL-STAR

"THE ONLY thing we ever talk about is moving the puck, going to the hole and getting it back," says Gretzky. And there are few players who can find the holes quicker than Kurri. Indeed, as Gretzky was held to four goals in the Chicago series, Kurri [who scored 12] was finding time and space to play his subtle game.

—Jack Falla, SI, May 27, 1985

9

BERNIE GEOFFRION

" Even if he only popularized the slap shot rather than invented it, as he always claimed to have done, his contribution to the game would be immense. The modern NHL was built on the glory of the slapper from the wing—and few did it better than Boom Boom. " —MARK BEECH

‣ 1961 HART TROPHY WINNER
‣ TWICE LED NHL IN GOALS

A PLAYER was practicing slap shots alone in the Montreal Forum. A reporter, hearing the continuous sound of a puck rebounding from the boards, knew the shooter was Bernard Geoffrion. Looking in, the reporter shouted: "Hey, I've got a nickname for you. Want to be called Boom Boom?" "Sure," said Geoffrion.

—Huston Horn, SI, March 27, 1961

Boom Boom broke his nose nine times.

PHOTOGRAPH BY YALE JOEL/TIME LIFE PICTURES/GETTY IMAGES

YVAN COURNOYER

CANADIENS 1963–1979

❝ He epitomized the Flying Frenchmen Canadiens, with his blinding speed and ability to control his body and the puck at a breakneck pace. ❞ —SARAH KWAK

- ▸ SIX-TIME ALL-STAR
- ▸ 1973 CONN SMYTHE TROPHY WINNER

"THE ROCKET was everything in hockey to me," Cournoyer says. "I guess it was the same for most kids in Montreal. You can't tell many people who grew up here that the Rocket wasn't the greatest that ever lived. How could I ever compare to him?" Actually, Cournoyer resembles the sainted Richard every time he takes a pass and begins a rush over the blue line. He skates swiftly down the right wing, looks to his left, then cuts sharply, without a wasted half-stride, and is suddenly in front of the goal, ready to fire his lefthanded shot. That kind of move was Richard's trademark. Few who have followed him have executed it as well as Cournoyer. Yvan is so anxious to use this talent that some hockey men have accused him of shooting too much. "There is no such thing as shooting too much," he replies to such criticism. "I think a player should shoot from everywhere, backhand or forehand, from any angle."

—Pete Axthelm, SI, April 3, 1967

The swift Cournoyer was nicknamed The Roadrunner.

PHOTOGRAPH BY JAMES DRAKE

10

THE

Best Defensemen

BOSTON HAS BEEN BLESSED WITH IMPRESSIVE SPORTS TRIOS THAT HAVE RATED WELL WITH SI PANELS. WHEN WE PUT TOGETHER OUR BASEBALL'S GREATEST BOOK, THE RED SOX LANDED THREE LEFTFIELDERS IN OUR TOP 10, INCLUDING THE NUMBER 1 MAN, TED WILLIAMS. A SIMILAR PATTERN EMERGED IN OUR BASKETBALL'S GREATEST BOOK, WHERE THE CELTICS HAD THREE OF THE TOP 10 SMALL FORWARDS, INCLUDING OUR BEST, LARRY BIRD. WITH HOCKEY DEFENSEMEN THE PATTERN REPEATS. SI HAS THREE BRUINS ON THE LIST, TOPPED BY BOBBY ORR.

ORR, WILLIAMS AND BIRD HAVE MORE IN COMMON THAN THEIR UNQUESTIONED EXCELLENCE IN COMPETITION. THEY ALL SEEMED TO EMBODY A CERTAIN TYPE OF MANLINESS. WILLIAMS WASN'T JUST A BALLPLAYER, HE WAS A DECORATED FIGHTER PILOT. BIRD EMERGED FROM SMALL-TOWN INDIANA AND BROUGHT A HEROIC SWAGGER AND CONFIDENCE TO THE COURT.

THEN THERE'S ORR, A MAN OF IMPENENTRABLY SOLID CHARACTER, AS DETAILED BY S.L. PRICE'S MAGNIFICENT PROFILE IN THIS SECTION. ONE NOTEWORTHY AND POSSIBLY SURPRISING EXAMPLE OF ORR'S METTLE IS THE WAY HE SUPPORTED FORMER TEAMMATE DEREK SANDERSON AS HE WAGED LENGTHY BATTLES AGAINST DRUG AND ALCOHOL ADDICTION. ORR PROVED HIMSELF TO BE STEADFAST AGAINST ALL MANNER OF OPPOSITION.

1

BOBBY ORR

BRUINS 1966–1976
BLACKHAWKS 1976–1977,
1978–1979

" He redefined how the game is played by creating so much offense from the defensive position. Bobby Orr was as good a skater as the league has ever seen, and he was the embodiment of composure under fire. " —PIERRE MCGUIRE

▸ EIGHT-TIME NORRIS TROPHY
WINNER
▸ THREE-TIME HART TROPHY
WINNER

WHAT HAS gotten into Bobby Orr? Already the National Hockey League's best defenseman—the alltime best, most people would say—the Bruins' superchild entered the new year leading the league in scoring. We can now expect a pitcher who will win a batting championship, a quarterback who will gallop for more yardage than Gale Sayers and a guard who will lead the NBA in rebounding. "Here's a kid who's only 21 years old," says Boston goalie Gerry Cheevers, "and he's keeping us all alive and well. He's got to win the Hart Trophy as the most valuable player, the Norris Trophy as the best defenseman and the Vezina Trophy as the best goaltender." Best goaltender? "Yeah," Cheevers said. "Bobby has stopped more shots this year than any goalie in the league."

—*Mark Mulvoy, SI, January 12, 1970*

Orr twice led the NHL in scoring.

PHOTOGRAPH BY JOHN G. ZIMMERMAN

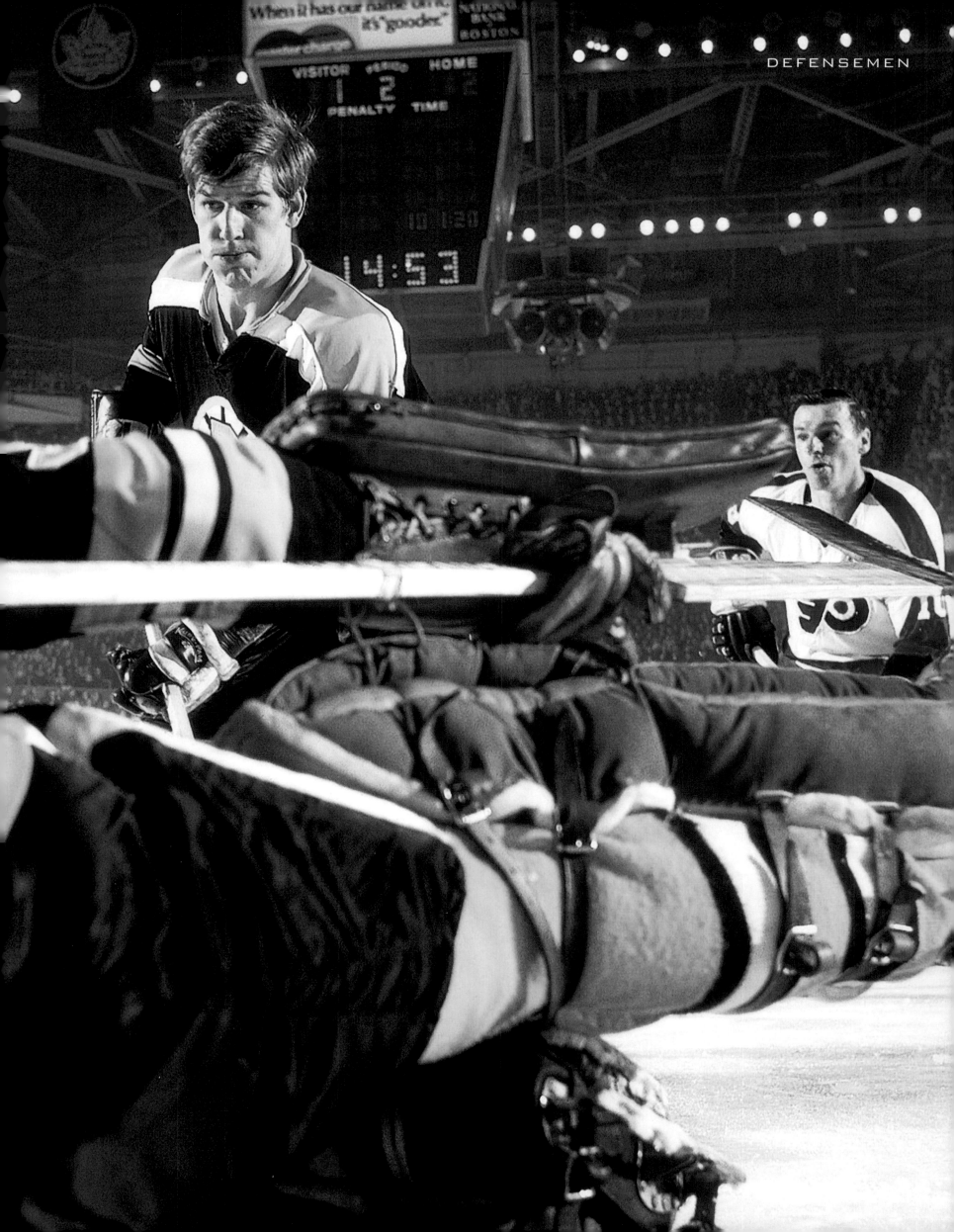

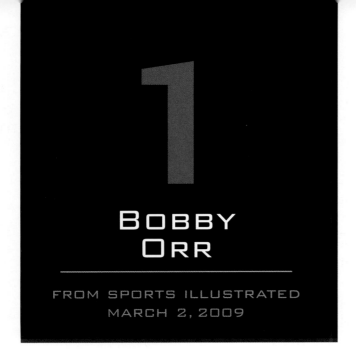

1

BOBBY ORR

FROM SPORTS ILLUSTRATED
MARCH 2, 2009

CALL HIM THE GODFATHER

*More than just a transformative player, Bruins great
Bobby Orr provided hockey nation with an example of
how to handle yourself, both on the ice and off*

BY S.L. PRICE

E RAN A TIGHT ROOM," former Bruins center Derek Sanderson likes to say about the man who helped saved his life, but that doesn't do the matter near enough justice—not with Bobby Orr's first Boston coach, Harry Sinden, calling him the Godfather and his last, Don Cherry, relating how teammates shortened it over the decade that Orr played a kind of hockey no one had ever seen. "God here yet?" the other Bruins would say, or "Where was God last night?" But not to Orr's face. Not once.

God came to Boston in 1966, 18 years old, and within two seasons the once-pathetic Bruins had been transformed into a spectacular, mean, winning bunch. Some of that was due to the '67 trade that brought in scoring machine Phil Esposito and forwards Ken Hodge and Fred Stanfield, but it was Orr, the working-class product of Parry Sound, Ont., who set the tone. His on-ice artistry—coupled with a willingness to hurl that 6-foot frame in front of any slap shot, into any opponent—endowed him with ultimate authority. He barely had to say a word.

Game days, Orr would arrive at 2:30 for a 7:30 start, play cards, bang around the emptiness, sort through the 144 sticks sent him every few weeks—weighing them, selecting two, maybe three, discarding the rest—getting himself ready. His teammates would file in at five or six o'clock. He'd wander about then with one stick weighted with lead or with pucks taped to the blade, shifting it from hand to hand. Locker room music rarely played. "I have never run into any player who brings

the intensity that he brought," says Sinden, who spent 45 years as a coach or front office executive. "His silence, his looks, were enough to tell you if he didn't like what was happening. And he made the rest of us the same way. You could not be around him without feeling that and getting in line."

If you had a bad period? Or dogged it? Sanderson's locker was by a pillar, and he'd set his chair so the pillar would block Orr's view from across the room. "Is he looking?" Esposito would whisper. Always, Orr would be staring lasers. Sanderson only felt worse when Orr would wait until he was alone, come over and mutter, "You got to pick it up. We need you."

Then Orr would hit the ice again, and it was wondrous to see—for the fans, yes, but even opponents found themselves entranced. During one penalty kill against the old Seals in Oakland, Orr swooped behind goal in possession, tussled with an opponent and lost a glove. "He went around by the blue line, came back, picked up his glove—still had the puck," Esposito says. "[Goalie] Gerry Cheevers was on the bench, and I'm standing there and I hear Cheesy say to me, 'Espo, you want *The Racing Form*?' I said, 'Might as well; I'm not touching the puck!' Bobby killed about a minute and 10, 20 seconds of that penalty—and then. . . " with even the Oakland players cheering now, ". . . he scored. Greatest thing I ever saw."

In 1969–70 Orr became the only player to sweep the league's top awards—MVP, defenseman, playoff MVP and scoring title—and capped it off by scoring the Stanley Cup–winning goal over St. Louis in overtime. The following season, the Bruins scored 124 more even-strength or shorthanded goals than they gave up when Orr was on the ice, and that remains his most lasting monument; the man most mentioned as Orr's rival for the title of greatest ever, Wayne Gretzky, never cracked +100.

Yet Orr bristled at the attentions of superstardom, would tell coaches to find reasons to bawl him out like the rest. His last good season, 1974–75, he scored 46 goals but probably gave away a half dozen more by insisting that teammates had deflected the puck in. It's no accident that his signature play—and the one that won the first of his two Stanley Cups, against the Blues—was a give-and-go. Orr's best rushes were never look-at-me affairs but a storm he brewed on one end of the ice, gathering in his fellow Bruins for the inexorable sweep forward. When he began to move, says former Montreal goalie Ken Dryden, the sensation was unique: All the Canadiens began backpedaling in a small panic, like beachgoers sighting a coming monster wave.

"Guys make fun of me because I'm always talking about him," says Cherry, whose second life as a hockey broadcaster gives him plenty of opportunity. "My son made [an Orr highlight] tape to Carly Simon—"Nobody Does It Better"—and I cry every time I see it. I don't know why."

It's no mystery. Orr did it all: blocked shots, dealt out punishing blows, endured the swooping hits of players desperate to stop him, somehow. When it came time to defend a teammate or himself, he fought. Gladly. "Too much," Esposito says. "He didn't have to, but he had a temper."

The fact is, despite his schoolboy haircut and shy grin, Orr was a killer on the ice. He laid out the Blackhawks' Stan Mikita with a perfect forearm cheap shot, hammered the hell out of Mikita's teammate Keith Magnuson at every opportunity, waited a year to get his revenge on Toronto's Pat Quinn—Orr jumped him in a brawl—after Quinn knocked him unconscious with a riot-sparking hit in the 1969 playoffs.

A game-changing talent, a taste for blood: Those were enough to make Orr a hockey hero for life. But vulnerability is what makes him resonate still. A recent TV ad shows Orr sitting silently while a lengthening scar on his famous left knee serves as a time line of victory, and loss; he played, really, only eight full seasons, and operations on both knees left him a near cripple at 30. His last hurrah, the 1976 Canada Cup series, provided the perfect, bittersweet coda: Orr in so much pain that he couldn't practice, beating the Russians on one leg, outplaying the Czechs single-handedly, "the most courageous that I've ever seen a hockey player," says Bobby Clarke, the captain. Hockey nation didn't disagree.

Orr's loyalty to the faithful is just as fierce. If he has refused to donate signed pictures or gear to a desperate fan, or refused a charity golf tournament or hospital visit, no one has heard of it. In 2006 a story ran in *The Boston Globe* about a high school hockey player, Bill Langan, who played in a regional title game on the day of his mother's wake; the kid mentioned that his mother used to watch Orr play. Orr called, asked if he could help. Langan asked him to come to a team dinner. Orr made no promises. But he showed up without warning and stayed an hour.

As for the big, bad—and now old—Bruins, Orr is, Sinden says, "still the Godfather." When the flamboyant and reckless Sanderson showed up in Chicago in the winter of '78 stoned and unable even to hold a

cup of coffee steady, Orr personally checked him into a hospital and was there when Sanderson woke up with three doctors staring at him. "Who's going to tell him?" one said.

"I'll tell him," Orr said and then leveled with Sanderson: "You're a full-blown alcoholic and a drug addict. It's over. You've got to go to rehab." Orr paid for that first stint. When Sanderson relapsed, he says, Orr paid to send him back. And then again. "He never left me," Sanderson says.

When Sanderson finally cleaned up, and began a new life as a financial adviser for athletes in the 1990s, Orr invested with him, gave Sanderson the chance to work with Orr's clients too.

In January, Orr returned to Oshawa, where he played as a junior, to coach against Cherry in the 2009 Top Prospects Game, the annual showcase for top junior talent.

On the morning of this year's game Orr and his team of prospects posed for the traditional team photo. Afterward, the coaches and players scattered to the locker room, leaving their chairs and platforms and mess behind. Orr didn't say a word. He grabbed two chairs and skated them off the ice. Then he went back for a riser, bent over, and shoved it slowly to one end of the empty rink: wrong door. He wheeled and shoved it the length of the ice again, leaving it at the right one so the arena crew would have a bit less work.

The players returned after a few minutes and began circling the ice counterclockwise. Orr joined in, dipping into the flow and skating hard again, reversing time if only for a few laps. Orr gathered up a puck and wristed it low into the empty goal, making the net shiver. He stopped, began feeding all the young men as they swooped past, clockwise now: Foligno, Holland, de Haan, Tavares, O'Reilly. He tapped gloves with one, cracked a joke with another. Now Eakin, McNabb, Roussel flashed past, and now Schenn, and Orr motioned with his stick, and Schenn passed back the puck, maybe three inches wide. "Hey!" Orr snapped, and banged his stick on the ice to say, right here, and Schenn got closer with the next one. Orr gave him a grin.

He came off the ice later, and the press gathered and someone asked if he remembered what it felt like to be that young. He spoke about playing as a kid, outdoors mostly, shooting through the fierce cold on the Seguin River, on Georgian Bay, scrapping on icy parking lots. "No coaches, no parents," he said. "Get the puck and just go.

"It was never a job for me. Even during my pro days, it was never, ever a job. That's what these kids have to understand: Just enjoy it, keep that love and passion for the game. I think what sometimes we do—we, the pressures, the coaches and parents—we just suck that love and passion from our kids. And I think that's wrong."

He and Cherry had a bet on the game, $100. That night Orr's side won 6–1, and Cherry gave it up at the handshake. "Money goes to money, you see that?" he said.

And then Orr raised the bill over his head and waved it in triumph. Thousands roared. Thousands laughed. Their Bobby was back, no limp, and eyes shining. It felt perfect, the way any church does when the ceremony goes off without a hitch and the light streams just so. ∎

He had a boyish smile, but Orr was as tough as they came.

2

NICKLAS
LIDSTROM

RED WINGS 1991–2012

Lidstrom captained Detroit for his final six seasons.

PHOTOGRAPH BY DAVID E. KLUTHO

"Dubbed the Perfect Human for his smooth and seemingly flawless game. Nicklas Lidstrom got to the right places at the right times, a recipe for seven Norris Trophies and four Stanley Cups." —KOSTYA KENNEDY

▸ 11-TIME ALL-STAR
▸ 2002 CONN SMYTHE TROPHY WINNER

THE RED WINGS' fourth Cup in 11 years would validate their claim to being the dominant NHL team of their era. But most important, a Detroit victory would dispel the hoary notion that a European-born-and-trained player—in this case, Lidstrom, a Swede—could not captain a Stanley Cup champion: the old myth and the C.

—Michael Farber, SI, June 9, 2008

3

DOUG HARVEY

CANADIENS 1947–1961
RANGERS 1961–1964
TWO OTHER TEAMS

"A few months before he died, I asked Tom Johnson, Harvey's defense partner in Montreal and later Bobby Orr's coach in Boston, how much better Orr was than Harvey. Johnson replied, 'I didn't say that.' Harvey wasn't quite Orr, but without Harvey, who dictated play from the back, there might not have been an Orr." —MICHAEL FARBER

▸ SEVEN-TIME NORRIS TROPHY WINNER
▸ 11-TIME ALL-STAR

"HARVEY'S THE best I've ever seen," says coach Hector (Toe) Blake, the Old Lamplighter of the Canadiens' famous Punch Line. "The biggest single asset a defenseman can have is ability to anticipate plays. In that Harvey is in a class by himself. Besides that, he can do everything else well—bodycheck, skate, stickhandle, shoot, get the puck out of our zone, set up plays." "A measure of Harvey's greatness," says Canadiens vice president Kenny Reardon, "is that he can break the rules now and then and get away with it. A defenseman is not supposed to carry the puck across the ice in front of the goal in his own zone. Harvey just glides along in there from time to time as if he's daring someone to try to take the puck."

—Kenneth Rudeen, SI, February 17, 1958

As a youth Harvey also excelled at baseball and football.

PHOTOGRAPH BY BRUCE BENNETT STUDIOS/GETTY IMAGES

4

RAY BOURQUE

" Few hockey moments won as much universal joy as the night Ray Bourque, a 21-year veteran with Boston, lifted the Stanley Cup on the final night of his NHL career, a season after he was traded to Colorado. " —BRIAN CAZENEUVE

▸ FIVE-TIME NORRIS TROPHY WINNER
▸ 19-TIME ALL-STAR

SAYS DEFENSEMAN Mike Milbury, "When Bourque was named co-captain (in 1985) he took the role to heart. He has become a leader. I asked him what he wanted to do after he was out of hockey, and he said he was thinking of working for the Department of Public Works. I think Ray just wants to be together with a group of other guys."

—*Franz Lidz, SI, March 9, 1987*

Bourque showed rare consistency and longevity.
PHOTOGRAPH BY PAUL BERESWILL/HOCKEY HALL OF FAME

The expansion Islanders matured quickly with Potvin.

PHOTOGRAPH BY TONY TRIOLO

5

DENIS POTVIN

ISLANDERS 1973–1988

" He was robust, physical, a tremendous leader and a four-time Stanley Cup champion. More than any statistical accomplishment, what will always stand out is how amazingly fierce a competitor he was. " —PIERRE MCGUIRE

▸ THREE-TIME NORRIS TROPHY WINNER
▸ FIRST DEFENSEMAN TO SCORE 1,000 CAREER POINTS

BILL TORREY knew that Potvin would do for the Islanders what Orr had done for the Bruins. That is, the GM knew Potvin someday would wipe the smirks from the faces of all those people who had ridiculed the Islanders, particularly those smug Rangers. What Torrey didn't know was that Potvin would do it so quickly.

—Mark Mulvoy, SI, March 31, 1975

6

LARRY ROBINSON

CANADIENS 1972–1989
KINGS 1989–1992

"At 6' 4", 225 pounds, 'Big Bird' blended size and agility like no one else in his era. Always defensively responsible, he was never a minus player, and holds the NHL career record in that category at +730." —SARAH KWAK

▸ TWO-TIME NORRIS TROPHY WINNER
▸ 1978 CONN SMYTHE TROPHY WINNER

ROBINSON PERSONALLY signaled the Canadiens' revival during the early moments of Game 5 at the Forum. He rattled two Bruins into the boards with hard bodychecks, and when some combative Bostonians tried to get at Guy Lafleur after he had hit one of them illegally with the butt end of his stick, Robinson rushed to the scene and put an end to all overt threats. Robinson fought regularly during his first few seasons with the Canadiens in the early 1970s, but he has not been challenged since one night two seasons ago when he came out of the dressing room with his skates untied and half-falling off and outpunched Philadelphia's Dave (Hammer) Schultz, then the NHL's heavyweight champion. "I don't want to fight and hit all the time," Robinson says. "If I do, I'll end up being only 4' 8"."

—*Mark Mulvoy, SI, June 5, 1978*

The Big Bird was a skilled puckhandler.

PHOTOGRAPH BY CRAIG MOLENHOUSE

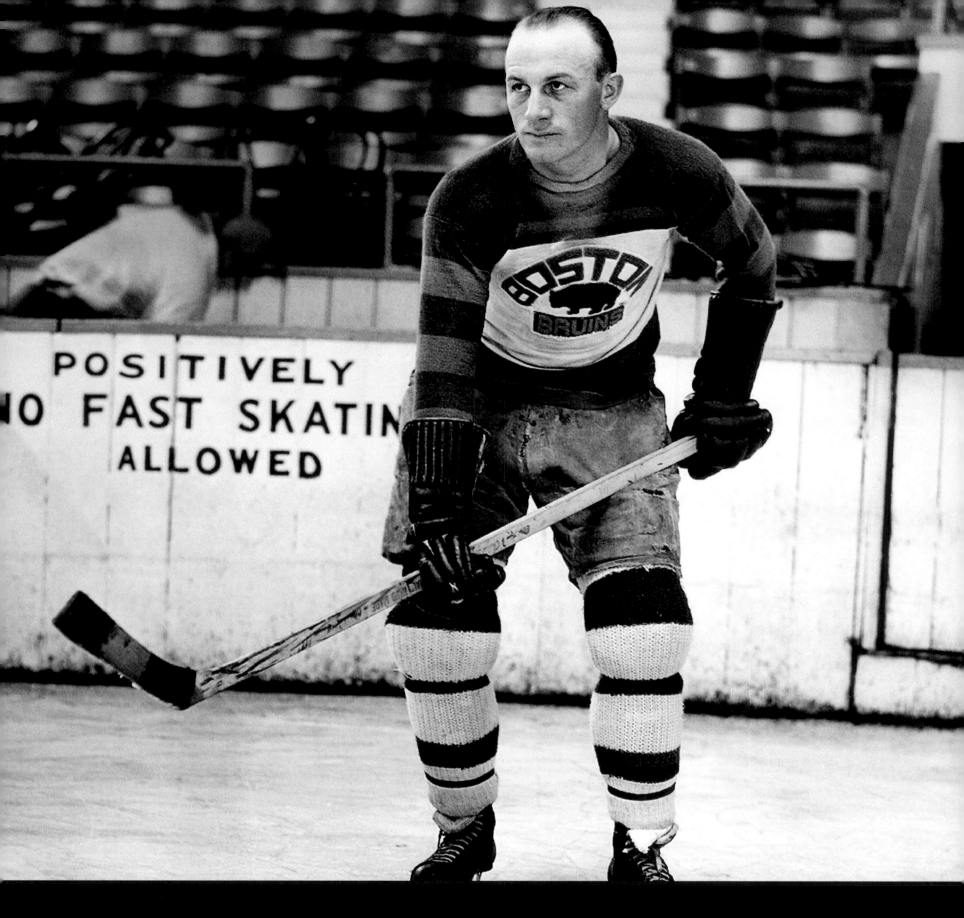

BRUINS 1926–1940
AMERICANS 1940

"The Edmonton Express was hockey's first great offensive defenseman. Shore was tough too, once refusing anesthetic when his ear had to be sewn back on—and watching the operation with a mirror." —MARK BEECH

► FOUR-TIME HART TROPHY WINNER
► EIGHT-TIME ALL-STAR

SHORE BROUGHT to the NHL a brand of rough and tumble that never has been equaled. He antagonized fans, fought opponents and stirred more controversy than any other man in the game. Opponents often teamed to cream him, owners sought to outlaw him and fans came to curse him. But when Shore played, the crowds came.

—Stan Fischler, SI, March 13, 1967

EDDIE SHORE

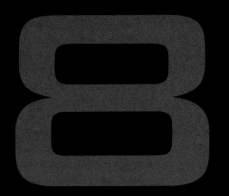

8

CSKA MOSCOW 1977–1989
DEVILS 1989–1995
RED WINGS 1995–1998

" He was, simply, the king of Soviet defenseman. When he entered the NHL with the first wave of Russians, he led Detroit to two Cups. " —E.M. SWIFT

SLAVA FETISOV

▸ CAPTAINED SOVIET NATIONAL TEAM
▸ SEVEN-TIME WORLD CHAMPION

"I HAVE so much respect for Slava," says former teammate Brendan Shanahan. "If he'd fought every guy who threw an extra elbow at him [in 1989], he would've been fighting every shift. For Russians, he was the Jackie Robinson of hockey. He opened doors. He took all the cheap shots and played with a smile on his face."

—*Michael Farber, SI, February 28, 2000*

Fetisov wrestled with Dallas's Pat Verbeek.
PHOTOGRAPH BY DAVID E. KLUTHO

Coffey's speed was an asset at both ends.

PHOTOGRAPH BY JERRY WACHTER

9

PAUL COFFEY

OILERS 1980–1987
PENGUINS 1987–1992
RED WINGS 1993–1996
SIX OTHER TEAMS

" Even his name suggests the caffeinated speed he showed off nightly. A savvy playmaker, he set the paradigm for offensive defensemen. " —SARAH KWAK

▸ THREE-TIME NORRIS TROPHY WINNER
▸ 14-TIME ALL-STAR

COFFEY'S 12 playoff goals were magnificent: blasts from the point, tap-ins from the crease, breakaways off feeds from Gretzky. Ted Green, a former Bruin and Oilers assistant coach, says "We leaned on Coffey the way the Bruins used to lean on Bobby Orr. No one could have risen to the occasion better. Not even 'himself.' "

—E.M. Swift, SI, October 14, 1985

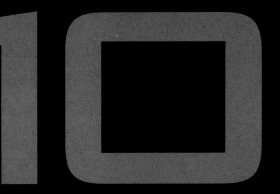

10

CHRIS CHELIOS

CANADIENS 1983–1990
BLACKHAWKS 1990–1999
RED WINGS 1999–2009
THRASHERS 2009–2010

“ The skilled but irreverent backliner treated rules as optional and never met a foe he wouldn't spear, slash or cross-check. ” —BRIAN CAZENEUVE

▸THREE-TIME NORRIS TROPHY WINNER
▸ 11-TIME ALL-STAR

"AFTER SUFFERING a ruptured spleen in 2001, Peter Forsberg of the Avalanche almost underwent emergency surgery again in Game 1 of the Western Conference finals, this one performed by Chris Chelios, M.D.—Mesozoic Defenseman. When Forsberg yanked his feet out from under him as Detroit celebrated a Brett Hull goal, Dr. Chelios steeled himself to remove a few more of Forsberg's internal organs. Say this for Chelios: He's so old school, he makes house calls. As Forsberg skated to the Avalanche bench, Chelios caught up with him and prepared to use his lumber to make an incision in Forsberg's gut. Before he could do so, a vigilant linesman interceded. Chelios later offered little comment about going *ER* on Forsberg, although eventually he did say, "Ah, I do what I want." Marcus Welby, he's not.

—*Michael Farber, SI, May 27, 2002*

Chelios made the playoffs 24 times in 26 seasons.

10

THE

BEST GOALTENDERS

IN 1997 E.M. SWIFT EXAMINED THE QUESTION OF WHY GOALIES HAD BECOME SO DOMINANT. SHUTOUTS WERE UP, SAVE PERCENTAGES WERE SKY-HIGH, AND VETERAN GOALTENDERS WERE HAVING CAREER YEARS. NO ONE HAD A DEFINITIVE EXPLANATION, BUT REASONS OFFERED INCLUDED: POORER OFFENSES, THE ADVENT OF GOALIE COACHES AND BETTER EXERCISE REGIMENS.

GLENN HALL, AN ALLTIME GREAT, THEORIZED THAT IT WAS ALL ABOUT IMPROVEMENTS TO THE GOALIE'S MASK. WITH EARLIER VERSIONS OF THE MASK, GOALIES COULD STILL SUFFER CAREER-ENDING EYE INJURIES. BUT BY THE MID-90S MASKS WERE BUILT MORE SOLIDLY, SO GOALIES NO LONGER HAD TO STRIKE A BALANCE BETWEEN EFFECTIVENESS AND PERSONAL SAFETY. "WITH THE MASKS THEY'RE USING NOW," HALL SAID, "GOALTENDING HAS GONE FROM ONE OF THE MOST DANGEROUS POSITIONS IN SPORTS, TO THE LEAST DANGEROUS POSITION IN HOCKEY."

ANOTHER POSSIBILITY WAS THAT THE MID-'90S SIMPLY ENJOYED A HISTORIC SURGE IN TALENT, AS HAPPENED IN THE ORIGINAL GOLDEN AGE OF GOALTENDING IN THE LATE '50S AND EARLY '60S. THAT THEORY MERITS CONSIDERATION, AS EACH OF THIS BOOK'S TOP FIVE GOALIES, AND SEVEN OVERALL IN THE TOP 10, COME FROM ONE ERA OR THE OTHER. BROADER TRENDS MATTER, BUT EXCEPTIONAL INDIVIDUALS HAVE BEEN KNOWN TO ALTER HISTORY AS WELL.

1

PATRICK ROY

CANADIENS 1984–1995
AVALANCHE 1995–2003

"He won 551 regular-season games and reached the playoffs 17 times in 18 years. In the postseason he immortalized himself. Yes, Saint Patrick was hot at times—tempestuous—but also exquisitely cool." —KOSTYA KENNEDY

- THREE-TIME CONN SMYTHE TROPHY WINNER
- THREE-TIME VEZINA TROPHY WINNER

ROY REDEFINED the position. He conquered the game with his pioneering butterfly style, but he also helped change the equipment by working with Koho, which manufactures his pads, to make them lighter. Any goalie who drops to his knees to cover the bottom of the net wearing six-pound leg pads rather than the old nine-pounders should genuflect to Roy. Even though he was not the original butterfly goalie, Roy made it the standard. The stand-up netminder and the reflex goalie are as anachronistic as a slide rule. Roy stands square to the shooters, playing the percentages by taking away shots along the ice and forcing them to beat him top shelf. Roy has taken goaltending from the realm of artistry to that of science. He is, in that sense, the first modern goalie.

—*Michael Farber, SI, April 8, 2002*

Roy has the second-most wins in NHL history.

PHOTOGRAPH BY DAVID E. KLUTHO

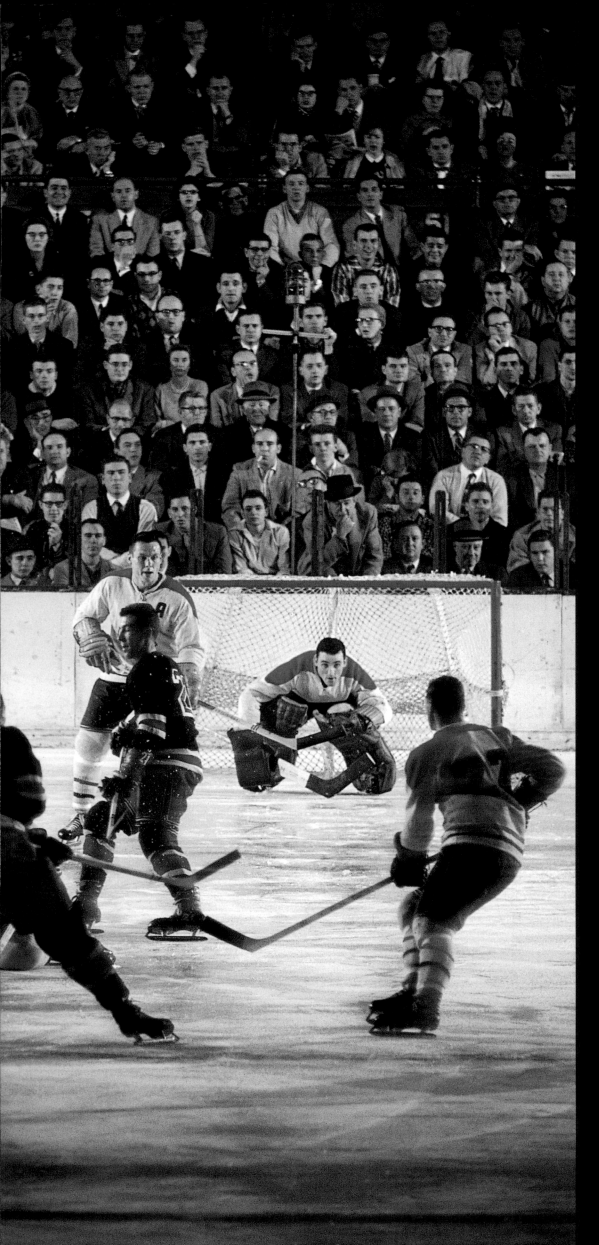

JACQUES PLANTE

" He is best remembered for his iconic protective mask, which changed the face of the game forever, but his play was also transformative. He was the first NHL goalie to venture outside his crease to handle the puck on a regular basis. " —MARK BEECH

‣ SEVEN-TIME VEZINA
TROPHY WINNER
‣ 437 CAREER VICTORIES

PLANTE HAD more than talent. He had genius. He shattered what for decades had been the first commandment of goaltending— thou shalt not bother a puck that is not bothering you. Goalies were supposed to wait for trouble, then try to deal with it as best they could. Thanks to Plante, goalies today can stop trouble before it happens. But, as with most innovations, it was not always well-received. "Réveille-toi! Wake up!" the Montreal crowd would yell at him on those rare occasions when his wanderings would result in a goal against. In 1960, when a cranky knee led to an early-season slump, Plante was booed by Forum fans. "After seven years all they see are my saves . . . not my work," he said. "I play pro hockey; I know what it is like. Most of them, they played school hockey. What do they know?"

—*Jack Falla, SI, November 17, 1986*

Plante, uncovered here, didn't don a mask until 1959.

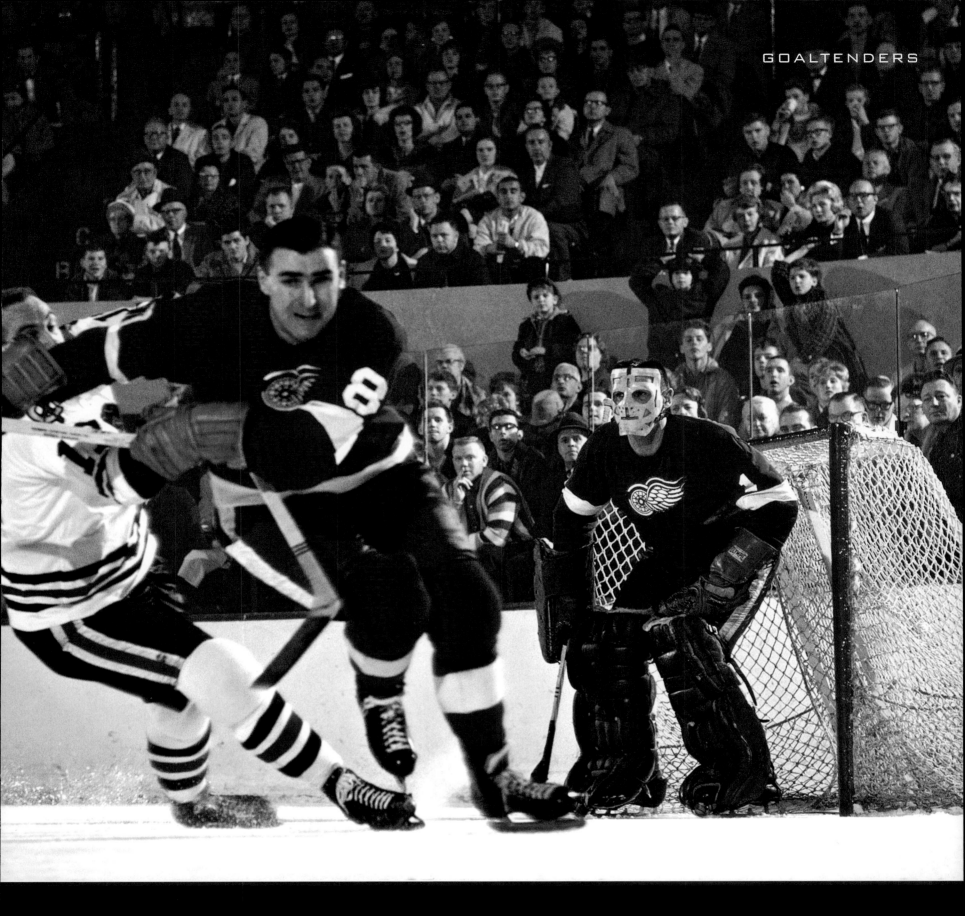

The intense Sawchuk won four Vezina trophies.

PHOTOGRAPH BY JOHN G. ZIMMERMAN

3

RED WINGS 1949–1955,
1957–1964, 1968–1969
FOUR TEAMS THROUGH 1970

" Sawchuk played through severed
tendons in his hand, ruptured disks in
his back and a collapsed lung, yet he won
four Stanley Cups and retired as the
NHL's career leader in both wins and
shutouts. " —BRIAN CAZENEUVE

▸ 447 CAREER VICTORIES
▸ 103 CAREER SHUTOUTS

SAWCHUK IS a marvelous
goaltender to behold. He exhibits
a special pride which makes him
a hated figure in many cities but a
hero in Detroit: He guards his net
not merely as an object four feet
high and six feet wide, but as if it
were a precious tapestry that only
he could protect.

—William Leggett, SI, January 18, 1960

TERRY
SAWCHUK

DEVILS 1991–2014
BLUES 2014–2015

4

"If he had played more outside of the swamps of New Jersey, where he backstopped a boring but effective defensive team, his legacy would reach mythical proportions." —SARAH KWAK

"HOCKEY ISN'T just a job for Martin," Devils coach Jacques Lemaire says. "It's his toy." He can be found outdoors sometimes, playing forward in street hockey games in St. Liboire during the off-season. Hardly a day goes by without a neighbor's child ringing the doorbell to ask, 'Can Martin come out and play?' "

—*Michael Farber, SI, October 6, 1997*

MARTIN BRODEUR

▸ NHL RECORD 691 CAREER VICTORIES
▸ FOUR-TIME VEZINA TROPHY WINNER

THE CALM TOPS THE STORM

The best goalies tend to be anxious sorts, which makes it all the more remarkable that Martin Brodeur rode a personal wave of serenity straight to the alltime wins record

BY MICHAEL FARBER

WHETHER FACING 90-MPH shots attracts or creates lunatics is a chicken-and-egg question, but the top goalies of the past six decades certainly are a rogue's gallery of the maladjusted, a list as suited to *Psychology Today* as to *The Hockey News*. Jacques Plante, a seven-time Vezina Trophy winner and the backbone of the Canadiens' 1950s dynasty, was a fretful man who liked to knit. It could never really be Happy Hour when Red Wings goalie Terry Sawchuk, who died in '70 at age 40 from complications sustained in an alcohol-fueled fight with a teammate, walked into a bar. The tempestuous Patrick Roy, who has a league-record 151 playoff wins, famously asked the Canadiens' president during a '95 game to trade him, was shipped to Colorado four days later and three years after that smashed TVs and a video machine in a coach's office after being yanked from a tie game and missing out on a win. The inscrutable Dominik Hasek, a two-time league MVP with Buffalo, barely knew some of his teammates' names, and Ed Belfour, third in career wins, had such obsessive prepractice routines that the Stars had to move their practice schedule back by 30 minutes to accommodate him.

Then there is the goalie perhaps destined to go down as the Greatest of All-Time. Three shy of Roy's mark of 551 regular-season wins and three shutouts behind Sawchuk's record of 103, the Devils' Martin Brodeur, now in his 16th NHL season, is surely the most balanced of the men who rank among the elite. He appears more than, in hockey's favorite phrase, "normal . . . for a goalie." He actually seems normal for almost anybody.

"There's Marty after the second period, having his Sprite and half a bagel, working on a shutout, and he's talking and joking with the guys in the room," says Oilers defenseman Sheldon Souray, a former New Jersey teammate. "Then he'll go out and stop 10 shots in the third. There's just this calmness about him. Maybe it's because he still thinks of hockey as a game."

The renewed appreciation of Brodeur, who, incidentally, has kicked a habit of drinking soda between periods and is in the best physical condition of his life, comes less than six years after the elegies surrounding Roy's retirement anointed him as the greatest. The blink of an eye in which Roy ruled the top of the goaltending world is indecent given his playoff successes and his role in establishing the modern norm—the butterfly—for the position. But as Devils president Lou Lamoriello says, "Greatest is a very difficult word. Tomorrow comes along awfully quick."

Despite all his shutouts, Brodeur says he never wakes up thinking he has to blank an opponent that night, just beat it. Roy's victory record is a brighter beacon because, as Brodeur says, "when you win, everybody's happy." He is guarded enough not to add that he also especially wants this record because it belongs to Roy.

Brodeur could have a chance to tie Roy's mark—and certainly to move to the precipice of it—in Montreal, Brodeur's hometown and St. Patrick's domain for two of his four Stanley Cups. Says New Jersey captain Jamie Langenbrunner, "A little ironic." With Roy's freshly retired number 33 jersey hanging above him, Brodeur might add another episode in the soap-operatic psychodrama between these goaltending titans.

"A rivalry between two French guys," one former NHL goalie says of the relationship between Brodeur and Roy, and while that assessment contains an element of truth, it barely hints at the complexity. To posit that they dislike each other is no more illuminating because they really don't, at least not in an easily digestible Carolina-Duke kind of way. "My relationship with Patrick is good," Brodeur says. "If we see each other anywhere, we'll take the time to go out of our way to say hi. But I don't have his number and he doesn't have mine."

Textbook Case A in the Brodeur-Roy Passive-Aggressive Handbook: When Roy was asked after his 2003 retirement to name the next great goalies, he mentioned Anaheim's Jean-Sébastien Giguère and Florida's Roberto Luongo but not Brodeur. "The reason," Roy says now, "is I thought Marty was already there." Brodeur claims not to recall the incident, but a former Devils teammate insists the goalie was stung by the perceived slight.

Textbook Case B: Brodeur never hesitates to express his disdain for the butterfly, a percentage-based technique that allows a splay-legged goalie to cover the lower part of the net. Brodeur is the antibutterflyer, tracking the puck and standing up, dropping to one knee or even stacking his pads to stop it, an amalgam so old-fashioned that Devils TV commentator Glenn Resch, a former Stanley Cup–winning goalie, likens it to a tennis player winning a Grand Slam with a wooden racket. Of course, whenever Brodeur, who as a teenager bolted the goalie school run by Roy's guru, goaltending instructor François Allaire, dismisses the butterfly style, he is also prodding its progenitor, Roy. "Actually Marty butterflies more than he lets on," says New Jersey backup Kevin Weekes. "We laugh about it. At a stoppage or when we come in the [dressing] room, I'll say, 'Nice butterfly.' He'll kinda giggle and say, 'You saw that? It wasn't really a full butterfly.'"

Roy and Brodeur—or should it be Brodeur and Roy?—will converge at 551, possibly in the wintry city so important to them. If the record is not matched then, it will be soon. And then Brodeur will wave goodbye, taking goaltending numbers to places over the horizon. ∎

5

DOMINIK HASEK

BLACKHAWKS 1990–1992
SABRES 1992–2001
RED WINGS 2001–2004, 2006–2008
SENATORS 2004–2006

" Pardon the cliché, but Hasek never actually stood on his head. The Gumby-like goalie, however, did snow angel, barrel roll, intentionally drop his stick and head-butt pucks. There never has been a more unconventional goaltender or, if all were measured at the top of their games, a better one. " —MICHAEL FARBER

▸ SIX-TIME VEZINA TROPHY WINNER
▸ TWO-TIME HART TROPHY WINNER

HASEK'S STAND in the shootout against Canada, in which he stopped all five shots, galvanized his homeland. When the shootout began, Hasek's mother, Marie, was sitting in front of the TV in the family's second-floor apartment [in the Czech Republic]. She became so anxious that she left the flat and started walking the stairs. "All I heard were people screaming from the other apartments" Marie says. Then her daughter came bursting out the door: "Mom, come back! We won!" When Hasek's mother left her building later that day, Marie found a sign stuck to the front door: HASEK NENI CLOVEK, HASEK JE BUH! (Hasek is not a human being, Hasek is God!)

—*William Nack, SI, August 10, 1998*

The Dominator had 81 career shutouts.

6

KEN DRYDEN

CANADIENS 1971–1973,
1974–1979

❝ His career was short but few have been so brilliant. Dryden won a Stanley Cup, a Calder and a Vezina. Cerebral both on the ice and off of it, he went on to serve in Canada's House of Parliament. ❞ —KOSTYA KENNEDY

▸ FIVE-TIME VEZINA TROPHY
WINNER
▸ WON CONN SMYTHE TROPHY
BEFORE HE WON THE CALDER

AT DINNER in Montreal's Café Martin, Dryden wanted to talk shop with Rohmann, the maître d'. He wanted to know all about the beef, the lobster bisque, the profit per plate, the freezer facilities, the help. How are serving sizes decided? Dryden's restless mind never stops probing, even when he is on the ice. Some nights, particularly when the Canadiens are playing one of those expansion teams that seem to shoot marshmallows instead of pucks, Dryden has plenty of time to case the arena. "I look at the scoreboard, read the message board, everything," he says. Afterward he briefs his teammates and the press on the outcomes of the other games. "Detroit tied Los Angeles on Dionne's goal in the late minutes of the game," he reported to one and all the other night. "The Wings were down 4–2 before they rallied."

—*Mark Mulvoy, SI, February 14, 1972*

Dryden had a career 2.24 goals-against average.

PHOTOGRAPH BY MANNY MILLAN

7

GLENN HALL

RED WINGS 1952–1953,
1954–1957
BLACKHAWKS 1957–1967
BLUES 1967–1971

❝ "Mr. Goalie" started 502 consecutive complete games, a record that will surely never be touched. ❞ —PIERRE MCGUIRE

▸ THREE-TIME VEZINA TROPHY WINNER
▸ 1968 CONN SMYTHE WINNER

A PUCK to the face was considered a hazard of the profession, not an excuse to sit out. Once Toronto's Jim Pappin hit Hall with a slap shot that left a 30-stitch gash across both lips and knocked out the only tooth Hall lost in his playing career. "The dentist told me how lucky I was," Hall says. "I said through my swollen lips, 'Ah don' fee' wucky.' "

—*E.M. Swift, SI Classic, October 27, 1992*

Hall was admired by teammates and opponents alike.

PHOTOGRAPH BY TONY TRIOLO

8

VLADISLAV TRETIAK

" He came to prominence in 1972, when at age 20 he nearly stole the historic first series between Canada and the USSR. Big and lightning quick, Tretiak dominated international hockey for a dozen years. " —E.M. SWIFT

▸ THREE OLYMPIC GOLD MEDALS
▸ FIVE-TIME SOVIET LEAGUE MVP

TECHNICALLY, WHAT sets Tretiak apart from other goalies is his skating ability—the single most important facet to goaltending. He flows about the crease seamlessly. "A goalie must be a virtuoso on skates," Tretiak wrote in his autobiography, *The Hockey I Love*. "He does not stand in the crease, he plays in the crease."

—*E.M. Swift, SI, November 14, 1983*

Tretiak averaged 1.78 goals against in international play.

PHOTOGRAPH BY MELCHIOR DIGIACOMO

9

BERNIE PARENT

BRUINS 1965–1967
FLYERS 1967–1971,
1973–1979
TWO OTHER TEAMS

" The Broad Street Bullies might have been consigned to NHL history as the barbarians at hockey's gate if not for the sublime Parent. He had shutouts in two Stanley Cup–clinching Game 6s, earning consecutive Conn Smythe trophies and one Philly bumper sticker: ONLY THE LORD SAVES MORE THAN BERNIE PARENT." —MICHAEL FARBER

- TWO-TIME VEZINA TROPHY WINNER
- TWICE LED LEAGUE IN GOALS-AGAINST AVERAGE

IN HIS SHUTOUT of the Islanders, Parent was a model of the goalie's craft. He rarely left his feet to block a shot, steered rebounds away from the New York attackers hanging around his crease and in all ways performed as if programmed by a computer. "It may look easy," he said afterward, "but it never is." Parent is a package of nerves during a game, but he hides his emotions by wearing his mask from the time he leaves the Flyers' dressing room until he returns. "I don't want people to see what I go through," he says. His only obvious nervous trait is a systematic cleaning away of the loose ice chips in front of his net even when there are no loose ice chips.

—*Mark Mulvoy, SI, April 15, 1974*

An eye injury ended Parent's career at 33.

PHOTOGRAPH BY HEINZ KLUETMEIER

GRANT FUHR

OILERS 1981–1991
FIVE TEAMS 1991–2000

"Say what you will about the good fortune of backstopping the most offensively talented teams in history; Fuhr was an undeniably important part of the Edmonton dynasty of the 1980s. While his team controlled the puck, they also didn't offer much defensive support." —SARAH KWAK

▸ 1998 VEZINA TROPHY WINNER
▸ 403 CAREER VICTORIES

THE PUCK is suddenly on the stick of Barry Pederson, a center for the Vancouver Canucks. Pederson is at the end of a breakaway, streaking toward the goal. Fuhr glides out to meet him, giving Pederson less of the net, more on the glove side. Fuhr has not thought about doing this. There was no time for a plan. He moves on instinct and reflex. Six feet away, Pederson slaps a shot that is traveling more than 90 mph when it finds the pocket in the blur that is Fuhr's glove. The crowd in the Coliseum groans in appreciation of the save.

"Bar none, Grant Fuhr is the best goalie in the league," Pederson will say later. "He has the fastest reflexes. Sometimes his concentration might drift during inconsequential games. But in the big-money games Fuhr is the best. He's the Cup goalie. It's sure not by luck."

—*Ralph Wiley, SI, January 11, 1988*

Fuhr was the first player of color to make the Hall of Fame.

PHOTOGRAPH BY ANTHONY NESTE

10

THE

Best Coaches

AMONG OUR TOP 10 COACHES ARE TWO PAIRS OF MEN WHO SUCCEEDED EACH OTHER WITH A TEAM. THE FIRST INSTANCE IS TOE BLAKE TAKING OVER FOR DICK IRVIN IN MONTREAL, AND THEY ESTABLISHED THE KIND OF CONGO LINE OF VICTORY YOU WOULD EXPECT FROM TWO ALLTIME GREATS. IRVIN'S TEAMS WON THREE STANLEY CUPS, AND BLAKE WON FOLLOWED HIM UP BY WINNING EIGHT MORE.

THE OTHER HANDOFF, LESS PROPITIOUS AND MORE CURIOUS, TOOK PLACE BETWEEN SCOTTY BOWMAN AND AL ARBOUR. THESE MEN WOULD GO ON TO WIN MULTIPLE CHAMPIONSHIPS WITH OTHER CLUBS, BUT THEY BEGAN THEIR COACHING JOURNEYS WITH THE ST. LOUIS BLUES.

BOWMAN WENT FIRST, TAKING OVER FOR THE EXPANSION CLUB WITH ITS INAUGURAL SEASON ALREADY IN PROGRESS. BOWMAN DEMONSTRATED HIS COACHING ABILITIES AS THE BLUES MADE THE FINALS EACH OF HIS FIRST THREE SEASONS. BUT AFTER CONFLICT WITH OWNERSHIP, BOWMAN LEFT TO GO TO MONTREAL AND BEGIN HIS STANLEY CUP COLLECTION. ARBOUR TRIED HIS HAND BEHIND THE BENCH, BUT AFTER PARTS OF TWO SEASONS HE WAS FIRED. HE WAS PICKED UP BY THE ISLANDERS, WHERE HE FOUND A TITLE GROOVE OF HIS OWN. MEANWHILE THE BLUES, WHO SHUCKED THESE TWO ALLTIME GREATS, HAVE YET TO WIN THEIR FIRST CHAMPIONSHIP.

1

SCOTTY BOWMAN

BLUES 1967–1971
CANADIENS 1971–1979
SABRES 1979–1980, 1982–1987
PENGUINS 1991–1993
RED WINGS 1993–2002

" Bowman holds career marks for games won in the regular season and playoffs. Known as the master of the line change, Bowman could outthink almost anyone else behind a bench and was a deft handler of both superstars and role players. " —BRIAN CAZENEUVE

▸ NINE STANLEY CUP TITLES
▸ 13 FINALS APPEARANCES

IN PROCLAIMING Bowman the best coach or manager in North American team sports, ever, we compared not only apples to apples, like Bowman to Toe Blake, but also apples to plums like Bowman to Red Auerbach and Joe McCarthy, and apples to peaches like Bowman to George Halas and Paul Brown. But you must accept two premises: 1) Winning championships with multiple teams as Bowman has is more difficult than winning them with a single franchise as most other storied coaches and managers have done, and 2) Coaching a team has never been more complex or perilous than it is today. The financial stakes are higher. The pressure is greater. The seasons are longer. Winning championships in the modern era is the ultimate tiebreaker.

—*Michael Farber, SI, June 29, 1998*

Bowman won titles with three franchises.

2

TOE BLAKE

" Rare is the great player who becomes a great coach, but the canny Blake was an exception. Wearing his trademark fedora, the former league MVP coached Montreal to eight Stanley Cup titles in 13 years, including five in a row. " —E.M. SWIFT

▸ 500-255-159 CAREER RECORD
▸ NINE FIRST-PLACE FINISHES
  IN REGULAR SEASON

DURING THE GAME Blake's teeth, like jackhammers, forever blast into a chunk of gum and at times, it appears, his lower lip. His head rolls like a cue ball with English on it, and his voice—constantly discharging epithets—is that of a foreman in a stamping mill. High-voltage moments send him bolting up and down in a jagged line but, when confronted with obvious defeat or victory or excruciating blunder, he somnambulantly stumbles about in tight little circles. Right now the thing most troubling Toe Blake, the Captain Bligh of the NHL and everybody's candidate for a long vacation in a nice, quiet country place with high walls around it, is the fact that the experts have once again picked his team to finish in first place. The long run with Blake toward success is never a tranquil trip. "It's the way I am," says Blake. "It's the only way I know how to get there."

—*Mark Kram, SI, November 22, 1965*

Every team Blake coached had a winning record.

PHOTOGRAPH BY HY PESKIN

3

AL ARBOUR

**BLUES 1970–1972
ISLANDERS 1973–1986,
1988–1994**

" Nicknamed "Radar" because, like the character on the TV series *M*A*S*H*, Arbour not only wore glasses, but also seemed to know what would happen before it actually did. " —MARK BEECH

▸ FOUR STANLEY CUP TITLES
▸ 782-577-248 CAREER RECORD

"HE'S A player's coach," says Islanders GM Bill Torrey. "He reveled in playing and enjoys being around players, and they feel that. They also know his basic honesty. Whether they agree with him or not, they know deep down that he's doing what's good for them and for the team."

—E.M. Swift, SI, May 24, 1982

4

IN ADAMS's formula for success there are several other ingredients as important as his indifference toward tradition. One is enthusiasm. After 40 years in top professional hockey, 10 as a star player and the last 30 as Detroit's general manager, Adams still comes up on his toes every time the Wings play.

—*Marshall Dann, SI, March 18, 1957*

" A Hall of Fame player, the boisterous Adams left his greatest mark as a coach. A big personality and a bigger talent, he's the only man to win a Cup as a player, coach and GM. " —KOSTYA KENNEDY

JACK
ADAMS

▸ THREE STANLEY CUP TITLES
▸ 413-390-161 CAREER RECORD

The NHL's coach of the year award bears Adams's name.

PHOTOGRAPH BY AP

Imlach was his teams' GM as well as its coach.

PHOTOGRAPH BY DOUG GRIFFIN/TORONTO STAR/GETTY IMAGES

5

PUNCH IMLACH

MAPLE LEAFS 1958–1969,
1979–1980
SABRES 1970–1972

" He was feared by his players, but he sure knew how to get their attention. Toronto was a very important market for the NHL, and Imlach did tremendously well there. " —PIERRE MCGUIRE

▸ FOUR STANLEY CUP TITLES
▸ 402-337-150 CAREER RECORD

"I BELIEVE you can do anything you want to do," growled supersalesman Imlach, his blue eyes glinting. "You can't just sit back and say you're losing because of circumstances. When I came here the team was down, and I said, 'The hell with it. I don't like these circumstances. Let's make new ones.'"

—Kenneth Rudeen, SI, March 13, 1961

THE DRIVE TO SUCCEED

No coach demanded more of his players than the ornery Punch Imlach, who made his teams put in the work it took to win whether they liked it or not

BY PETE AXTHELM

EVERY MAN REACTS A LITTLE BIT differently to the grim routine of a Toronto Maple Leafs hockey practice. The older ones skate evenly, lips pressed tightly together and eyes fixed on the ice. The younger ones may yell at one another or curse quietly at no one in particular as they gather the energy for another rush across the rink. George (Punch) Imlach, the bald, 48-year-old coach, stands near the blue line, in the middle of the action, with one hand in his pocket and the other holding a whistle. His crisp voice echoes through the empty Maple Leaf Gardens, goading his players to work longer and harder than any others in the National Hockey League. "That's it," he yells when a few men battle unusually hard for a loose puck. "I want you guys to get mad."

And many of the Maple Leafs do get mad—at each other, at the teams they are preparing to face and, often, at their coach. Few Toronto players will tell you that they like Punch Imlach. They say they "respect him" or "understand him" or "get used to him." Some have even said that they disliked him and thought he was hurting the club—but the ones who said those things in public are no longer playing hockey in Toronto. Those who remain have learned to keep quiet and concentrate on hockey. And in the seven years since the energetic, intense Imlach took over a last-place team in midseason and drove it into the Stanley Cup finals, his players have done well enough to make him one of the game's most successful men.

That is all Imlach demands. "I don't give a damn if each player likes me personally, as long as he's loyal to the club and does his best," he says. "In fact I try to avoid getting too close to the players. After all, I'm the general manager, so I've got to talk salary with them, too."

Imlach's history of tough and intransigent salary negotiations has made it very clear that he is not worried about being liked. Bobby Baun played on a broken leg to help the Leafs win the final game of the playoffs two years ago; a year later Imlach refused to grant his salary demands and Baun was a bitter holdout. Eddie Shack, an eight-year major leaguer, scored 26 goals last season while earning a modest $13,500. This past summer he wheedled a $5,000 increase out of Punch—and Imlach took the first opportunity he found to order Shack to the Leafs' Rochester farm club for the training season.

Imlach's feats in the 1958–59 season are legendary in Toronto. He came to the floundering club as general manager, and fired its coach within a month. Taking over himself, he immediately began claiming that his last-place team would make the playoffs. With a furious drive in the last two weeks of the season, the Leafs did—and then went on to upset the Boston Bruins in the semifinal round and fight the mighty Montreal Canadiens through five games before losing the finals.

The Leafs won the Stanley Cup in 1962 and repeated for two more years, making Imlach the only combined general manager–coach ever to win three straight Cups.

Imlach spells out what he calls his "formula" as if he were reading from Norman Vincent Peale, whose positive-thinking creed has sometimes been distributed as a textbook to Toronto players. Hard work. Complete control of the club. Positive thinking. Loyalty. "Technical ability," adds Punch, "is only about the fifth most important thing. Good physical and mental shape can make up for a lot of technical deficiencies." It all sounds very simple, but the formula is more complex than it appears—and so is the man who preaches it.

"Every coach may try to use psychology on his players," says George Armstrong, the Toronto captain. "But what Punch does is really amazing. It's almost impossible to sustain a mood or spirit over a 70-game season, but somehow he did it in the 1958–59 season—and he's come pretty close to doing it ever since."

While Imlach's psychological approach varies, his commitment to hard work remains immutable. Most teams go through four weeks of training camp, practicing once a day, before the NHL season; the Maple Leafs practice twice a day for five weeks. "I know some guys find it awfully hard," Imlach says. "Especially ones who come from other teams like Detroit, where Sid Abel doesn't believe in working them too much. I know that some are going to complain, but there's nothing I can do for them. This is the way I believe in doing things."

Goalie Terry Sawchuk, who did come from Detroit, says, "It was very hard at first. But you just have to get used to it. Then you realize that Punch is doing a lot for you."

Center Red Kelly's approval is slightly more qualified. "I agree with him that hard work is important," says Red. "But I also believe that a man can drive himself. And if you drive yourself, you knew just what's good for you and when to stop." If Imlach has sometimes pushed Kelly beyond the point where Red thought he should have stopped, it has apparently brought results. Kelly came to Toronto in 1960 as a once-great defenseman who appeared to be fading. Imlach switched him to center, and Kelly suddenly and incredibly found new life.

Imlach permits himself to gloat a little about his best deals, but he always points out that his trades are all dependent on another part of his formula. "Nobody second-guesses me around here," he says. "I make the decisions myself, and I take full responsibility. The owners of this club know that as soon as they want to make the decisions, all they have to do is fire me. I always remember what Conn Smythe once told me: Be sure to make your own mistakes." ∎

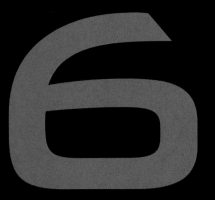

6

FRED SHERO

" The legendary coach won two Stanley Cup titles and earned the first Jack Adams Award. He also ushered in the modern era of NHL coaching, introducing systems, film study and full-time assistants on the bench. " —SARAH KWAK

▸ 390-225-119 CAREER RECORD
▸ HIS FLYERS DEFEATED RED ARMY TEAM IN 1976 EXHIBITION

"SOMETIMES I DON'T think he knows the difference between Tuesday and Wednesday, and sometimes I think he is a genius who has us all fooled," said Scotty Bowman. The real secret of Shero's success was that he simplified and made enjoyable what he called "a little boys' game played by men."

—*Jay Greenberg, SI, December 3, 1990*

The oft-bumbling Shero was nicknamed Freddy the Fog.

PHOTOGRAPH BY HEINZ KLUETMEIER

7

ANATOLI TARASOV

" From the detritus of World War II, Tarasov took a fledgling sport in his homeland and built a dynasty. The godfather of Soviet hockey was creative in reimagining the game, emphasizing team play. " —MICHAEL FARBER

▸ THREE OLYMPIC GOLD MEDALS
▸ NINE CONSECUTIVE WORLD CHAMPIONSHIPS

U.S. COACH Lou Vairo remembers [Tarasov's advice]: "Borrow from all schools, look at the nature of your people, and use their strengths to let them express themselves. Use your imagination, don't be afraid to try something new, and don't pick up the pucks after practice."

—E.M. Swift, SI, December 17, 1982

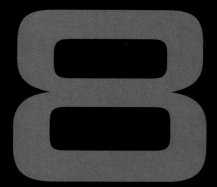

8

MIKE BABCOCK

DUCKS 2002–2004
RED WINGS 2005–2015
MAPLE LEAFS 2015–PRESENT

“ In the modern NHL, coaches are far more expendable than their marquee players, but Babcock has been an exception. The second-fastest coach to reach 500 wins, he is near the top of every NHLers' list of coaches they'd like to play for. ” —SARAH KWAK

▸ WON 2008 STANLEY CUP TITLE
▸ GOLD MEDALS WITH TEAM CANADA IN 2010, 2014

ANAHEIM ROOKIE coach Mike Babcock, 40, reached the finals in his first NHL season, matching the feat of New Jersey coach Pat Burns, who did it with Montreal in 1989. Babcock's veneer of cockiness often camouflages his greatest asset: He is confident enough to admit he doesn't have it all figured out. "It's been said that nobody asks more questions than I do," says Babcock, who was a defenseman for McGill University in the mid-1980s. He has learned to coach by osmosis and strews credit like rose petals for every set play or practice drill he has appropriated; he dutifully labels them in homage. In the lexicon of Babcock's Ducks, there is the Detroit chip, the Dallas tap back, the Minnesota push-the-pace, the (Todd) Bertuzzi power-play play, and the Jacques Lemaire forecheck drill.

—Michael Farber, SI, June 2, 2003

Babcock has won five national team titles.

9

DICK IRVIN

BLACKHAWKS 1928–1929,
1930–1931, 1955–1956
MAPLE LEAFS 1931–1940
CANADIENS 1940–1955

" The World War I veteran was the Blackhawks' first captain and coached the Maple Leafs to a title in 1932, but he is best known as the coach who guided the Canadiens to three titles, as the franchise was just becoming hockey's premier dynasty. Irvin was the career leader in coaching wins when he retired in '56. " —BRIAN CAZENEUVE

▸ FOUR STANLEY CUP TITLES
▸ 692-527-230 CAREER RECORD

"IF THE TEAM is stale, that's easy. You give them a rest. If the team is lazy, that's easy too. You give them more work. If the team simply cannot do what is asked of it, the answer is to try and get new players who are more capable. Ah, and here's the toughie—if the team will not do what is asked of it, then the man who is in trouble is the coach. Management isn't in the habit of firing the whole team when it is relatively simple to let the coach go." Irvin popped the last piece of muffin into his mouth and smiled for the first time in several hours. "So you see," he said, while slipping into his overcoat, "the coach must be more than a coach in a technical sense. He must be a psychologist too."

—*Whitney Tower, SI, February 13, 1956*

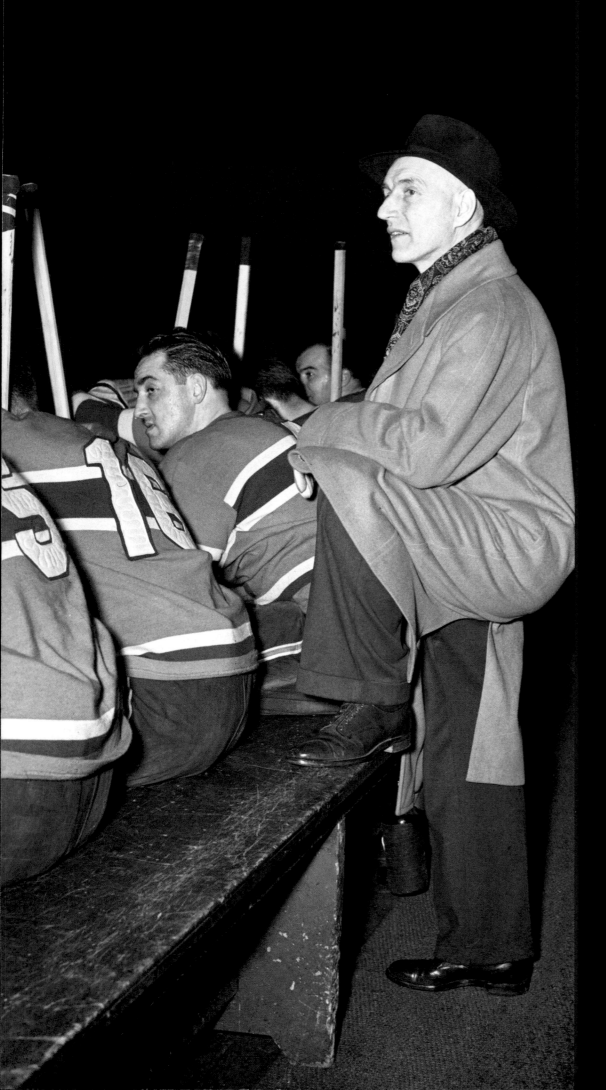

Irvin quickly had Montreal on a winning track.

Gretzky and Sather were a winning combination.

10

OILERS 1977–1994
RANGERS 2002–2004

" In 1977 he scored a goal in his first game as player-coach of the Edmonton Oilers, who were then in the WHA. It was a sign of things to come—Sather mentored Wayne Gretzky while guiding the greatest scoring teams in NHL history. " —MARK BEECH

"AROUND THE LEAGUE, people interpret [Sather's] actions as arrogance," says Gretzky. "But he believes in the best of everything: the best effort, the best refereeing, wearing the best clothes. He expects a lot from people. He had to work hard to stay in this league, and that's what he wants out of everyone."

—E.M. Swift, SI, April 1, 1985

GLEN SATHER

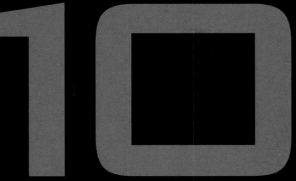

▸ FOUR STANLEY CUP TITLES
▸ 592-383-128 CAREER RECORD

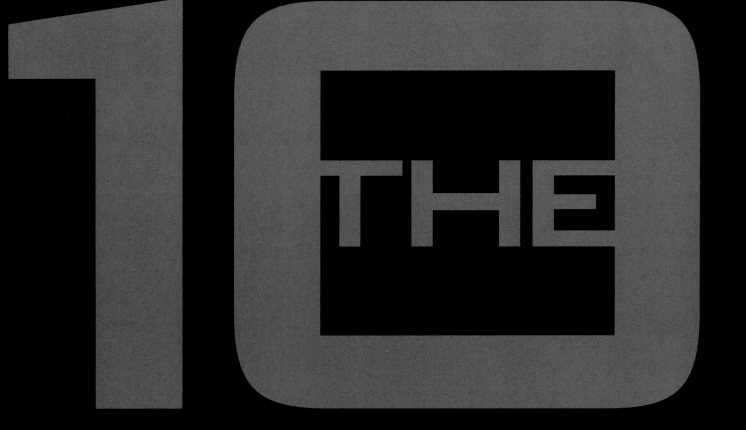

THE 10

Best Enforcers

MANY OF THE MEN ON OUR LIST OF TOP ENFORCERS MADE THEIR NAMES BY VIRTUE OF A LINK TO STARS WHO ARE HONORED ELSEWHERE IN THIS BOOK. JOHN FERGUSON HELPED MAKE LIKE EASIER FOR JEAN BÉLIVEAU WITH THE CANADIENS. CLARK GILLIES PROTECTED MIKE BOSSY FOR THE ISLANDERS. WAYNE GRETZKY BECAME THE GREAT ONE THANKS TO THE SERVICES OF NOT ONE BUT TWO TOP 10 ENFORCERS.

BUT IF YOU FOCUS IN ON THE ENFORCERS THEMSELVES, SOMETIMES THE PICTURE IS NOT SO GREAT. TOP-RANKED ENFORCER BOB PROBERT HAS AS TROUBLED A STORY AS ANY PLAYER IN THIS BOOK. AFTER A CAREER THAT WAS INTERRUPTED BY A TERM IN PRISON FOR COCAINE POSSESSION AND ALSO A DRUNKEN MOTORCYCLE CRASH, HIS HEART GAVE OUT AT AGE 45.

THEN THERE'S MARTY MCSORLEY, WHOSE TIME IN THE NHL ENDED WITH A YEARLONG SUSPENSION AFTER HE CLUBBED THE CANUCKS' DONALD BRASHEAR IN THE CLOSING SECONDS OF A GAME. BRASHEAR WAS KNOCKED OUT AND MISSED 20 GAMES. MCSORLEY WAS NOT ONLY SUSPENDED, BUT ALSO FOUND GUILTY OF CRIMINAL ASSAULT. "YES, I MEANT TO SLASH HIM," MCSORLEY TOLD SI AFTER THE CONVICTION. "DID I MEAN TO HURT HIM WITH MY STICK? NO." BUT HE DID. THE TRICK OF PLAYING ROUGH IS, YOU CAN'T BE SURE HOW IT WILL END.

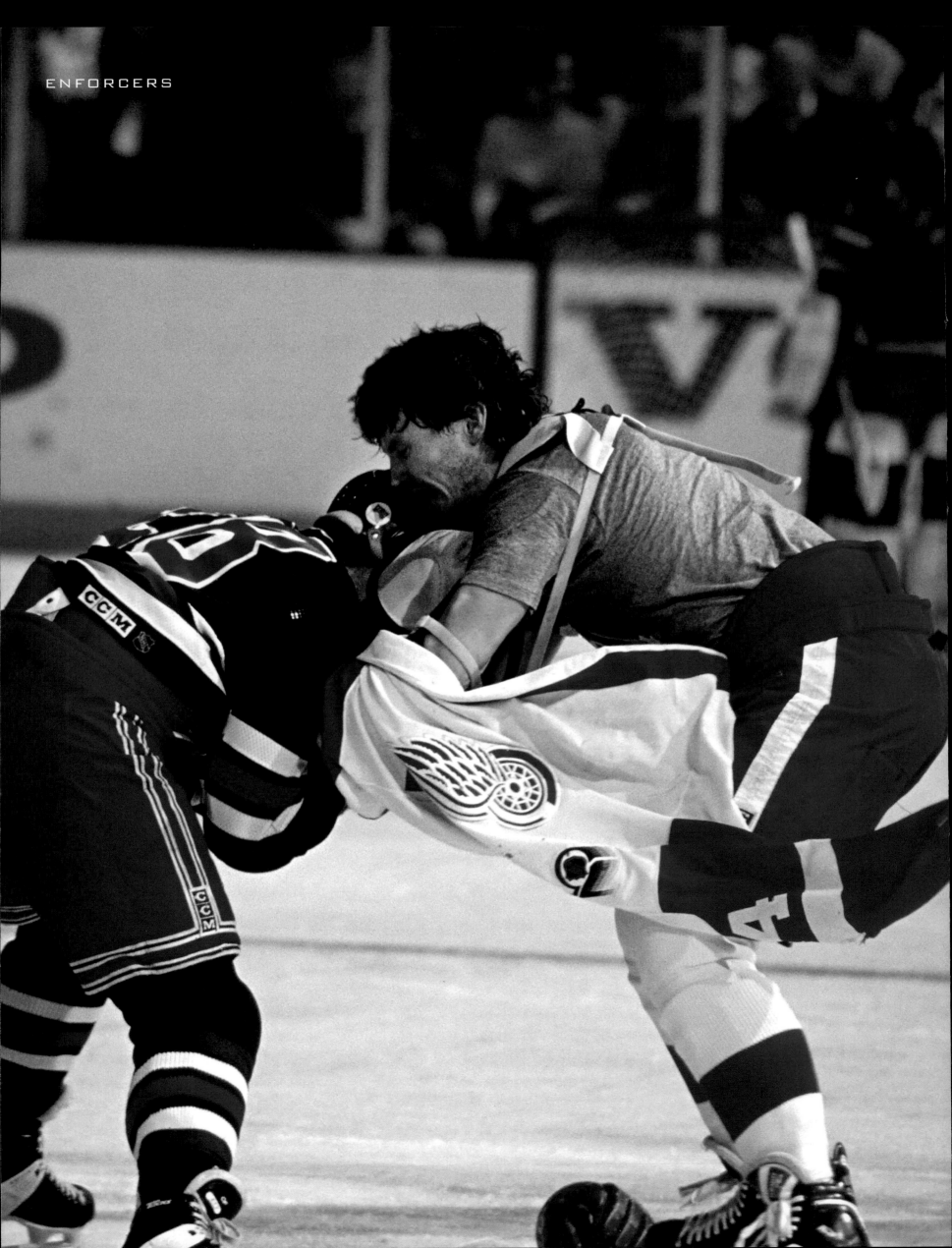

1

BOB PROBERT

RED WINGS 1985–1994
BLACKHAWKS 1995–2002

" The beloved Probert really could play —he had a 29-goal season—but principally he was the undisputed, albeit not undefeated, heavyweight champion of his era, the Paul Bunyan by which all NHL enforcers measured themselves. The only things Probert couldn't lick consistently were personal demons, drugs and booze. " —MICHAEL FARBER

▸ 3,300 CAREER PENALTY MINUTES
▸ 1987–88 NHL PENALTY MINUTES LEADER

THESE PLAYOFFS have turned out to be the worst of times for the league; ugliness erupted in every series. In Game 2 of Detroit–St. Louis, Red Wings forward Bob Probert drew a one-game suspension for high-sticking Blues defenseman Garth Butcher and punching goalie Vincent Riendeau on the same play. St. Louis general manager Ron Caron, who has a long history of press box tantrums, responded to Probert's attack by saying, "[Probert] should be in jail," within earshot of several scratched Detroit players who were sitting in the press box. Probert, who spent six months in jail last year for cocaine possession, was defended by Red Wings goalie Glen Hanlon, who grabbed Caron by his tie.

—Jay Greenberg, SI, April 22, 1991

Probert tangled with the Rangers' Tie Domi (left).

DAVE SCHULTZ

FLYERS 1971–1976
THREE OTHER TEAMS

> " The baddest of Philadelphia's notorious "Broad Street Bullies," Schultz still holds the single season record for penalty minutes with 472. " —E.M. SWIFT

- ▸ 2,294 CAREER PENALTY MINUTES
- ▸ LED NHL IN PENALTY MINUTES FOUR TIMES

ALTHOUGH COACH Fred Shero tends to regard Schultz's 20 fighting penalties this season as the true measure of the Hammer's worth, the fact is that Schultz also scored 20 goals, while becoming the most accomplished enforcer since John Ferguson. "Hockey is a contact sport for men," Schultz says. "It's not an ice ballet or the Ice Follies." Schultz grew up in a Mennonite Brethren community in Saskatchewan and used to spend part of his summers at Bible camp. "The Bible says not to be afraid of anything mortal," he says, "because you can be here today and gone tomorrow. I'm not afraid of anything. I'm not even afraid of losing a fight. I never want to hurt anybody in a fight. Oh, I like to beat them up and leave them with some bruises and some bumps, but I don't want to hurt them. One night I cut Bryan Hextall during a fight in Atlanta, and when I saw the blood I told him I hadn't intended to cut him. I meant it."

—Mark Mulvoy, SI, May 6, 1974

Schultz cross-checked the Bruins' Wayne Cashman.

PHOTOGRAPH BY JOHN D. HANLON

CANADIENS 1963–1971

Ferguson traded blows with Bobby Hull in 1968.

3

"He did a lot of heavy lifting playing with Jean Béliveau. He was a phenomenal athlete, a great lacrosse player too. He knew how to get people's attention quickly, and he really understood the game." —PIERRE MCGUIRE

› 1966–67 NHL PENALTY MINUTES LEADER
› TWO-TIME ALL-STAR

HE IS the Canadiens' cop, the bodyguard for the smaller players on the team. When Ferguson plays, the fleet Montreal forwards skate recklessly, knowing he is around to protect them. When he does not play, these same forwards look as though they are out for a quiet afternoon of public skating.

—Mark Mulvoy, SI, March 23, 1970

JOHN FERGUSON

4

TIGER WILLIAMS

MAPLE LEAFS 1974–1980
CANUCKS 1980–1984
THREE OTHER TEAMS

❝ He'd fight before the game, after the game or anytime in between. The NHL's career leader in penalty minutes at 3,966—the equivalent of more than 66 complete games—could also score, potting 241 goals. Still, there was never a doubt that the inveterate brawler did his best work with his gloves off. ❞ —KOSTYA KENNEDY

▸ LED NHL IN PENALTY MINUTES THREE TIMES
▸ 1980–81 ALL-STAR

"WHEN I first came into the league [Islanders goalie Billy Smith and I] went at it every game," says Williams. "I had a stick swinging fight with him one time—I've still got a picture of it hanging on my wall." Smith recalls the Williams incident well. "Tiger almost broke my neck that night," he says. "I whacked him around the ankles, and he swung his stick baseball-bat style as hard as he could. I put my head down, but he caught me right behind the ear and shoved my head all the way across to my other shoulder. My neck was stiff for about three days, but I held no grudge against Tiger. I laughed. Today we have sort of an unspoken agreement to give each other a little extra room."

—*E.M. Swift, SI, May 3, 1982*

Williams scored 513 career points.

PHOTOGRAPH BY BORIS SPREMO/TORONTO STAR/GETTY IMAGES

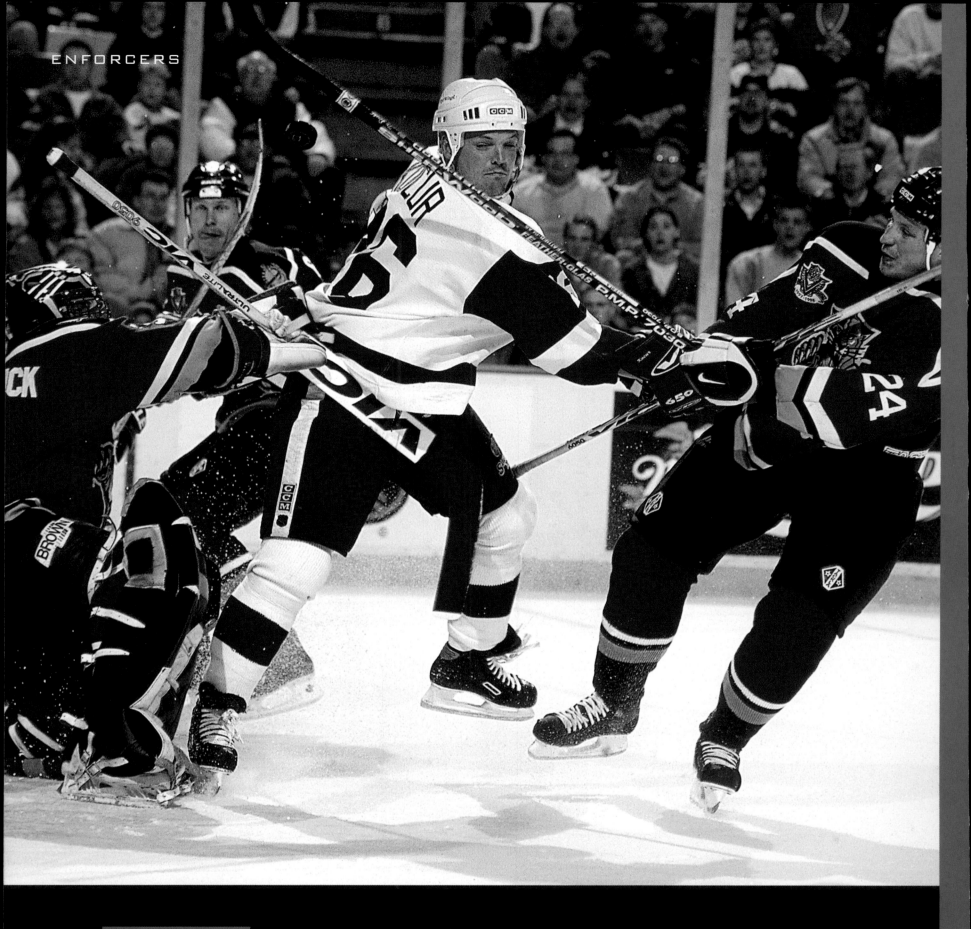

5

JOEY KOCUR

RED WINGS 1984–1991, 1996–1999
RANGERS 1991–1996
CANUCKS 1996

❝ Half of the Red Wings' Bruise Brothers, along with Bob Probert, he was a feared administrator of the game's unwritten rules. ❞ —MARK BEECH

▸ 1985–86 NHL PENALTY MINUTES LEADER
▸ THREE STANLEY CUP TITLES

In Detroit, Kocur trained at boxing mecca Kronk Gym.
PHOTOGRAPH BY DAVID E. KLUTHO

"RANGERS GM Neil Smith, who was a Detroit scout in 1983, drafted Kocur. Kocur followed Smith to New York in a '91 trade. Smith recalls, "Joey took some bad penalties, got suspended, and the fans screamed, 'Why did we get this goon?' Of course here we are three years later, and they're all chanting, 'Joey! Joey! Joey!'"

—Tim Crothers, SI, June 22, 1994

6

STU GRIMSON

SEVEN TEAMS 1988–2002

"With his 6' 5", 240-pound frame and a short fuse, "The Grim Reaper" struck a fearsome figure on the ice, clashing with the league's heavyweights more than 200 times." —SARAH KWAK

▸ 2,113 CAREER PENALTY MINUTES
▸ CAREER-HIGH 235 PENALTY IN 2000–01

AFTER CAPITALS tough-guy Craig Berube gave Ducks left wing Paul Kariya a mild bump in the second period, Grimson sought out Berube. "[The hit] was hard enough to elicit a response," Grimson says. "Why not send a message early? Not so much for the league as for the kid, that I'm going to do my best to make sure he's allowed to play his game."

—*Michael Farber, SI, October 19, 1998*

Grimson went at it with the Penguins' Krzysztof Oliwa.

PHOTOGRAPH BY MARK HUMPHREY/AP

7

MARTY McSORLEY

PENGUINS 1983–1985, 1993–1994
OILERS 1985–1988, 1998–1999
KINGS 1988–1993, 1994–1996
THREE OTHER TEAMS

" McSorley— aka Wayne Gretzky's bodyguard—protected The Great One with his fists in both Edmonton and Los Angeles. But he could play both forward and defense, and led the NHL with a +48 plus-minus rating in 1990–91. " —E.M. SWIFT

▸ 3,381 CAREER PENALTY
MINUTES
▸ 1992–93 NHL PENALTY
MINUTES LEADER

WHEN THIS dark and gloomy game finally drew to a close, the Kings were on top (of the Oilers) by a score of 4–2. "I think it got a little out of hand," says Los Angeles assistant coach Cap Raeder. "But sometimes [fighting] can bring a team closer together. Everyone stuck up for everyone else, and that's what it's all about." Added McSorley, who received an automatic three-game suspension for collecting his fourth and fifth game-misconduct penalties of the season, "When you win a real emotional game, with a lot of fights, you go home and you feel a little closer to your teammates. I thought the fights made it a real spiritual game."

—Jay Greenberg, SI, March 12, 1990

Undrafted, McSorley fought his way to the NHL.

PHOTOGRAPH BY ROBERT BECK

A FAMILY OF FIGHTERS

*When you hear how the McSorley brothers go at each other
on the golf course, you'll understand why Wayne Gretzky
brought Marty along with him to Los Angeles*

BY RICHARD HOFFER

MARTY MCSORLEY AND HIS older brother Chris—a former minor league player who now coaches for Toledo in the East Coast Hockey League—were playing golf a few summers ago. There were some bucks involved. Chris was trying to get out of the rough, and Marty broke into a somewhat distracting karaoke act. Chris is not a man to distract. In the minors he once bit the tip off the nose of a player who tried to distract him, which is all the more astonishing if you know that Chris did not play the game with a full complement of teeth. He must have had to *gnaw* the poor fellow's schnozz off. ("I'm not proud of that," Chris says.) Anyway, back on the golf course, Chris drilled Marty in the leg with a three-iron shot, and Marty crumpled onto the fairway. Then he straightened up, ran for Chris's bag and threw it into the water hazard. They shrugged and went for ice cream.

About all that can be said of the outing is, good thing they weren't driving carts, what with lost security deposits and everything. But Marty is surprised to hear something like *that*. He's dealing with someone who doesn't know the McSorley boys. "Oh, we could never rent a cart," he says. "We'd have fought all day over who'd drive."

So maybe the golf story gives you an idea of what the rest of the NHL is up against. A McSorley is insanely competitive, brooks no nonsense, reacts swiftly and inappropriately, sometimes bites off more than he can chew. A McSorley is dangerous to be around.

What McSorley does is not complicated, although it's not as simple as it sometimes looks. He is not a goon, a firebomb lobbed onto the ice to enliven the occasional dull game. He is not an assassin. It's true—every once in a while he'll become so unhinged that he plunges the league into a self-righteous funk. "We're disturbed about the number of fights," a league official said after a McSorley rampage in 1990 that included a vicious slash. ("I'm not proud of that," Marty says, ever a McSorley.) But mostly his violence is calculated.

"Listen," says McSorley, who is so boyish looking and mild-mannered as to invite doubt concerning his league-leading 399 minutes in penalties last year. "I would love to go out there and just play the game. But what you have sometimes is a condition of unbalanced talent. You'll have a less-talented guy, who's trying to make a living, after all, trying to check a Wayne Gretzky or a Mario Lemieux, harassing him, slashing him, intimidating him. A big guy can step up and shift that balance of power, keep everybody honest. If there's a fast game, a finesse game, you'll rarely see a fight. Last year there was a fight in every 1.24 games—really not that many fights."

Of course, as one of the four or five genuine heavyweights in the league, McSorley was in many of those fights. At 6' 1", 235 pounds, he is a capable regulator, a forceful reminder that his team's goal scorer is off-limits. No wonder Gretzky insisted on taking McSorley with him in his famous trade from Edmonton to Los Angeles in 1988. "Do I need a guy like that?" asks Gretzky. "Everybody needs a guy like that. You have to have a presence out there so they don't take that extra liberty."

When McSorley observes that liberty being taken, he is deeply disappointed. He would rather it never came to this, but. . . . "I'll have to call, say, Wayne's rightwinger off the ice, and all of a sudden the guy checking Wayne has me beside him for 10 or 15 seconds, and he doesn't know where I came from," McSorley says. "And then, just as suddenly, I'm back on the bench."

McSorley believes the game's purity is actually restored after each melee. "A lot of times there's a fight on the ice, and you'll find the game will become clean," he says. "A fight has the ability to remind everyone that there are big guys out there, and if you want to keep messing around, the big guys will know where to find you. I just wish it didn't have to happen."

The way McSorley tells you this, you almost feel sorry for him. The reluctant enforcer, the dutiful destroyer.

Then again, you're talking about a brood that has turned everything but contract bridge into a collision sport. Chris admits to contact golf, among other family pastimes. "You know," he says, "when you're leaning over a four-footer and you get slashed across the forearms with a nine-iron?"

Marty admits that "getting dirty" was instinctive to him. It had to do with survival among six brothers, maybe playing tennis-ball hockey in a converted chicken coop and not finishing one game—not one, ever. "A team would be losing," McSorley sighs, "and something would happen."

Still, the miracle is that through all this carnage McSorley has become a solid player. While leading the league in penalty minutes last season, he had 15 goals and 26 assists—and another 10 points in the playoffs. "He's the best at what he does," says Gretzky, "because first of all, he can play. He can play right wing or defense, kill penalties, play a bit on the power play."

This represents quite a leap in McSorley's game. Gretzky likes to say, "I knew Marty before he could skate," but it was even worse than that. When Pittsburgh first signed Marty—the guy voted least likely to twirl Dorothy Hamill in the Ice Capades—the idea was so galling for the McSorley household that Chris, who was working in a steel mill at the time, threw his lunch bucket away and went to the NHL draft to insist on a tryout, which he got with the Philadelphia Flyers.

"You see, everybody in my family had so much respect for the NHL," says Marty, "until I got in."

∎

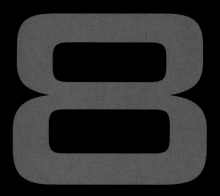

TIE DOMI

MAPLE LEAFS 1989–1990,
1995–2006
RANGERS 1990–1992
JETS 1992–1995

" For an undersized guy, Domi was amazingly tough. He never shied away from anyone. " —PIERRE MCGUIRE

▸ 3,515 CAREER PENALTY MINUTES
▸ 1993–94 NHL PENALTY MINUTES LEADER

"[REFEREE KERRY] Fraser came up to me and said, 'Don't touch him. I know his act, and I'm not going to call anything, but don't touch him,' " reported Toronto roughneck Tie Domi, who most certainly touched Dominik Hasek in the dying seconds of [Game 3 of the conference final], skating into the crease and ramming him into the post. The bump touched off some predictable shenanigans that featured Sabres coach Lindy Ruff striding in the direction of the Toronto bench and screaming, "You're one f------ dead man." Ruff and Domi were roommates on the 1990–91 New York Rangers. "We used to call him Ruff at home and Lindy on the road," Domi recalled with sly satisfaction. After being told of Domi's remarks, Ruff countered by reciting this bit of doggerel he dreamed up when Domi was a rookie: You touch me, you go me. My name is Tie Domi.

—Michael Farber, SI, June 7, 1999

The 5' 10" Domi punched the Devils' Lyle Odelein.

PHOTOGRAPH BY DAMIAN STROHMEYER

The Islanders' Duane Sutter felt Semenko's onslaught.

DAVE SEMENKO

" His Edmonton teammate, Kevin Lowe, once proclaimed Semenko as the "Gretzky of tough guys." The 6' 3", 215-pounder mostly squared off with other heavyweights, rarely dropping down in class. " —MICHAEL FARBER

▸ 1,473 CAREER PENALTY MINUTES
▸ TWO STANLEY CUP TITLES

HE'S DISLIKED by rival teams, who mockingly called him "cement head," But Semenko knows his role. "I've seen it a couple of times with us," says Vancouver Canucks coach Harry Neale. "Gretzky just kind of rolls his head in the direction of a guy who just hit him, and Semenko moves in."

—Mike Delnagro, SI, February 15, 1982

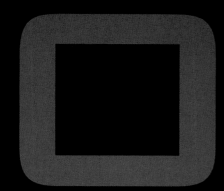

10

CLARK GILLIES

ISLANDERS 1974–1986
SABRES 1986–1988

"So mean was Gillies's reputation that after he twice beat Flyers' enforcer Dave Schultz early in his career, few rivals dared to challenge him. Gillies never amassed 100 penalty minutes in a single season, but his reign as heavyweight champ—see his brutal knockout of Rangers defenseman Ed Hospodar—was unquestioned." —BRIAN CAZENEUVE

‣ 1,023 CAREER PENALTY MINUTES
‣ FOUR STANLEY CUP TITLES

GILLIES'S FACE looked like a topographical map of the Laurentians—the mountain range in Quebec to which many of the Canadiens will soon be headed for golf—after the Islanders clinched their Stanley Cup semifinal series with Montreal. The forward's left eye had two cuts between the lid and the brow, and the bridge of his nose was swollen and scraped to a shine. From previous encounters over the past 10 seasons, he also had a network of scars on his forehead and jaw. How battered was he? "I don't know when I've felt better," said Gillies, grinning. "Mentally or physically." It was Gillies's immovable presence in front of the Montreal net that ultimately led to the demise of the Canadiens in six rugged games.

—E.M. Swift, SI, May 14, 1984

Gillies had 319 career goals and 378 assists.

PHOTOGRAPH BY BRUCE BENNETT/GETTY IMAGES

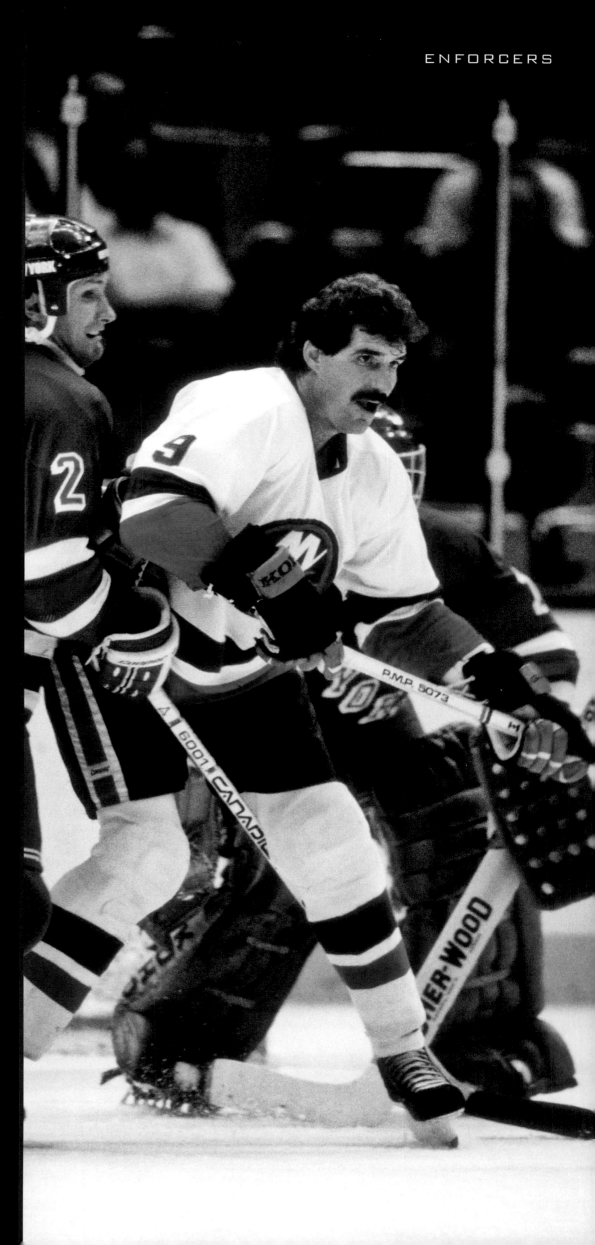

THE 10

MOST ENTERTAINING PLAYERS

THE LIST OF MOST ENTERTAINING PLAYERS IS DOMINATED, UNDERSTANDABLY, BY THE MEN WHO PUT THE PUCK IN THE NET. THE REASON IS OBVIOUS: MAKE THAT RED LIGHT ON TOP OF THE GOAL TURN ON, AND YOU'VE GIVEN THE FANS A REASON TO STAND UP AND CHEER.

BUT THE TOP 10 FOUND ROOM FOR ONE PLAYER WHO KEPT THE LIGHT OFF. DOMINIK HASEK IS THE LONE GOALIE TO MAKE THE MOST ENTERTAINING LIST, COMING IN AT NUMBER 8. THIS FROM THE SAME PANEL THAT VOTED HASEK ONLY THE FIFTH-BEST GOALIE.

HASEK'S METHODS HELP EXPLAIN WHY, WHEN IT CAME TO SHOWMANSHIP, HE TOPPED ALL 'TENDERS. IN A 1997 STORY ON THE SABRES' HIGH ENTERTAINMENT VALUE, MICHAEL FARBER PRAISED HASEK'S GYRATIONS AND THEN DESCRIBED A PARTICULAR HASEK MANEUVER IN WHICH "HE WILL DROP HIS STICK TO THE ICE AND COVER THE PUCK WITH HIS BLOCKER. THERE'S COMPELLING LOGIC IN THE MANEUVER, ESPECIALLY WHEN THE PUCK IS TO HIS RIGHT, OR STICK SIDE. UNLIKE THE CLUMSY CATCHING GLOVE, THE BLOCKER HAS FINGERS THAT ALLOW HIM TO SNATCH A PUCK EASILY—AS LONG AS THOSE FINGERS AREN'T OCCUPIED HOLDING ON TO THE STICK." IT WAS A HIGH-RISK PLOY, AND ONE OF THE REASONS THE GREAT CZECH WAS MORE OF A SHOW THAN THE MEN WHO WERE ATTACKING HIM.

1

BOBBY ORR

BRUINS 1966–1976
BLACKHAWKS 1976–1977,
1978–1979

" With his dazzling end-to-end rushes, Orr changed both the role of the defenseman and the way the game itself was played, sometimes eluding all five opposition skaters with a wizardry that forever altered the way we looked at the hockey. " —BRIAN CAZENEUVE

ORR REMAINS the pivot figure in the game, the single charismatic personality around whom the entire sport will coalesce in the decade of the '70s, as golf once coalesced around Arnold Palmer, baseball around Babe Ruth. Three years ago the NHL reproduced like an amoeba and became 12 teams instead of six, and this season two more clubs were added. Orr is the fixative that binds this unstable mess together. Orr's style makes him the perfect player to lure fans to expansion hockey games. His coach, Tom Johnson, says, "Bobby has all the tricky moves, the fakes and blocks that excite the experts. He does things that no other hockey player can do, and a lot of people just take it for granted. But he also does the things that excite the newcomer: the rink-long rushes, the hard body checks and that whistling slap shot of his. The puck is on his stick half the time. If you're looking at your first hockey game—and lots of people are nowadays—all you do is watch Orr and you catch on fast."

—Jack Olsen, SI, December 21, 1970

Orr worked magic at both ends of the ice.

PHOTOGRAPH BY JOHN G. ZIMMERMAN

2

WAYNE GRETZKY

OILERS 1978–1988
KINGS 1988–1996
BLUES 1996
RANGERS 1996–1999

" You never knew what you'd see. Gretzky understood space—and used it—like no one else. He might bat in a goal out of mid-air, score five times in a game, spin past a row of defenders or backhand a pass through three sets of legs. When he was on the ice, you did not turn away. " —KOSTYA KENNEDY

HE IS BOTH hockey's greatest scorer and its greatest ambassador, the man who almost single-handedly made the NHL viable in California, which now has three teams. He leaves the game with a mind-numbing 61 NHL records. Scoring patterns in the NHL have changed so dramatically since he was tearing apart the league in the 1980s that some of his numbers seem to come from a different sport. During the six seasons from 1981–82 through '86–87, Gretzky averaged 203 points per year. What was he doing, bowling? But Gretzky admits, with a rueful smile, that even though he scored 894 career goals, "10 years from now they won't even talk about my goal scoring; it'll just be my passing." That was his genius. Gretzky's vision and imagination were such that he routinely created plays no one had ever seen. He played hockey like a chess master, several steps ahead of everyone else.

—E.M. Swift, SI, April 26, 1999

Fans flocked to be in the presence of Greatness.

PHOTOGRAPHS BY DAVID E. KLUTHO

3
MAURICE RICHARD

CANADIENS 1942–1960

" "The Rocket" was a pure goal scorer and awesome competitor. "When he came flying toward you with the puck on his stick," said goalie Glenn Hall, "His eyes were all lit up, flashing and gleaming like a pinball machine. It was terrifying." " —E.M. SWIFT

GALLICLY HANDSOME and eternally intense, he is regarded by most aficionados as the greatest player in the history of hockey. Whether he is or not, of course, is one of those sports arguments that boil down to a matter of personal opinion. However, as Richard's supporters invariably point out, hockey is in essence a game of scoring, and here there can be no argument: The Rocket stands in a class by himself. It is not simply the multiplicity of Richard's goals nor their timeliness but, rather, the chronically spectacular manner in which he scores them that has made the fiery rightwinger the acknowledged Babe Ruth of hockey. "There are goals and there are Richard goals," Dick Irvin, the Canadiens coach, remarked. "He doesn't get lucky goals. Let's see, he's scored over 390 now. Of these, 370 have had a flair. He can get to a puck and do things to it quicker than any man I've ever seen—even if he has to lug two defensemen with him, and he frequently has to. And his shots! They go in with such velocity that the net and all bulges."

—Herbert Warren Wind, SI, December 6, 1954

The NHL's goal-scoring award is named for Richard.

A MOTORCAR COMING AT YOU

Maurice Richard played with both intensity and integrity, the kind of man who could terrify goalies and then go skate at a park with the neighborhood kids

BY GILBERT ROGIN

WHAT MAKES TORONTO tick?" asked the TV announcer. "What makes Toronto dead?" Maurice (the Rocket) Richard asked back. Richard sat, his shoes off, in a dark room in the Royal York hotel, laughing at Red Skelton and smoking a cigar—a burly man of 38 with an erect carriage, tilted, somber, devout face, inflexible eye, abundant black hair which also thickly mats his chest and back, making him look like a mangy bear. "If he had another hair on his back, he'd be up a tree," says Kenny Reardon, who is vice president of the Canadiens. Richard's roommate in Toronto, Marcel Bonin, who once wrestled a toothless, suffering bear in a carnival ("I never win," he admits) was out somewhere in the cold, solid city. The Ontario Good Roads Association made roisterous marches up and down the long, dim hotel corridors, X's on the backs of their red necks and violent apocalypses on their broad neckties. One of them hammered on Richard's door.

"Go to bed, damn it!" Richard shouted. "That's my whole life trouble," he said, "trying to sleep. My mother was the same way. If I sleep four or five hours a night, it's good. TV puts me to sleep every time. Where would we be without TV, eh? And what did we do before?

"Eighteen years of this," he said. "In the town. Out of the town. I really get tired of all these trips." He got up and closed the transom, shutting out the racket. "People bother me," he said. "The young ones, they're all right. It's the old ones who have had a drink or two too much, yelling at you, asking all sorts of questions." He made a face. "I was at this sports banquet. A famous person got up to speak. He had too much to drink. He kept on talking and no one knew how to stop him. It was embarrassing. I'll never be like that."

And no one, certainly, will ever be quite like Maurice Richard. Not even himself. "You should have come up five years ago," he had said in the men's room of a Montreal-Detroit sleeper several days before. "It's getting to be my time now. I'm getting near the end."

"He was a wartime hockey player," says Frank J. Selke, the 66-year-old managing director of the Canadiens. "When the boys come back, they said, they'll look after Maurice. Nobody looked after Maurice. He looked after himself. When the boys come back, they said, they'll catch up with him. The only thing that's caught up with Maurice is time."

"I first saw him in 1942," says Reardon. "I was playing for an Army team. I see this guy skating at me with wild, bloody hair the way he had it then, eyes just outside the nut house. 'I'll take this guy,' I said to myself. He went around me like a hoop around a barrel."

"When he's worked up," says Selke, "his eyes gleam like headlights. Not a glow, but a piercing intensity. Goalies have said he's like a motorcar coming on you at night. He is terrifying. He is the greatest hockey player that ever lived. I can contradict myself by saying that 10 or 15 do the mechanics of play better. But it's results that count. Others play well, build up, eventually get a goal. He is like a flash of lightning. It's a fine summer day, suddenly. . . . "

"Holy Dirty Dora!" says Montreal coach Toe Blake. "You got to give it to the fellow. The fellow was fantastic. That's why you got to give it to the fellow. That will!"

"In all my experience in athletics, academic pursuits, business," says NHL president Clarence Campbell, "I've never seen a man so completely dedicated to the degree he is. Many people who prosper take prosperity for granted. He doesn't to this day. He is the best hockey player he can be every second. You know, he is the eldest of a fairly extensive family raised in relative poverty. Back of it all, somehow or other, he was going to lift himself. He has an inner urge to transcend."

"He is not the Pope. . . . " says Camil Des Roches, the Canadiens' publicity man, wistfully.

"He is God," says Selke.

Richard is regarded in Canada as no athlete is in the United States. He is not only a sports idol, he is the national idol, particularly among the French-speaking people of Montreal and the province of Quebec. But adulation sits on him like an uneasy crown.

"Nothing goes in my head," he says. "I don't believe in anything. It's nice. I like to forget about it. I don't think I deserve it. That's my whole trouble all the years. It's just the way it went. There are better hockey players but they don't work as hard. I like to win."

Richard adores children and is perhaps most at ease with them. He always carries postcards with his picture on them which he signs and gives away. Children adore Richard. Richard often skates with kids or referees their games. "The kids all call this one place where we skate Maurice Richard Park," he says. "That's not the real name. In Montreal most of the people things are named after are dead people. Parents should spend more time watching their kids play," he says. "I come out after the game starts and stand hidden in a corner. I like to play with them in the park. The kids get such a kick out of it. They talk of nothing else for a week afterward."

At the NHL meeting last year there was some facetious talk of the end, the day when Richard would get so old Montreal would no longer protect him and he would be available for the $20,000 waiver price. "I'd pay $20,000 for him," said Phil Watson, coach of the New York Rangers. "I'd put him in a glass case in Madison Square Garden and say, 'Pay your money and take a good look at the great Maurice Richard!' " ∎

4

MARIO LEMIEUX

PENGUINS 1984–1994,
1995–1997, 2000–2004,
2005–2006

" Game 2, 1991 Stanley Cup final. Lemieux grabs the puck at the right face-off circle in Pittsburgh's zone and goes coast-to-coast, flummoxing North Stars defenders and beating goalie Jon Casey with a backhand. On CBC, Harry Neale, who has a gift for précis, says, "One against the world. And he dekes the whole world." " —MICHAEL FARBER

THE PENGUINS are no longer regarded by Pittsburgh as comic relief after the Steelers pack up and go home. Last season, attendance increased 46%, from an average of 6,839 to 10,018. This season there has been another 18% gain, to 11,864. How much of that increase is due to Lemieux? "I'd say 90 percent," says Paul Steigerwald, the Penguins' director of marketing. "No, actually I'd have to say 100 percent. He's meant everything to this organization." Including its continued existence in Pittsburgh. It was only last summer that Edward J. DeBartolo, owner of the Penguins and the Major Indoor Soccer League's Pittsburgh Spirit, threatened to disband or move both franchises. The Penguins were said to be going north across the border to Hamilton, Ont. Now, with Lemieux leading a renaissance, the moving vans have been called off. "We're staying right here," says general manager Eddie Johnston.

—*Bob Kravitz, SI, March 3, 1986*

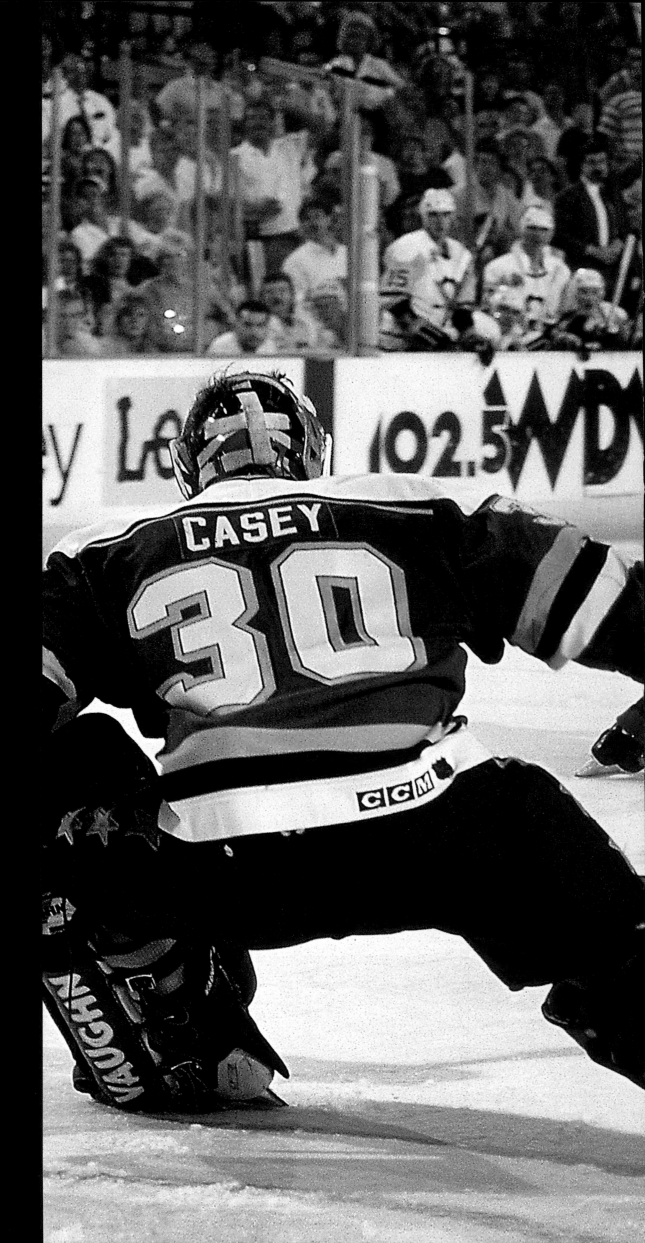

Lemieux lit up both the lamp and a city.

Lafleur is the Canadiens' alltime leading scorer.

PHOTOGRAPH BY JOHN IACONO

CANADIENS 1971–1985
RANGERS 1988–1989
NORDIQUES 1989–1991

"When he had the puck on his stick people would stand up out their seat just to watch him as he was sailing down the ice with his hair flying behind him. His right hand shot down the lane was devastating, and he was one of the few players of his era who could score from long range." —PIERRE MCGUIRE

"WHEN I FIRST saw him, I thought he was an average player," says linemate Steve Shutt. "Then in Chicago he gave us a taste of what was inside that shyness. He simply deked the entire Blackhawks team—skated through them like they weren't even on the ice. Henri Richard said, 'Did you see that? No one can do that.' "

—J.D. Reed, SI, March 22, 1976

5

GUY LAFLEUR

6

BOBBY HULL

BLACKHAWKS 1957–1972
JETS 1972–1980
WHALERS 1980

"With his infectious grin and Herculean physique, the Golden Jet filled arenas wherever he played. He would shrug off defenders as he streaked end-to-end, then finish with his trademark 95 mph slap shot." —E.M. SWIFT

NOT ONLY one of hockey's finest, Bobby Hull is also its handsomest player. His hair is blond, his eyes blue and his smile uncommonly forthright and ingratiating. From the neck down he has the sculptured musculature of a Muscle Beach playboy. Hockey is not a game of giants, and at 5'10" and 190 pounds Hull is literally a big man on the ice. Some of the most effective players in hockey are unspectacular. A novice spectator, for instance, can easily overlook Gordie Howe because the fabulous Detroit wing does everything so economically and with so little fuss. But it would be impossible to overlook Bobby Hull. When he is on the ice he moves excitingly and with the grace and fluency of a figure skater. There is a cheerful, vivid, freewheeling recklessness about him. He picks up the puck and sprints toward the enemy goal with jack-rabbit acceleration. Head up, eyes unblinkingly calculating, he seems almost visibly deciding whether to try to roughhouse past the defense or feed one of his linemates.

—Kenneth Rudeen, SI, November 14, 1960

Hull made the cover of TIME magazine in March 1968.

PHOTOGRAPH BY ART RICKERBY

7

PAVEL BURE

"One of the fastest skaters in NHL history, the Russian Rocket also possessed marvelous puck-control skills. He was nearly unstoppable—when he wasn't lingering at the blue line watching his teammates play defense. He scored 59 goals in 2001–02, and finished that season at –2." —MARK BEECH

CITIZENS OF this coniferous jewel of a city had never seen Bure's like in a Canucks uniform: a game-breaker, a dangerous, attacking player capable of scoring from anywhere without help from anyone. "He can take the puck from behind our net, carry it down the ice and score," says Vancouver captain Trevor Linden. "That's rare."

—*Austin Murphy, SI, December 7, 1992*

Bure led the NHL in goals scored three times.

PHOTOGRAPH BY DAVID E. KLUTHO

8

DOMINIK HASEK

" He patrolled the crease with a brilliant, acrobatic style. Flopping, sliding, twisting, diving, he used every inch of his body and his equipment to parry the puck. That Hasek faced so many shots, and made so many, many saves, kept the crowd on perpetual, disbelieving edge. " —KOSTYA KENNEDY

Hasek was first in save percentage for six seasons.

PHOTOGRAPH BY DAVID E. KLUTHO

HASEK IS the human Gumby. When he was a 10-year-old in Pardubice, Czechoslovakia, Hasek was so flexible that doctors thought something was wrong with his knees. "I could do the butterfly 180 degrees," says Hasek, describing a perfect split. "Now I can't make it 180 degrees, but my butterfly is still very good."

—Michael Farber, SI, February 10, 1997

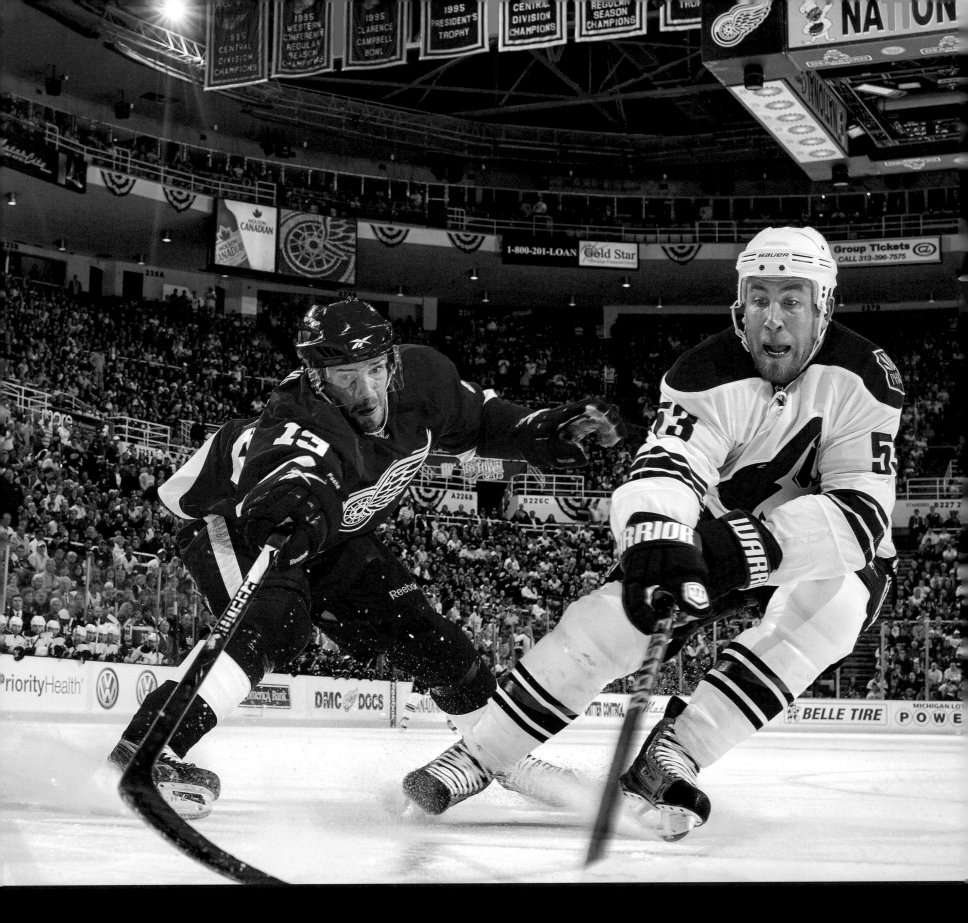

Datsyuk has won four Lady Byng Awards.

PHOTOGRAPH BY DAVID E. KLUTHO

9

PAVEL DATSYUK

" With awe-inspiring dekes and dangles, Datsyuk is a YouTube favorite of his peers, who have dubbed him "The Magician." Performing slight of hand with his incomparable stickhandling skills, he slips pucks through defenders' skates and pickpockets puck-carriers so fast, he's scored before they know the puck's gone from their blade. " —SARAH KWAK

THIS IS what Datsyuk can do: stickhandle, pass, shoot, win face-offs, kill penalties and steal a puck from an opposing player as efficiently as a jackal can strip a carcass. This is what Datsyuk can't, or won't, do: Dance the hokey-pokey after he scores. There is no self-aggrandizement, no preening. Just hockey.

—Michael Farber, SI, April 13, 2009

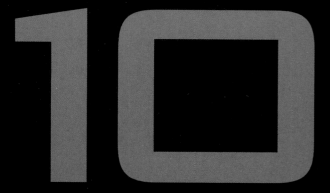

10

ALEX OVECHKIN

CAPITALS 2005–PRESENT

" The Great 8's jack-o'-lantern grin is the perfect complement to his hard-charging, ebullient playing style. But while his joy and energy are what captivate fans, it's his rocket shot from the wing that brings them to their feet. " —MARK BEECH

THIS IS a halting attempt to describe the nearly indescribable six seconds of astonishing, mind-stretching hockey that will always live in online video and highlight reels: the Impossible Goal. Midway through the third period in Phoenix, Ovechkin gathered the puck at the red line and burst down the right flank. Four strides over the blue line, retreating Coyotes defenseman Paul Mara checked him, but Ovechkin made an inside move that took him partway around Mara and pitched Ovechkin at a 45-degree angle toward the left corner of the rink. Stumbling because of Mara's persistent checking, Ovechkin, now perhaps 10 feet from goaltender Brian Boucher's net, at the lower edge of the left face-off circle, corkscrewed himself onto his back, took his left hand off his stick, cradled the puck with the hook of his blade and then, over his shoulder, shoved the puck into the short side of the net past a stunned Boucher. "I don't know what was more amazing," says Phoenix coach Wayne Gretzky. "That goal or him blowing a kiss to me that day. . . . That goal was one of the prettiest I've ever seen. "

—Michael Farber, SI, December 25, 2006

Ovechkin is one who seems to enjoy his talents.

PHOTOGRAPH BY ROBERT BECK

10 THE

BEST GAMES

IN THE UNITED STATES HOCKEY IS NOT THE MOST POPULAR SPORT IN THE COUNTRY, NOT NEARLY. BUT IF YOU WERE TO ASK AMERICANS TO NAME THE GREATEST SPORTS EVENT OF THE 20TH CENTURY, THE U.S. HOCKEY TEAM'S WIN OVER THE SOVIET UNION AT THE 1980 OLYMPICS WOULD BE AT THE TOP OF THE LIST. THE TEAM'S CAPTAIN, MIKE ERUZIONE, NEVER PLAYED AN NHL GAME AND WASN'T EVEN DRAFTED, BUT 35 YEARS LATER, EVERY SPORTS FAN OVER A CERTAIN AGE KNOWS HIS NAME.

THE POPULARITY OF THAT GAME SPEAKS TO THE SCALE OF THE UPSET AND ALSO THE POLITICAL TENSIONS OF THE ERA, BUT IT ALSO SHOWS HOW NATIONAL-TEAM GAMES CAN UNITE AN AUDIENCE ABOVE ITS PAROCHIAL DIVIDES. THE TREND CARRIES THROUGH THE CATEGORY, WITH FIVE OF THE TOP 10 GAMES, INCLUDING ALL OF THE TOP FOUR, COMING FROM INTERNATIONAL PLAY.

THESE GAMES RESEMBLE COLD WAR—ERA SPY MOVIES IN THAT, IN MOST INSTANCES, THE RUSSIANS ARE CAST AS THE VILLAINS. SOME OF THIS OWES TO THE ROLE THE FORMER SOVIET UNION PLAYED IN WORLD POLITICS, BUT IT IS ALSO A TRIBUTE TO THE SOVIET HOCKEY PROGRAM. PLAYERS FROM THE U.S.S.R. NATIONAL TEAMS ARE HONORED AS INDIVIDUALS THROUGHOUT THIS BOOK AS RATING AMONG THE BEST OF THE BEST. THESE GAMES WEREN'T JUST JINGOISTIC RALLIES, THEY WERE GREAT HOCKEY.

1

1980 OLYMPIC SEMIFINAL

USA 4, SOVIET UNION 3

"The greatest win in U.S. sports history—a completely unforeseen toppling of the fearsome, beyond formidable Soviet Union. Steeped in symbolism and heavy with political weight, this was also a dang good hockey game in the Lake Placid barn: Down 3–2 after two periods, the U.S. scored twice, then withstood Soviet pressure for 10 minutes. Miracle." —KOSTYA KENNEDY

- ▸ MIKE ERUZIONE SCORED THE GAME-WINNER
- ▸ JIM CRAIG STOPPED 36 OF 39 SOVIET SHOTS

THE IMPACT was the thing. One morning they were 19 fuzzy-cheeked college kids and a tall guy with a beard, and the next . . . . WE BEAT THE RUSSIANS! In Babbitt, Minn., hometown of forward Buzzie Schneider, guys went into their backyards and began firing shotguns toward the heavens. *Kaboom! Kaboom!* WE BEAT THE RUSSIANS! In Santa Monica a photographer heard the outcome of the game and went into his local grocery store, a mom-and-pop operation run by an elderly immigrant couple. "Guess what," he said. "Our boys beat the Russians." The old grocer looked at him. "No kidding?" Then he started to cry. "No kidding?"

—E.M. Swift, SI, December 22–29, 1980

Craig's toughness set the stage for American elation.

PHOTOGRAPHS BY HEINZ KLUETMEIER (2) AND ERIC SCHWEIKARDT (BOTTOM LEFT)

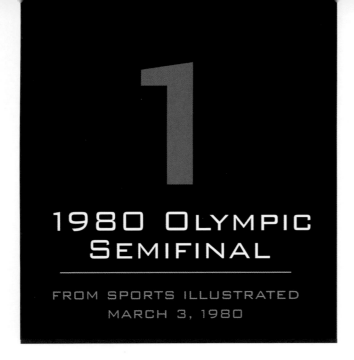

1

1980 OLYMPIC SEMIFINAL

FROM SPORTS ILLUSTRATED
MARCH 3, 1980

RALLY 'ROUND THE FLAG

A charismatic group of underdogs toppled the Soviet favorites and became a national phenomenon in a country that had not been known to put hockey first

BY E.M. SWIFT

FOR MILLIONS OF PEOPLE, THEIR single, lasting image of the Lake Placid Games will be the infectious joy displayed by the U.S. hockey team following its 4–3 win over the Soviet Union last Friday night. It was an Olympian moment, the kind the creators of the Games must have had in mind, one that said: Here is something that is bigger than any of you. It was bizarre, it was beautiful. Upflung sticks slowly cartwheeled into the rafters. The American players—in pairs rather than in one great glop—hugged and danced and rolled on one another.

The Soviet players, slightly in awe, it seemed, of the spectacle of their defeat, stood in a huddle near their blue line, arms propped on their sticks, and waited for the ceremonial postgame handshakes with no apparent impatience. There was no head-hanging. This was bigger, even, than the Russians.

"The first Russian I shook hands with had a smile on his face," said Mark Johnson, who had scored two of the U.S. goals. "I couldn't believe it. I still can't believe it. We beat the Russians."

In Lake Placid and across the country, it was more of the same. A spontaneous rally choked the streets outside the Olympic Ice Center, snarling bus traffic for the umpteenth time since the start of the Games. A sister of one of the U.S. hockey players—in between cries of "The Russians! I can't believe we beat the Russians!"—said she hadn't seen so many flags since the '60s. "And we were burning them then," she added.

So move over, Dallas Cowboys. The fresh-faced U.S. hockey team had captured the imagination of a country. This was America's Team. When the score of the U.S.–Soviet game was announced at a high school basketball game in Athens, Ohio, the fans—many of whom had probably never seen a hockey game—stood and roared and produced dozens of miniature American flags. In a Miami hospital, a TV set was rolled into the surgical intensive care unit and doctors and nurses cheered on the U.S. between treating gunshot wounds and reading X-rays. In Atlanta, Leo Mulder, the manager of the Off Peachtree restaurant, concocted a special drink he called the Craig Cocktail, after U.S. goalie Jim Craig, whose NHL rights belong to the Atlanta Flames. What's in a Craig Cocktail? "Everything but vodka," Mulder said. Impromptu choruses of "The Star-Spangled Banner" were heard in restaurants around Lake Placid, while down in the U.S. locker room—you still doubt this is America's Team?—the players leather-lunged their way through "God Bless America"!

"Someone started it as a joke, I think," said Dave Silk, the right wing who had set up the tying goal. "But all of a sudden we were all singing. We got to the part after '*land that I love . . .*' and nobody knew the words. So we kind of hummed our way to ' . . . *from the mountains, to the prairies . . .*' and we finished it. It was great."

Great as it was, there was still a little matter of the gold medal to take care of. Going into their game against Finland, it was possible for any of the four medal-round teams—the U.S., Finland, Sweden, the U.S.S.R.—to win the gold. Despite its astonishing string of upsets and its 5-0-1 record, the U.S. wasn't even assured of a bronze. But America's Team had come too far to lose.

"To be one game away from the gold medal is the dream of a lifetime," said forward John Harrington. "There was no way we were going to blow it."

They didn't, but it wasn't easy. Finnish goalie Jorma Valtonen made 14 stops in the first period as Finland took a 1–0 lead. Steve Christoff tied the game in the second period, but the Finns scored a power-play goal two minutes later.

So, after two periods, this U.S. squad found itself in almost the same position that another American Olympic hockey team had been in 1960 at Squaw Valley. After having beaten the Soviets the day before, the '60 team was trailing Czechoslovakia 4–3 with one period to play. The U.S. players then came out and scored six unanswered goals. One of the leaders of that comeback was Billy Christian, and 20 years later it was his son, David, who sparked the decisive rally.

With just under 2½ minutes gone in the third period, Christian broke up-ice and slid a pass to Phil Verchota, who broke around the defense and beat Valtonen to tie the game at 2–2. Then, at 6:05, Christian backhanded a shot from the point that the ubiquitous Johnson picked up behind the net and passed out front to Rob McClanahan. After waiting calmly for Valtonen to make the fatal first move, McClanahan slipped the puck between the goaltender's legs for a 3–2 U.S. lead.

The drama built as the Americans were called for three penalties between 6:48 and 15:45 and the Finns pressed the attack. Finally, with 3½ minutes to play, the U.S. scored perhaps its most spectacular goal of the entire tournament—a shorthanded one at that. Christoff slammed a startled Finn against the boards and centered a pass to Johnson.

"I was going to shoot it right away but the puck was bouncing, so I pulled it around, went in and took a backhand," Johnson said. Valtonen sprawled and blocked Johnson's shot, but with two defenders on him, the 5' 9", 155-pound Johnson rapped the rebound into the net. It was his team-high 11th point of the tournament. "We knew we'd never be in this situation again," Johnson would say. "I just sit here in awe."

It was the only time all week that any of the U.S. players had been in awe of anything. Coach Herb Brooks had told them so many times over the past few months that Soviet captain Boris Mikhailov looks like Stan Laurel that, well, it was impossible for them to treat Mikhailov, or any of his teammates, with reverence. "Every time we watched a film of the Russians," said Harrington, "he'd keep saying, 'Stan Laurel, Stan Laurel, look at Stan Laurel.'"

Harrington, Silk and captain Mike Eruzione have compiled a 16-page booklet entitled "Brooksisms"—and "Stan Laurel" is an entry. An old-fashioned motivator, Brooks repeats favored aphorisms with enough regularity that they make an impression. Among them:

—You're playing worse every day, and right now you're playing like the middle of next month.

—Gentlemen, you don't have enough talent to win on talent alone.

—Boys, in front of the net it's bloody-nose alley.

—Don't dump the puck in. That went out with short pants.

—Throw the puck back and weave, weave, weave. But don't just weave for the sake of weaving.

—Let's be idealistic, but let's also be practical.

—You can't be common because the common man goes nowhere. You have to be uncommon.

The U.S. hockey team was anything but common. Even before the Americans beat the Soviets, Lake Placid restaurant managers sent over complimentary bottles of wine, and New York state troopers asked for autographs. At one point, Silk's mother, Abigail, who was housed with 40 other hockey parents and relatives in an abode they called the Hostage House, was riding a bus when she heard a young man tell the girl he was embracing that he was on the hockey team.

"Really? And who are you?" Mrs. Silk asked, cruelly.

"I'm Dave Silk," he said, undaunted.

"I'm Dave Silk's mom," she replied. The girl fled.

So it was that people actually sensed the impending upset of the Soviets, as if wishing could make it so. It was such an unreasonable hope—virtually unthinkable for anyone who had seen the U.S.S.R.'s 10–3 rout of the U.S. at Madison Square Garden three days before the Olympics opened. Tickets for the rematch were scalped for as much as $340 a seat, and Johnson heard of one lady who had offered $600. "Are you telling me it wasn't worth it?" he said two hours after the upset, while watching a replay of the game with teammates in the Holiday Inn. "I'd have paid a thousand to have been in that atmosphere."

It was electric. Craig, superlative throughout the Olympics, gave up two first-period goals but made 16 saves, most of them tough ones. Indeed, he kept the U.S. alive. Then, with three seconds remaining in the period, the U.S. made the key play of the game. Christian took a 100-foot slap shot from beyond center ice that goaltender Vladislav Tretiak let rebound off his pads. Johnson, busting toward the net, weaved through the two Soviet defensemen and picked up the puck. He feinted, dropping his shoulder as if to shoot,

Brooks used humor to boost his young team's confidence.

and Tretiak went to his knees. Johnson pulled the puck back, moved to his left a bit and slid the puck behind Tretiak and into the net just before time expired. That was all for Tretiak, who was promptly yanked from the game in favor of Vladimir Myshkin. And when Aleksandr Maltsev made it 3–2 at 2:18 of the second period, that was all the scoring for the Soviets.

All told, the U.S. outscored its opponents 27–6 in the second and third periods, testimony to the team's depth and conditioning. Charged up by the chants of "U.S.A.! U.S.A.!" the Americans tied the score at 8:39 of the third period. Silk sent a pass through two defensemen to Johnson, who picked the puck off a Soviet skate and fired it under Myshkin. The game winner came 1:21 later, Eruzione beating Myshkin through a screen. Eruzione means "explosion" in Italian, and his goal sent repercussions rinkwide, nationwide, indeed, worldwide.

After it was all over on Sunday, and the U.S. players were wearing their gold medals, it was left to Harrington to find a fitting Brooksism for the whole improbable series of upsets. He didn't have to think about it long. "Boys, we went to the well again, and the water was colder and the water was deeper."

It was sweeter too. ∎

2

1972 SUMMIT SERIES GAME 8

"The pride of a nation at stake, Canada overcame a 5–3 third-period deficit to score the series' final three goals, and Paul Henderson, who tallied with 34 seconds left, became a national hero." —E.M. SWIFT

▸ SERIES WAS THE FIRST MEETING OF NHL AND USSR PLAYERS
▸ GAMES 5–8 WERE IN MOSCOW

HENDERSON, A nine-year man who had given no previous intimations of immortality, scored his third successive game-winning goal, the one that gave Canada a desperate 4-3-1 series edge and spared the NHL All-Stars a Siberian reception at home. "Henderson saved Canada and the NHL," said Toronto owner Harold Ballard.

—Mark Mulvoy, SI, October 9, 1972

Henderson (right) capped Canada's comeback.
PHOTOGRAPH BY DENIS BRODEUR/NHLI/GETTY IMAGES

This was Game 3 of what was called the Super Series.

PHOTOGRAPH BY DENIS BRODEUR/NHLI/GETTY IMAGES

3

1975 New Year's Eve Exhibition

CANADIENS 3, CENTRAL RED ARMY 3

"The greatest game that never counted, unless national pride and geopolitics are on your scoreboard. The Soviets were outshot 38–13 but, backstopped by Vladislav Tretiak, escaped the Forum with a 3–3 result." —MICHAEL FARBER

▸ TOUR WAS THE FIRST MEETING OF NHL AND SOVIET CLUBS
▸ RED ARMY SCORED FINAL GOAL IN THIRD PERIOD

OFFICIALLY, CHIEF coach Boris Kulagin's Moscow party line for the historic hockey games between club teams of the U.S.S.R.'s Major League and the National Hockey League is that they are "true friendlies." No way, Boris. "We have been told it would be very bad for us not to win," says left wing Valery Kharlamov.

—*Mark Mulvoy, SI, January 5, 1976*

4

2010 OLYMPIC GOLD MEDAL GAME

CANADA 3, USA 2 (OT)

❝When the underdog U.S. Olympic men's team tied it up with 25 seconds left in regulation, the game went from good to great. But when Canada's golden child, Sidney Crosby, slipped in the overtime winner to secure gold in front of the home crowd in Vancouver, it became legendary.❞ —SARAH KWAK

▸ ZACH PARISE SCORED GAME-TYING GOAL FOR USA
▸ MOST-WATCHED BROADCAST IN CANADIAN HISTORY

AMERICAN GOALIE Ryan Miller is late on his butterfly. Five hole. The puck is in the net. Pandemonium. Crosby flings his gloves skyward in a spasm of joy, an emotion that overwhelms rational thought. He is elated not for having scored a goal but for having won a game, even if the two are inextricable. Can you understand? He knows this is about something larger than one player, no matter how prepared or how gifted. What's the cliché? There's no I in Canada. Jarome Iginla hears rather than sees the goal. A wave of relief washes over him. He is a sensitive man. He knows that no matter what, the sun will rise Monday morning. He also knows that now it will shine that much brighter on a country whose identity is welded to the sport.

—Michael Farber, SI, December 6, 2010

Crosby's Olympics had been middling until his clincher.

5

1979 CONFERENCE FINALS GAME 7

CANADIENS 5, BRUINS 4 (OT)

"Up a goal with 2:34 to play in regulation, Boston was assessed a minor penalty for having too many men on the ice. Montreal tied the game on Guy Lafleur's goal with 1:14 to play and clinched the series on Yvon Lambert's overtime goal." —BRIAN CAZENEUVE

▸ BRUINS LED 3–1 AFTER TWO PERIODS
▸ MONTREAL WON '79 CUP

THIS WAS the most significant penalty in the history of major sports in North America. [Linesman John] D'Amico's call allowed the Canadiens to burnish their reputation as hockey's premier franchise and turned Montreal's merely impressive run of three consecutive Cups into a dynastic four.

—*Michael Farber*, SI, May 12, 2014

Boston's Gilles Gilbert mourned the winning goal.

CANADIENS 3, BLACKHAWKS 2

Richard's goals capped Montreal's comeback.
PHOTOGRAPH BY JOHN F. JAQUA

6

1971
STANLEY CUP
GAME 7

" Down 2–0 in the second, the Canadiens' Jacques Lemaire scored from center ice and changed the dynamic of the game. Most people thought Montreal would lose in first round that year, not win the Cup. " —PIERRE MCGUIRE

▸ HENRI RICHARD SCORED TWICE FOR MONTREAL
▸ ROOKIE GOALIE KEN DRYDEN WAS THE SERIES MVP

DRYDEN ENTERED the playoffs as the veteran of only six NHL games—all victories. Just up from the minors, he carried the Canadiens past the Bruins and Minnesota, and then thwarted the Blackhawks. "It's incredible," Dryden said on the Canadiens' champagne flight home. "I never dreamed I'd be here this year."

—Mark Mulvoy, SI, May 31, 1971

7

1987
CANADA CUP
FINALS GAME 3

CANADA 6, SOVIET UNION 5

" In the final act of the 6–5 Trilogy—
every game in the best-of-three final
ended with that score—Mario Lemieux
and Wayne Gretzky, linemates born of
necessity, combined on the late winning
goal. The conceit is that Gretzky taught
Lemieux how to win in the tournament.
Nonsense. " —MICHAEL FARBER

▸ FINALS WERE CONCLUSION
OF SIX-TEAM TOURNAMENT
▸ CANADA AND U.S.S.R. SPLIT
FIRST TWO GAMES

LEMIEUX'S CLIMACTIC goal was his
11th of the tournament—with Wayne
Gretzky assisting on nine of them—
and eradicated the doubts of his
countrymen about him. Before this
competition, Lemieux had drawn
criticism for declining to represent
Canada in international competition.
In addition, the effortlessness with
which he has played for the Penguins
had led observers to believe that he
does not go at full throttle. But he
and the rest of Team Canada were
certainly going all-out. The U.S.S.R.
jumped off to 3–0 and 4–2 leads in
the first period. Team Canada coach
Mike Keenan said afterward, "The
mood in the room (after the first
period) was that we were about to
participate in the greatest comeback
in the history of the game."

—Austin Murphy, SI, September 28, 1987

Lemieux (right) had 18 points in the tournament.

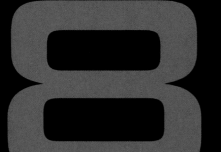

8

1982
MIRACLE ON
MANCHESTER

KINGS 6, OILERS 5 (OT)

" Trailing 5–0, the Kings scored six goals in the third period and overtime to win Game 3 of their first-round playoff series against the top-seeded Oilers. It remains the biggest comeback in postseason history. " —MARK BEECH

‣ KINGS FINISHED 48 POINTS BEHIND OILERS IN STANDINGS
‣ KINGS WENT ON TO WIN SERIES 3–2

THE SERIES is tied at one game each. Score: 4–0 Oilers in the second period. The Kings are struggling during a man-up situation. Suddenly the Edmonton bench begins booing the Los Angeles power play. Cocky? You bet. Immature? You said it. After giving up yet another goal, the Kings come back to win.

—*E.M. Swift, SI, October 11, 1982*

L.A.'s locker room was ebullient after the upset.
PHOTOGRAPH BY JAYNE KAMIN-ONCEA/LOS ANGELES TIMES

2013 STANLEY CUP GAME 6

BLACKHAWKS 3, BRUINS 2

❝ With Boston less than 80 seconds from forcing a seventh game in the Stanley Cup finals, Chicago forwards Bryan Bickell and Dave Bolland scored goals 17 seconds apart to lift the Blackhawks to a stunning 3–2 victory and a second title in four years. ❞ —BRIAN CAZENEUVE

‣ CHICAGO PULLED GOALIE BEFORE BICKELL'S SCORE
‣ BOLLAND'S GOAL SET RECORD FOR LATEST CUP- WINNING SHOT

IN THE center of the ice after the final horn sounded, Chicago captain Jonathan Toews mouthed the words, "I can't believe this," to teammate Corey Crawford. The goalie's answer, give or take a forgivable unprintable, was: "Never, no way." The 2013 Stanley Cup finals was a triumph not just for Chicago. Five months ago, as the NHL crawled out of the rubble of its third lockout in two decades, nobody could have drawn up anything as perfect as this series, a matchup between two Original Six franchises that turned out to be one of the most competitive and compelling finals in recent memory. The cuticle-shredding drama and fierce pace of play all added up to exactly what the NHL needed.

—*Brian Cazeneuve, SI, July 1, 2013*

Bolland hit his game-winner with 59 seconds remaining.

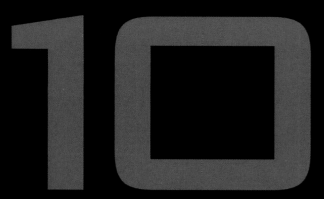

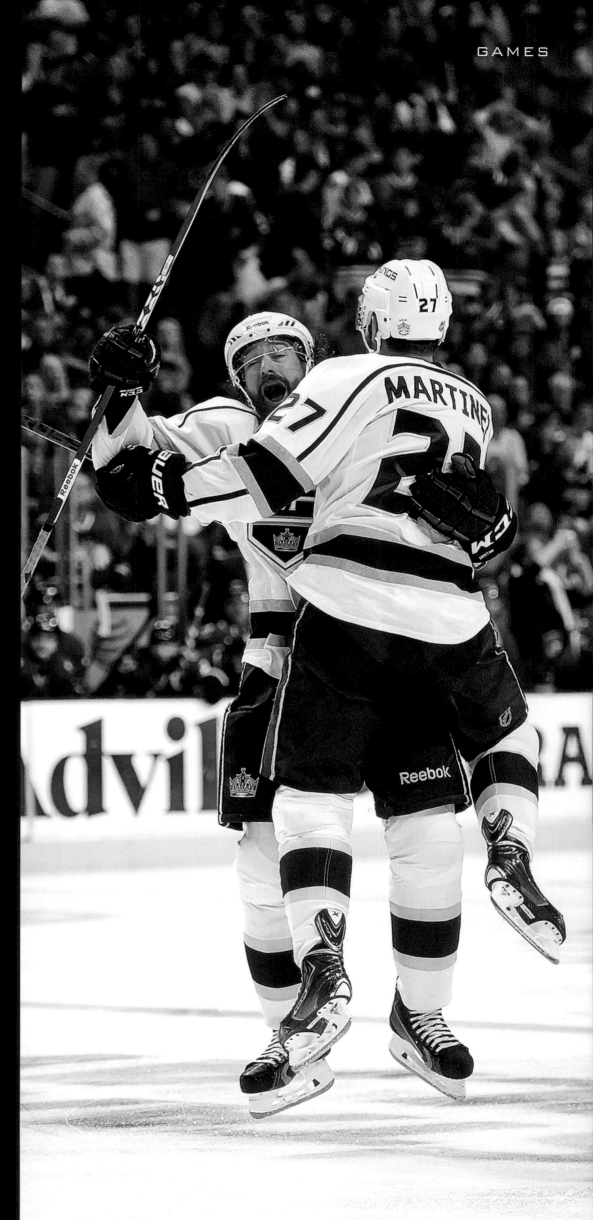

10

2014 CONFERENCE FINALS GAME 7

KINGS 5, BLACKHAWKS 4 (OT)

" After each game of the series, you asked, "Could this get any better?" And each time it did. The de facto Cup final— an underwhelming Rangers team awaited the winners—culminated in this unforgettable Game 7, in which the Kings erased two Blackhawks leads before defenseman Alec Martinez sailed in the winner in overtime. " —SARAH KWAK

▸ BLACKHAWKS BEAT KINGS IN 2013 CONFERENCE FINALS
▸ SERIES' LAST THREE GAMES DECIDED BY ONE GOAL

THE SERIES ended breathlessly, as it had to, with an Alec Martinez blast skimming off a Chicago Blackhawks sweater and into the net for a 5–4 overtime win and the opportunity for the Kings to win a second championship in three seasons, in the finals against the New York Rangers. No other club in history had won three Game 7s away from its building in one postseason. To do so, the Kings game back to tie this decisive contest not once, not twice, but thrice, their first lead coming on the winning score a little less than six minutes into the extra session. That was the answer to the Blackhawks threatening to become only the second team ever to eradicate a 3–1 series deficit in the conference final.

—*Brian Hamilton, SI.com, June 2, 2014*

Martinez's goal ended a tightly fought series.

PHOTOGRAPHS BY DAVID E. KLUTHO

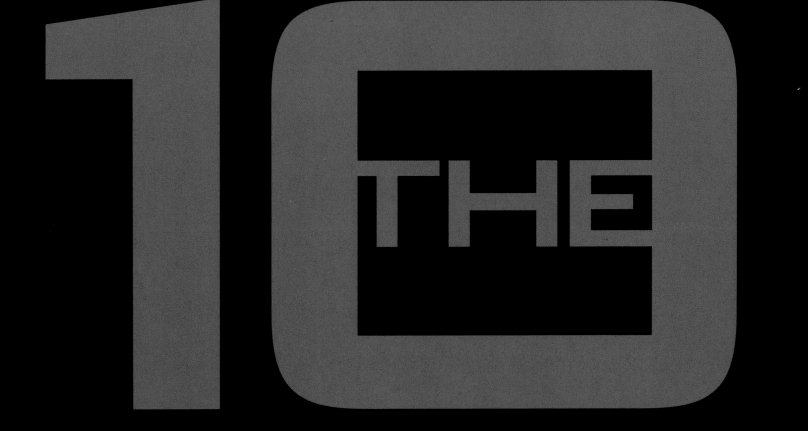

10

THE

BEST RIVALRIES

THE TWO KEY DETERMINING FACTORS IN A RIVALRY ARE HISTORY AND PROXIMITY, AND IF YOU LOOK THROUGH OUR TOP 10 YOU'LL SEE PLENTY OF EXAMPLES OF TEAMS THAT ARE PHYSICALLY CLOSE. THERE'S ALSO THE RARE EXCEPTION OF COLORADO-DETROIT, IN WHICH THE BRUTALITY AND THE STAKES MADE IRRELEVANT QUESTIONS OF BREVITY AND DISTANCE.

ONE RIVALRY WHICH DID NOT RECEIVE A SINGLE VOTE IS MONTREAL-DETROIT, AND THAT IS CURIOUS BECAUSE THESE TEAMS WERE RANKED 1-2 ON NEARLY EVERY BALLOT IN OUR BEST FRANCHISE CATEGORY. BUT IN RIVALRIES, THE CANADIENS WERE MATCHED UP WITH BOSTON AND TORONTO WHILE DETROIT HAS GREATER HISTORY WITH CHICAGO AND THE AFOREMENTIONED AVALANCHE.

WHY AREN'T THESE FRANCHISES MORE LIKE, SAY, THE CELTICS AND LAKERS IN BASKETBALL? THE PROBLEM IS THAT IT'S BEEN AGES SINCE THEY HAVE MET WITH ANYTHING ON THE LINE. AS A RIVALRY MONTREAL-DETROIT PEAKED IN THE 1950S, WHEN MAURICE RICHARD AND GORDIE HOWE DUELED FOR SCORING TITLES AND THE TEAMS MET IN THE FINALS FOUR TIMES. BUT AFTER NHL EXPANSION BEGAN IN '67, THE TEAMS RARELY CROSSED PATHS IN THE PLAYOFFS, AND THEY HAVEN'T SEEN EACH OTHER AT ALL IN THE POSTSEASON SINCE '78. THEY NEARLY MET IN THE SECOND ROUND IN 2015, BUT HERE CLOSE IS NOT ENOUGH.

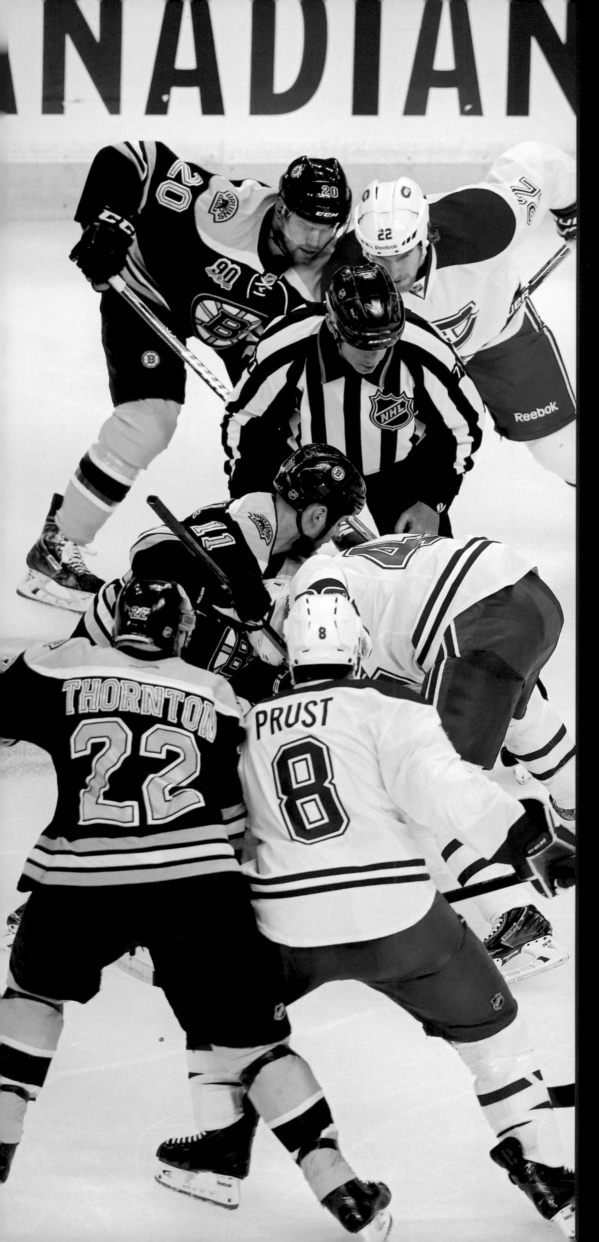

1

BOSTON-MONTREAL

FIRST MEETING: 1924

" The proximity is four-and-a-half hours, and many fans make the drive. The Bruins have had a lot of Francophone players, which only adds to the rivalry. But the skill and speed of the players, their great goalies, and the blood that been shed on the ice have made it amazing. " —PIERRE MCGUIRE

▸ REGULAR-SEASON:
355-264-103-7 (MONTREAL)
▸ POSTSEASON SERIES:
25–9 (MONTREAL)

APRIL IS a time for young love, tax deadlines and the Boston Bruins meeting the Montreal Canadiens in the playoffs. Bruins-Canadiens is the granddaddy of playoff rivalries— assuming your grandfather is a grumpy guy who keeps trying to stick a smelly glove in your face the way Montreal defenseman Mike Komisarek and Bruins rookie Matt Hunwick did to each other during a scrum at the end of Game 1. Hunwick emerged with a discolored eyelid and nasty scratches around his right eye, which proved to be the least of his worries—he was taken by ambulance for a splenectomy, hours before the Bruins went up two games to none in the series with a 5–1 win. This is one of those series that, as your mother once warned, can poke an eye out.

—*Michael Farber, SI, April 27, 2009*

Boston and Montreal have played nine Game 7s.

2

CHICAGO-DETROIT

FIRST MEETING: 1926

"Unlike most rivalries, theirs is rooted in respect. They traveled similar paths—the revival of the Dead Things in the '90s, the righting of Black Hawk Down two decades later—and now they take the high road in lockstep." —MICHAEL FARBER

▸ REGULAR SEASON:
366-266-84-13 (DETROIT)
▸ POSTSEASON SERIES:
9-7 (CHICAGO)

THE RED WINGS were trailing 4–2 with 51.8 seconds left when Damien Brunner scored for Detroit. "Datsyuk to Brunner!" Ken Kal shouted over the radio. "SCORES!" Those final, frenetic seconds were enough to give even a neutral observer an ulcer, if any neutral observer ever existed where the Red Wings and the Blackhawks are concerned.

—*Steve Rushin, SI, June 10, 2013*

The Norris family once owned both teams.

PHOTOGRAPH BY DAVID E. KLUTHO

3

MONTREAL-TORONTO

FIRST MEETING: 1917

" The embodiment of English vs. French-speaking Canada, this confrontation is the NHL's oldest continuous rivalry. Between 1956 and '69, the teams combined to win 13 Cups in 14 years. " —BRIAN CAZENEUVE

▸ REGULAR SEASON:
347-285-88-8 (MONTREAL)
▸ POSTSEASON SERIES:
8-7 (MONTREAL)

Since '79 the teams have only met in the regular season.

PHOTOGRAPH BY DAVE SANDFORD/GETTY IMAGES

AGAINST THE favored Canadiens, Punch Imlach's old men fully vindicated his faith in them. Marcel Pronovost, 36, was the best defenseman in the series. Toronto center Red Kelly, 39, and wing George Armstrong, 36, the captain, called on unflagging courage in what may have been the final Cup of their careers.

—*Pete Axthelm, SI, May 15, 1967*

4

COLORADO-DETROIT

FIRST MEETING: 1995

" Littered with fights and full-on brawls *(see: Bloody Wednesday, 1997)* the rivalry drew heat from a hit in the '96 playoffs, when Avalanche forward Claude Lemieux slammed the Wings' Kris Draper face-first into the glass, shattering his cheek. " —KOSTYA KENNEDY

‣ REGULAR SEASON:
42-19-1-7 (DETROIT)
‣ COLORADO WON THREE OF
FIVE POSTSEASON SERIES
BETWEEN 1996 AND 2002

COLORADO HAD beaten Detroit in its three previous regular-season meetings, but nobody could question the Red Wings' courage following their brutal 6–5 overtime victory. Said Detroit coach Scotty Bowman, "I don't think all that stuff that went on in the game"— 148 penalty minutes, Detroit's Darren McCarty pummeling Claude Lemieux, the Mike Vernon–Patrick Roy fight—"would have mattered if we hadn't won that game." "That game helped make us a team," Brendan Shanahan says. The teams' records following what is routinely called the March 26 Bloodbath are testimony to that game's significance: Including Monday night's result, The Red Wings were 15-7-3, while the Avalanche was 13–11.

—Michael Farber, SI, June 2, 1997

Physicality quickly elevated this rivalry.

5

PHILADELPHIA-
PITTSBURGH

FIRST MEETING: 1967

" When Philadelphia beat cross-state foe Pittsburgh in the first round of the 2012 playoffs, the teams combined for 72 penalty minutes in the first period of Game 3. " —MARK BEECH

> ▸ REGULAR SEASON:
> 150-85-30-8 (PHILADELPHIA)
> ▸ POSTSEASON SERIES:
> 4-2 (PHILADELPHIA)

FEAR HAD trumped loathing for two clean games—"Both teams understand there's two of the best power plays here, and you don't want to be killing penalties," Flyers center Danny Brière said after Game 1 of the first-round series—but the antipathy between the rivals, which spasmed during a 6–4 Philadelphia victory on April 1 when Flyers coach Peter Laviolette and Penguins assistant Tony Granato engaged in a screaming match while perched menacingly atop the dasher boards at their respective benches, was simply too dyspeptic to ignore. In the final five minutes, with Pittsburgh winger James Neal running amok, charging Sean Couturier and then slamming into Claude Giroux, more skirmishes erupted, including one between Scott Hartnell and Sidney Crosby. This was vitriolic hockey at its best—and worst.

—*Michael Farber, SI, April 23, 2012*

This rivalry has heated up in recent years.

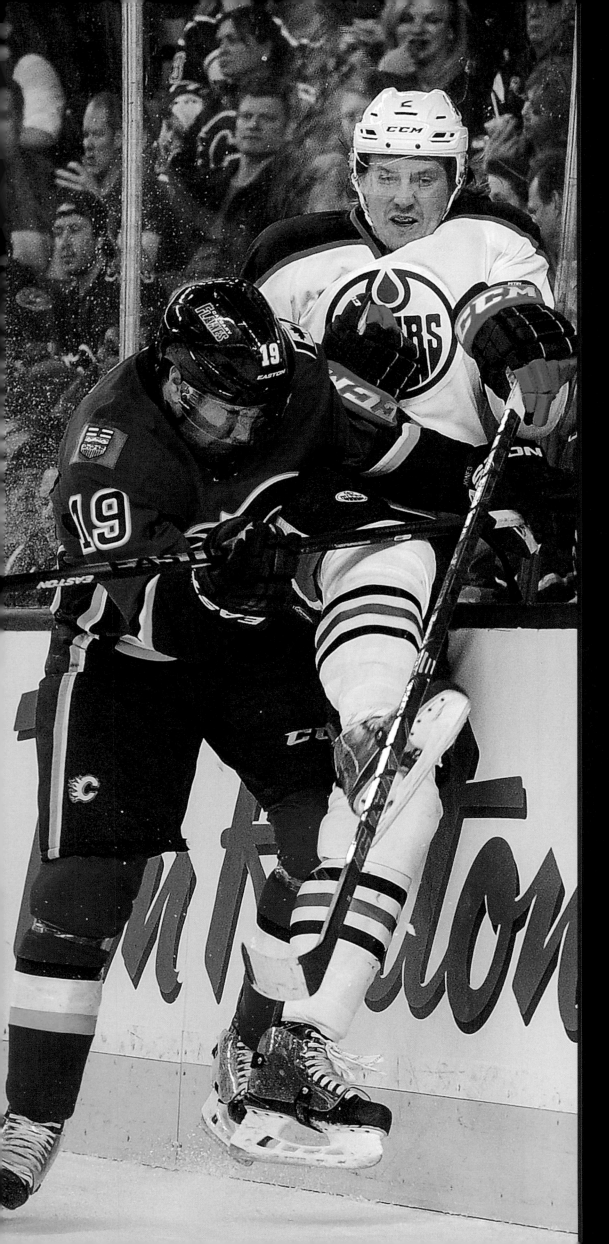

6

CALGARY-EDMONTON

FIRST MEETING: 1980

> *"One is disparaged as Deadmonton; one dismissed as Cowtown. But when these teams play, the resulting inferno is the Battle of Alberta, dating back to when Gretzky, Messier, Lanny McDonald and Dan Quinn annually locked horns in the playoffs."* —E.M. SWIFT

> ▸ REGULAR SEASON:
> 112-87-18-3 (CALGARY)
> ▸ POSTSEASON SERIES:
> 4–1 (EDMONTON)

USUALLY BRILLIANT, occasionally absurd, the Calgary-Edmonton series shaped up as a playoff classic from the very start, contested as it was in an atmosphere of unbridled ill will. The two cities, separated by 180 miles, can't stand one another. "We're the City of Champions and the Oil Capital of Alberta," crowed Oilers forward Dave Lumley on the eve of the series that became aptly known as the Uncivil War. Before last week was over, writers for Alberta's two major tabloids were slinging mud at each other. "In Cowtown, a two on one is what happens when your wife and your dog go after the same piece of meat," opined the *Edmonton Sun*. The *Calgary Sun*'s rejoinder: "If five kids are playing in a sandbox, it's easy to pick out the one from Edmonton. He's the one the cats keep trying to cover up."

—E.M. Swift, SI, May 5, 1986

Calgary's David Jones checked Jeff Petry in 2015.

FIRST MEETING: 1972

" Fueled by testy playoff meetings, numerous brawls and Denis Potvin's tough check that broke the ankle of Rangers forward Ulf Nilsson in 1979, the cross-island hatred has stood the test of time. " —BRIAN CAZENEUVE

▸ REGULAR SEASON:
124-104-19-7 (RANGERS)
▸ POSTSEASON SERIES:
5-3 (ISLANDERS)

Claude Lapointe scored on Mike Richter in 1999.
PHOTOGRAPH BY LOU CAPOZZOLA

THE POTVIN CHANT is not a staple in the Garden only when the Islanders play there. Potvin told me he had heard it while watching a New York Knicks game on television. To Rangers fans, Potvin's check cost their team the Cup, and the incident has remained as pronounced in their collective minds as an ax murder.

—George Plimpton, SI, April 3, 1989

7 ISLANDERS-RANGERS

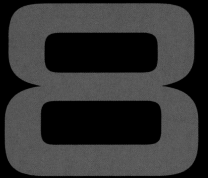

Quebec's Andrei Kovalenko escaped a Canadien crunch.

PHOTOGRAPH BY DAVID E. KLUTHO

"To borrow from Hobbes, this rivalry was nasty, French and short. From 1979 through '95, these teams engaged in a brutal provincial war. The highlight, or lowlight, was the Good Friday Massacre in 1984." —MICHAEL FARBER

▸ REGULAR SEASON:
62-39-12 (MONTREAL)
▸ POSTSEASON SERIES:
3-2 (MONTREAL)

8

MONTREAL-QUEBEC

A FREE-FOR-ALL began with Quebec's Dale Hunter and Montreal's Guy Carbonneau. Then Chris Nilan went after Quebec's Randy Moller, cutting him above the right eye with a series of punches. "I've been cut worse shaving," said Moller. He must shave with a jackhammer; his face was a bloody mess.

—Jack Falla, SI, April 30, 1984

HERE'S TO THE BAD OLD DAYS

A relatively civil edition of this rivalry had the writer missing the times when the Battle of Quebec inspired an enmity that spilled from the arenas into the taverns

BY E.M. SWIFT

OMEDAY THE YOUNG, talented Quebec Nordiques—everybody's pick as the Stanley Cup team of the future—will thank archrival Montreal for the character lesson they were handed last week by the Stanley Cup team of the past. Someday. Maybe. If they don't end up choking on the memory of it.

The Nordiques waltzed into the hallowed Montreal Forum last Thursday with a two-games-to-zip lead and with *Les Habitants* on the run in the NHL's most eagerly anticipated opening-round playoff series. But after surveying the 22 Stanley Cup banners hanging from the rafters, the Nordiques were outchecked, outhustled and outshot by their supposedly less-skilled opponents.

"They're playing like it's the 10th game of the year," Quebec coach Pierre Pagé railed. "If they don't want to lose, they have to give a lot more than that."

The Nordiques are the youngest team in the league, with an average age of 23½. This is Quebec's first appearance in postseason play since 1987, and most of its players have never participated in the NHL playoffs before. Heck, on a roster that includes four Russians, a Swede and a Czech, an appreciable number have never *seen* the NHL playoffs before. Still, that Pagé should feel compelled to plead for increased effort speaks volumes about the changed nature of this once storied rivalry that in the 1980s was as fierce as any in sports. Something was missing last week in this so-called Battle of Quebec that can be summed up in a single word—*enmity*.

Oh, how these two teams used to hate each other! The Canadiens and the Nordiques met four times in the playoffs between 1982 and '87, with each side winning twice. Some called it hockey, but it was closer to full-scale war, spilling over onto the streets and into the taverns across the province. No Quebecois was able to stand on the sidelines in bemused detachment. Everyone became a fanatic.

Sportswriters from Quebec and Montreal stopped speaking to one another. Carling O'Keefe, which owned the Nordiques, and Molson, which owned the Canadiens, declared beer war on each other and saw their sales affected by the outcome of the series. French separatists embraced the Nordiques; Anglophiles cheered for the Habs. "Those series were highly politicized, blown way out of proportion," says Steve Shutt, who played for the Canadiens from 1972 to '84 and now does radio and TV commentary for the team. "And they were the most brutal, dirty games I've ever played in. It was scary. They took so much out of you physically and emotionally that if you won, it didn't matter if you

went any further in the playoffs. The fans cared more about that series than if we won the Cup."

"We had 13 French Canadians, they had 13 French Canadians," says former Nordiques coach Michel Bergeron. "And tough players. We had Dale Hunter; they had Chris Nilan. These guys would always make something happen if they were behind by a couple of goals."

Hockey fans understand what those code words mean, particularly when linked to the likes of Hunter and Nilan: blood on the ice, preferably someone else's. "Now the breweries, Molson and O'Keefe, have merged," laments Bergeron, a radio talk-show host in Montreal. "Most of the people in the province, even Montreal fans, they're happy for Quebec because it's been so long since they've been in the playoffs. Both teams want to play a real clean series. I don't think the rivalry will ever be the same as it was."

Indeed, through the first five games, these kinder, gentler Nordiques and Canadiens did not engage in a fistfight, and sticks, by and large, remained down. One of the few cheap shots—an overtime slash to the forearm of Brian Bellows by Quebec defenseman Curtis Leschyshyn—led to the winning goal on a power play in Game 3. "The reporters would like it to get nasty so they'd have more to write about," Bellows said afterward. "But it hasn't been a nasty series."

In Montreal, after going down 0–2 the hometown fans had pretty much written off the Habs. With a 6–9 record over the last month of the season, Canadiens coach Jacques Demers's charges had limped into the playoffs. Demers, who a few weeks before had banned all newspapers (except *USA Today*) from the Montreal dressing room because he believed critical press reports were hurting his team, now found himself lampooned on a daily basis by Montreal's *La Presse*. A full-page caricature on April 21 depicted Demers as a downcast Napoleon, retreating to Montreal after the back-to-back drubbings in Quebec. The next day Pagé was drawn coming into town on a steamroller, wearing a Viking helmet, flattening Canadiens who fled in terror before the barbarians at their gates.

Unfortunately for Nordiques fans, Pagé's helmeted hoards played more like they were waging the battle of Sesame Street than the Battle of Quebec after they arrived in Montreal. The most vicious territorial struggle of Game 3 came during the pregame warmup, when Montreal's Mario Roberge stood his ground over the center-ice dot. It seems the superstitious Hextall must skate over the aforementioned dot before every game. Twice as Hextall approached it, Roberge slashed him on the pads. Jawboning ensued. Threats were made. Then Roberge was jostled by Quebec's Owen Nolan—his hardest hit of the night. In the old days, a bench-clearing brawl would have erupted, and 600 minutes in penalties would have been assessed. Not in the '90s. Hextall touched his dot, and the prospective combatants dispersed to their sandboxes. ■

FIRST MEETING: 1954

Wayne Gretzky fed Mario Lemieux in the '87 Canada Cup.

PHOTOGRAPH BY BRUCE BENNETT STUDIOS/GETTY IMAGES

" Hockey may be considered Canada's birthright, but it also came to represent more than a game in Soviet Russia. It was ideological warfare against the West, and their showdowns were a series of epic battles. " —SARAH KWAK

▸ RUSSIA LEADS 9–2 IN OLYMPICS MEETINGS
▸ RUSSIA LEADS 34-13-4 AT WORLD CHAMPIONSHIPS

CANADA-RUSSIA

HAS THERE ever been a more dominant performance by a Canadian team than its 7–3 Olympic quarterfinal trashing of Russia? If you said the 5–2 win over the Americans in 2002, you have support, but it was not a tour de force to match this humiliation of Canada's archnemesis.

—*Michael Farber, SI Presents, March 11, 2010*

10

CANADA-USA WOMEN

" They are the two best women's teams in the world, and their hostility is deliciously palpable. "The rivalry with Canada is a nasty one," says U.S. forward Kelli Stack. "We don't like them, plain and simple." **"** —E.M. SWIFT

‣ CANADA HAS FOUR OLYMPIC GOLDS, 10 WORLD TITLES
‣ USA HAS ONE OLYMPIC GOLD MEDAL, SIX WORLD TITLES

TO DRUM UP fan awareness, the U.S. and Canada played each other 13 times in the 3½ months leading up to Nagano. Canada won seven games, the U.S. six. "We played them too many times," says Canada forward Vicky Sunohara. "They learned from us and got better and better." And the games got rougher and rougher.

—*Kostya Kennedy, SI, February 19, 2002*

The two teams have won every Olympic gold medal.

PHOTOGRAPH BY DAVID E. KLUTHO

10 THE

BEST SINGLE-SEASON TEAMS

HOCKEY, MORE THAN ANY SPORT, HAS BEEN RULED BY DYNASTIES. FROM THE 1950S THROUGH THE 1980S, ESPECIALLY, TEAMS WON TITLES IN CHUNKS, FROM DETROIT'S TAKING FOUR STANLEY CUPS IN SIX YEARS AT THE BEGINNING OF THAT STRETCH, TO EDMONTON'S GRABBING FIVE IN SEVEN SEASONS, ENDING IN 1988–89. THE MAPLE LEAFS AND ISLANDERS HAD DYNASTIC RUNS IN THOSE DECADES, AS DID THE CANADIENS, MORE THAN ONCE.

IN CHOOSING THE GREAT SINGLE-SEASON TEAM PANELISTS WERE USUALLY ABLE TO FOCUS ATTENTION ON A PARTICULARLY OUTSTANDING TEAM WITHIN A DYNASTY, EVEN THOUGH LESSER EDITIONS DID DRAW THE OCCASIONAL STRAY VOTE.

IN TWO INSTANCES, TWO CLOSELY CLUSTERED TEAMS LANDED IN OUR TOP 10. ONE SET CAME FROM THE CANADIENS THAT WON FOUR STRAIGHT TITLES IN THE LATE '70S. THE OTHER SET WAS, INTERESTINGLY, THE RED WINGS TEAMS OF '95–96 AND '96–97. THE CURIOUS DETAIL THERE IS THAT THE '95–96 TEAM, THOUGH IT WON A RECORD 62 REGULAR-SEASON GAMES, DID NOT TAKE THE CUP THAT YEAR, LOSING TO COLORADO IN THE WESTERN CONFERENCE FINALS. THAT POSTSEASON FAILURE TAKES SOME BURNISH OFF WHATEVER DYNASTIC CLAIMS DETROIT MIGHT HAVE HAD, BUT THE RECORD WAS ENOUGH TO ELEVATE THAT TEAM TO A PLACE AMONG THE ALLTIME GREATS.

1

1976–77
CANADIENS

60-8-12 REGULAR SEASON

"With 10 future Hall of Famers on the team, including coach Scotty Bowman, the '76–77 Canadiens faced their toughest competition in scrimmages at practice. Setting the NHL record for most team points, these Canadians outscored opponents by 2.7 goals per game, and lost just twice in the postseason." —SARAH KWAK

- SWEPT BRUINS IN STANLEY CUP FINALS
- LED NHL IN GOALS FOR AND GOALS AGAINST

JUST HOW good are these Canadiens? In 94 regular-season and playoff games they outscored the opposition 440 goals to 194. They had the leading goal scorer (Steve Shutt), the leading point maker (Guy Lafleur) and the best goaltending tandem (Ken Dryden and Bunny Larocque). They have swept the last two finals, and their two-year playoff record is a remarkable 24–3—they lost only to the Islanders, twice this season and once a year ago. Says Tom Johnson, who played defense for the 1956–60 Montreal clubs and now is the Bruins' assistant GM, "These Canadiens have every element a team needs, and it's the hardest-working, best-checking great team I've ever seen."

—Peter Gammons, SI, May 23, 1977

Montreal had a 14-week stretch in which it lost once.

PHOTOGRAPH BY CO RENTMEESTER

2

1983–84
OILERS

57-18-5 REGULAR SEASON

" Besides Wayne Gretzky, the team that won the first of Edmonton's five Stanley Cups boasted a raft of outrageously talented and carefree young players, including Jari Kurri, Paul Coffey, Mark Messier, Glenn Anderson and Grant Fuhr. It may not have been the best team ever, but it was the sexiest. " —MARK BEECH

▸ DEFEATED ISLANDERS 4–1 FOR STANLEY CUP
▸ ISLANDERS HAD WON PREVIOUS FOUR TITLES

IN WRESTING the Cup from the Islanders four games to one with a 5–2 victory, the Oilers proved that creative and high-scoring offense can win big over an orthodox bump-and-grind defense. Edmonton may well have launched a new era in the pro game. The sleek may yet inherit the ice. Besides being the highest-scoring team ever to win the Cup, the Oilers are also the first NHL team to take the Cup west of Chicago and the youngest modern-era expansion team to win the title. "I hope we're an influence on the game," said Wayne Gretzky after emerging from the rollicking chaos of the Edmonton locker room. "We proved that an offensive team can win the Cup. That can't do anything but help hockey. We showed that you can win by skating and being physical without having to fight all the time."

—Jack Falla, SI, May 28, 1984

The Oilers achieved greatness in only their fifth NHL season.

PHOTOGRAPHS BY JOHN IACONO

3

1977–78
CANADIENS

59-10-11 REGULAR SEASON

" Montreal won its third of four straight
Stanley Cups with no apparent
weaknesses. The team featured the
league's leading scorer (Guy Lafleur), top
goaltender (Ken Dryden) and the best
defensive forward (Bob Gainey). The
Canadiens went unbeaten in 28
consecutive games and never trailed in a
playoff series. " —BRIAN CAZENEUVE

▸ DEFEATED BRUINS 4–2
FOR STANLEY CUP
▸ LED NHL IN GOALS FOR AND
GOALS AGAINST

ON THEIR record-breaking 23-0-
5 tear, the Canadiens enjoyed the
streak while it lasted and talked
about keeping it going as long as
possible—"so no other team will
ever break our record," as Guy Lafleur
said. In the course of their stunning
streak, the Canadiens played every
NHL rival except Minnesota at least
once. And they pulled it off despite
a staggering succession of ailments.
All-Star defenseman Guy Lapointe
missed 23 of the 28 games, checking
specialist Bob Gainey was lost
for nine, and injuries and illnesses
briefly sidelined Lafleur, captain
Yvan Cournoyer and center Pierre
Larouche. But flaunting Montreal's
enviable depth, coach Scotty
Bowman kept replacing the lame
and halt with fresh troops.

—Jerry Kirshenbaum, SI, March 6, 1978

This Montreal team went 12–3 in the postseason.

PHOTOGRAPH BY MANNY MILLAN

4

1971–72
BRUINS

54-31-11 REGULAR SEASON

"As colorful as they were dominant, the Big Bad Bruins would outscore you, outfight you and later outparty you. In addition to future Hall of Famers Phil Esposito, Johnny Bucyk and Gerry Cheevers, they featured Bobby Orr in his scintillating prime." —E.M. SWIFT

▸ DEFEATED RANGERS 4–2 FOR STANLEY CUP
▸ 12–3 POSTSEASON RECORD

Orr won the '72 Hart, Norris and Conn Smythe trophies.

PHOTOGRAPH BY NEIL LEIFER

ONE ASPECT of Orr's genius is not to let the spotlight stray from him at the big moments. Here he was against the Rangers, hockey's best player, Bobby Bad Knee, personally settling the bloody war between the sport's top teams—just as he had in the final Stanley Cup game against St. Louis two years ago.

—Mark Mulvoy, SI, May 22, 1972

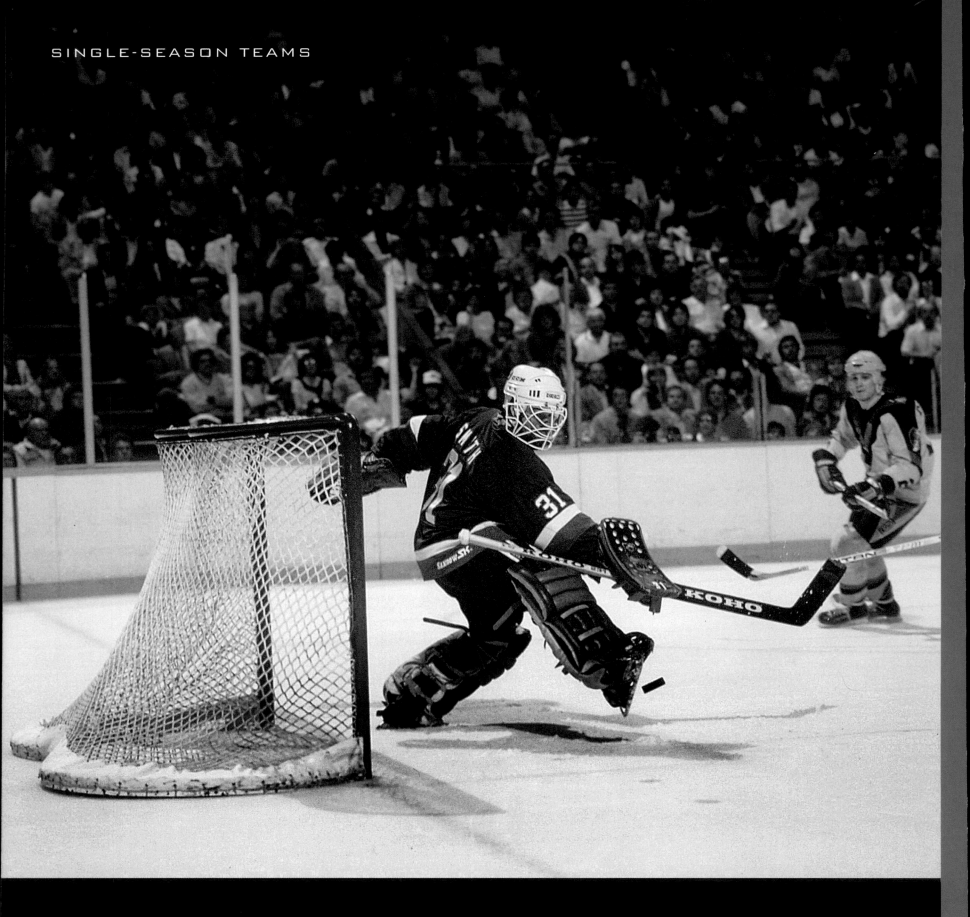

54-16-10 REGULAR SEASON

Goaltender Billy Smith was that season's Vezina winner.

PHOTOGRAPH BY PETER READ MILLER

5

" The Islanders needed a rally in the deciding game to survive their opening-round playoff series against Pittsburgh, but finished the postseason with nine straight wins. " —BRIAN CAZENEUVE

‣ SWEPT CANUCKS IN STANLEY CUP FINALS
‣ THIRD OF FOUR CONSECUTIVE TITLES

1981–82
ISLANDERS

THE ISLANDERS had been dominant in the series. Indeed, they have been that dominant for the past three years. Said coach Al Arbour. "The first year they said it was a fluke, the next we proved it wasn't, and this year we proved that we are a great team."

—E.M. Swift, SI, May 24, 1982

6

1951–52 RED WINGS

> " Seven future Hall of Famers formed the heart of this Detroit team that was led by a young Gordie Howe. They cruised through the regular season, then won all eight of their playoff games, four by shutout. " —E.M. SWIFT

▸ SWEPT CANADIENS IN STANLEY CUP FINALS
▸ LED NHL IN GOALS FOR AND GOALS AGAINST

HOCKEY HAS never pretended to imitate Major League Baseball. But last week, as the NHL opened its season, fans sensed that hockey, too, has its New York Yankees. Their names: the Detroit Red Wings, who have won the NHL [regular-season] title six years running. In three of those years the Wings have also won the Stanley Cup.

—*Sports Illustrated, October 18, 1954*

Terry Sawchuk (left) and Sid Abel were Cup comrades.

PHOTOGRAPH BY PRESTON STROUP/AP

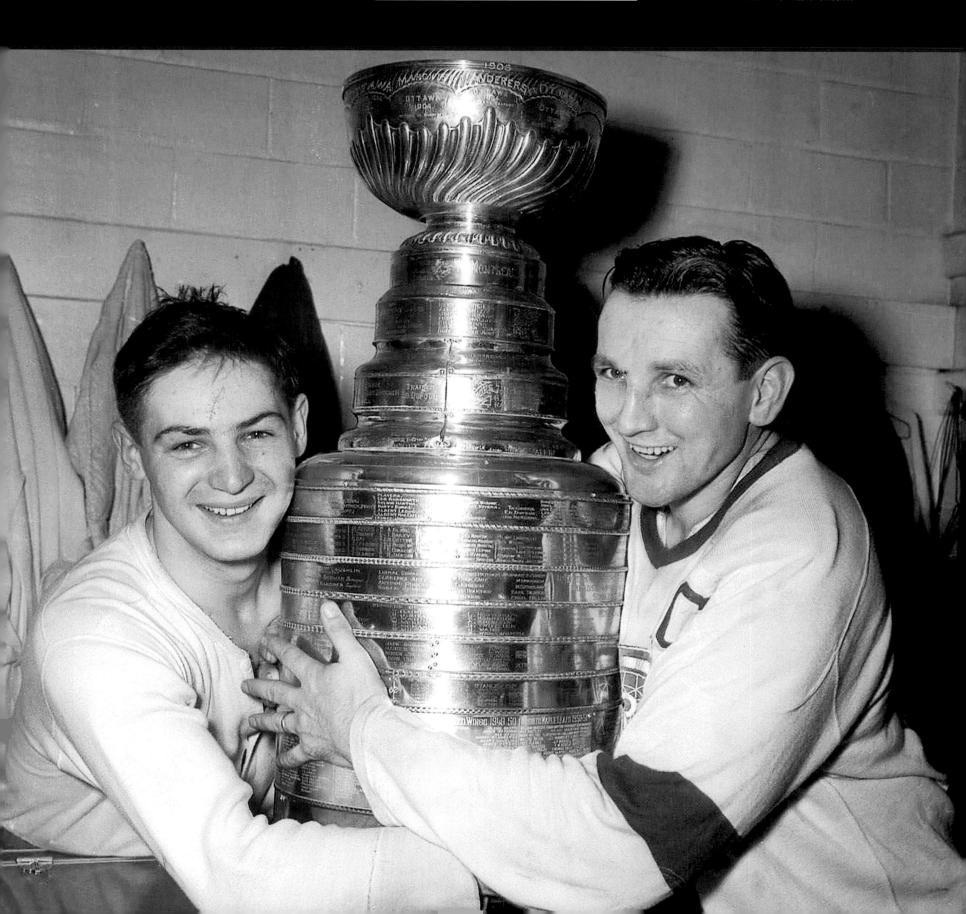

7

1955–56
CANADIENS

40-15-10 REGULAR SEASON

" The dynasty starts, the first of five straight Stanley Cups. The Rocket had not begun his slow fade into twilight. Along for the ride were some of the best, and most important, players in history: Plante, Béliveau, Geoffrion, Moore, Doug Harvey. That is basically a Hall of Fame wing. " —MICHAEL FARBER

▸ DEFEEATED RED WINGS 4–1 FOR STANLEY CUP
▸ LED NHL IN GOALS FOR AND GOALS AGAINST

IT IS quite possible that no hockey team in history has ever been led by two such brilliant craftsmen. It is likewise probable that no two stars on the same team were ever so exactly opposite in temperament as are Maurice Richard and Jean Béliveau. "With Maurice," said managing director Frank J. Selke, "his moves are powered by instinctive reflexes. Maurice can't learn from lectures. He does everything by instinct and with sheer power. Béliveau, on the other hand, is a perfect coach's hockey player because he studies and learns. He's moving and planning all the time. The difference between the two best hockey players in the game today is simply this: Béliveau is a perfectionist, Richard is an opportunist."

—*Whitney Tower, SI, January 23, 1956*

Jacques Plante backed up a stingy defense.

PHOTOGRAPH BY HY PESKIN

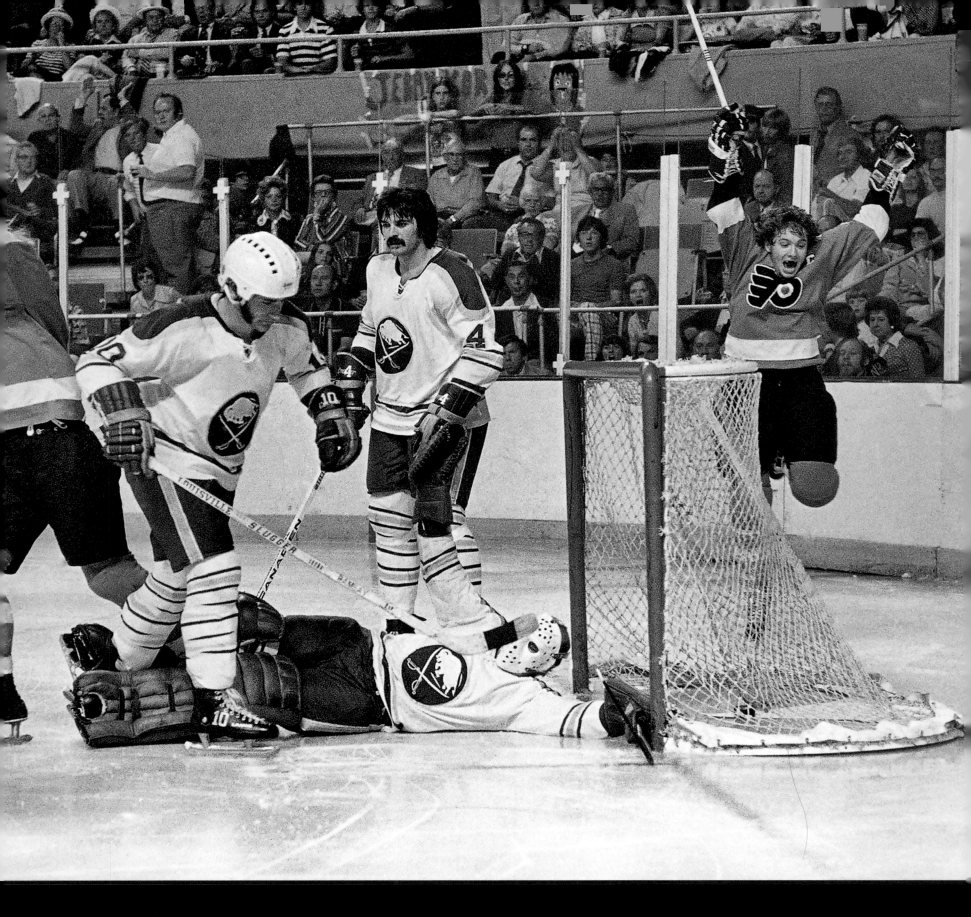

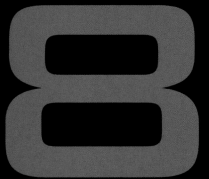

8

1974–75 FLYERS

51-18-11 REGULAR SEASON

"A Hart winner (Bobby Clarke), a Vezina winner (Bernie Parent) and the league's most wins led to a second straight Cup. The Flyers were deep, colorful and talented and if they weren't just beating you, the Bullies were knocking you silly." —KOSTYA KENNEDY

▸ BEAT SABRES 4–2 FOR CUP
▸ LED NHL IN GOALS AGAINST

Clarke's Flyers rose above Buffalo in the Cup finals.

WILL KATE SMITH arrive just before game time, sing "God Bless America," and then cheer the Flyers to another victory? Or will she do it on tape? In living color Kate the Great had a perfect record. "If she really means that much," coach Fred Shero grumbled, "I think we ought to put her on the payroll."

—*Mark Mulvoy, SI, May 26, 1975*

FIGHTING FOR RESPECT

*As the Broad Street Bullies captured their second consecutive
Stanley Cup, they showed there was more to their
game than the rough play that earned them their nickname*

BY MARK MULVOY

T'S ALL OVER, THE 1974–75 HOCKEY SEASON. *Finis!* After 254 days and 97 games, the Flyers concluded the longest season in pro sports history last week by winning their second straight NHL championship. They beat the Sabres 2–0 behind Bernie Parent's impeccable goaltending in the climactic sixth game in steamy Buffalo.

After the Flyers had short-circuited Buffalo's French Connection, after they had guzzled the bubbly from the Stanley Cup and after they had been cheered by 2.3 million delirious Philadelphians on their triumphant parade through the city, it was impossible to forget a message that coach Freddie (The Fog) Shero had once written on their dressing-room blackboard:

Fame is a vapor/Popularity an accident/Riches take wings/Only one thing endures/and that is character.

No one can deny that the Flyers have character. Lots of it. Take that character, add a generous portion of Parent's wizard goaltending, plus a good measure of captain Bobby Clarke's fanatical desire, have it rise to special occasions with Rick MacLeish's inspired play, season with a few sprigs of Kate Smith's golden tones, pour it all into Shero's disciplined system—and you have your basic Stanley Cup champion.

Last season the Flyers were called the Broad Street Bullies from the City of Brotherly Mug because of the coarse manner in which they played hockey. Ask who personified the Flyers' style of play in other NHL cities and Clarke, even Parent, would probably have taken a back seat to hockey's top-seeded bad boy Dave Schultz. "Nobody likes us," Shero admitted. "Nobody outside Philadelphia, that is. In fact, the *nicest* thing people say about us is that we are a bunch of muggers."

So they were. This spring, though, the Flyers suffered and survived a surprising metamorphosis. While their intrinsic natures will never permit them to be mistaken for so many Frank Merriwells, the Flyers disdained their standard rough-house tactics and beat the harried Sabres with pure, clean, fundamental hockey, just the way they had defeated the Toronto Maple Leafs and the New York Islanders in earlier playoff rounds. Unbelievably, the Flyers were involved in only two fights—one loss and one draw—during the six games against Buffalo. "We used to have at least two fights in every period," says Clarke.

Sticking to hockey, the Flyers limited Buffalo's alleged power play to just three goals in 32 attempts; held the French Connection line of center Gilbert Perreault and wings Richard Martin and Rene Robert—which had scored a total of 18 goals in 11 previous playoff games against Chicago and Montreal—to a paltry four goals in the finals; and thoroughly neutralized the normally elusive Perreault with their adroit checking maneuvers. In fact, Perreault, hockey's flashiest forward, managed but a single goal and one assist against the Flyers,

and for all of his one-on-one bobbing and weaving, the Philadelphia defensive umbrella stubbornly refused to collapse.

Terry Crisp was one of the five Philadelphia centers who shared the assignment of harassing Perreault. More analytical than most of his teammates, Crisp offered the best assessment of what the Flyers had just accomplished. "When people think of hockey," he said, "they think of everything being graceful and flowing. The Flying Frenchmen, the French Connection, all that. Then we came along. They used to call us goons because we weren't very fancy, but now they have no excuses—none—because there was no gooning in these playoffs. Or put it this way: The point we proved is that a working man's hockey team can win."

Call that character. Bob Kelly certainly is a working man with character. Affectionately known as Hound or Mutt to his teammates, Kelly is Philadelphia's designated hitter who usually steps onto the ice only when Shero feels the pace of a game has become too humdrum. "Kelly doesn't know how to put on his brakes," says Shero. "He shakes up both teams. He's the most dangerous 11-goal scorer in hockey."

Character, too, is the stamp of the Philadelphia defense, particularly Andre (Moose) Dupont, Ed Van Impe and the Watson brothers, Jimmy and Joe. They have never been popular with All-Star voters, but the Philadelphia Four provide Parent with the sturdiest protection in hockey. Parent says he can count the breakaways he faced this season on the fingers of one hand. "Those guys make it easy for me."

Clarke, in particular, was physically spent after the final game in Buffalo. A diabetic, he seemed to lose his skating élan as the playoff season closed in on the month of June, but even at 80% speed he was the most intimidating presence on the ice, aside from Parent. He killed penalties, worked the power play, shadowed Perreault perfectly and proved once more that he is the sport's most tireless performer. Although Clarke's natural skills hardly rival Bobby Orr's or Guy Lafleur's, or Perreault's for that matter, right now he is the dominant skater in the game because, as Shero says, "He has shown he is a winner."

So, in his position, is Parent, who was voted the MVP of the playoffs for the second straight year. Parent had four shutouts and allowed only 29 goals in 15 games. "That bumper sticker everyone has down in Philadelphia, the one that says 'Only the Lord saves more than Bernie Parent,' really isn't true," said Buffalo's Jerry (King Kong) Korab. "God couldn't have made all the saves that Parent made against us."

After the boisterous parade through Philadelphia, Parent was called to the microphone to address the 100,000 people who had crammed into John F. Kennedy Stadium. His words were brief—and to the point. "I'll see you again right here next May 27, O.K.?" he said. Whatever you say, Bernie. Everyone in Philadelphia is ready and waiting. ∎

9

1995–96
RED WINGS

62-13-7 REGULAR SEASON

> " Just an overwhelming group of players, led by Scotty Bowman, the best coach in the NHL history. " —PIERRE MCGUIRE

- ▸ NHL RECORD FOR MOST REGULAR-SEASON WINS
- ▸ LOST TO AVALANCHE 4–2 IN CONFERENCE FINALS

ON THE EVE of the playoffs Bowman told reporters, "There's nothing so uncertain as a sure thing. Good night." He said that at two o'clock in the afternoon. But the regular season showed that the Red Wings are the deepest, most versatile team in the NHL. The Detroit lineup is replete with unsung heroes like Kris Draper, Tim Taylor, Greg Johnson and penalty-killing specialist Doug Brown are all fourth-liners who do more than take up space. The depth makes the Red Wings tougher to shut down than one-line teams like the Blues. It also makes them less vulnerable to injuries than a team dependent on one player, as the Rangers are on Mark Messier. "Detroit has a lot of guys who can do a lot of things, but it also appears they have a lack of egos," Winnipeg GM John Paddock says. "They've seemed to put those other things— contracts, ice time—aside and concentrated on winning. That's why they won 62 during the season."

—*Michael Farber, SI, April 29, 1996*

Detroit scored in every regular-season game.

PHOTOGRAPH BY TIM DEFRISCO

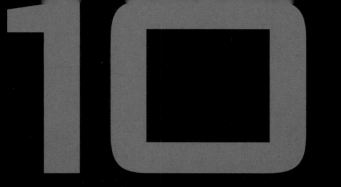

10

1996–97
RED WINGS

" They weren't overpowering but were a team of great grit and great grace. Laden with alltime stars—Steve Yzerman, Brendan Shanahan, Nicklas Lidstrom, Sergei Fedorov—the Wings delivered Detroit the Cup it had been waiting for since 1955. " —KOSTYA KENNEDY

▸ SWEPT FLYERS IN FINALS
▸ DETROIT'S FIRST CUP IN 42 YEARS

YZERMAN WAS slowly circling the ice, smiling as brightly as the 19,983 faces in the arena. "I'm glad the game is over," Yzerman said. "But I wish it had never ended. Since I was five years old, I've watched the Stanley Cup. I have stayed up, made a point of watching it being presented and always dreamed of the day that maybe I would get there."

—Michael Farber, SI, June 16, 1997

Fedorov led Detroit with 20 postseason points.

PHOTOGRAPH BY DAVID E. KLUTHO

10

THE

Best Franchises

"THE ORIGINAL SIX IS ABOUT THE FABRIC OF FAMILY," BLACKHAWKS GM STAN BOWMAN TOLD SI'S MICHAEL FARBER IN 2013. "THERE ARE HOCKEY FANS IN SOME OF THE NEW MARKETS WHO ARE INTENSE. BUT IT SEEMS THERE'S AN EXTRA LAYER OF PASSION FROM PEOPLE WHO'VE HAD IT PASSED ON FROM THEIR GRANDPARENTS AND PARENTS AND WHO NOW PASS IT ON TO THEIR CHILDREN. WHEN OUR TEAM STRUGGLED HERE, THERE WAS ALWAYS A GROUP WAITING FOR THINGS TO TURN AROUND. WHEN THERE'S NOT A LONG TRADITION OF HOCKEY AND A TEAM STRUGGLES FOR A TIME, I'M NOT SURE THEY COME BACK IN FULL FORCE. THAT'S THE REAL SIGNIFICANCE OF THE ORIGINAL SIX."

EACH OF THOSE ORIGINAL SIX, WHO COMPRISED THE ENTIRETY OF THE NHL FROM 1942 TO '67, MAKES THE LIST OF TOP FRANCHISES. THE RANGERS ONLY MADE IT NARROWLY, THOUGH, EDGING THE AVALANCHE FOR THE 10TH SPOT.

THE YOUNGEST FRANCHISE TO MAKE THE TOP 10 IS EDMONTON, WHICH BEGAN IN THE WHA AND JOINED THE NHL IN 1979. THOSE OILERS WON MORE TITLES IN THEIR FIRST 11 SEASONS IN THE LEAGUE THAN THE RANGERS HAVE IN THEIR FIRST 88. STILL, EDMONTON'S CUP COLLECTION HAS STALLED SINCE THAT EARLY RUSH. NEW YORK FANS KNOW ALL TOO WELL THAT ONE SPELL OF SUCCESS DOES NOT MEAN A DROUGHT WILL NEVER COME.

1

THE CANADIENS

FOUNDED 1909

" You probably call them the Habs. In French, they are also known as Les Glorieux and La Sainte-Flanelle. (Without irony.) Professors teach courses on the Canadiens as religion. Le Club du Hockey Canadien hasn't won the Stanley Cup since 1993, but now, in its second century, it remains the colossus. " —MICHAEL FARBER

▸ 24 STANLEY CUP TITLES
▸ 85 PLAYOFF SEASONS

IT IS DOUBTFUL if there is any group of sports addicts anywhere which supports its team with quite the supercharged emotion and lavish pride expended so prodigally by the citizens of bilingual Montreal on their hockey team, Les Canadiens— the Canadians. Hockey is deep in the Montrealer's blood. After a fine play, the Forum reverberates from the rinkside to the rafters with sharp enthusiastic applause. But many volts above this in feeling and many decibels above in volume is the singular and sudden pandemonium that shatters the Forum, like thunder and lightning, whenever the incomparable star of Les Canadiens, Maurice (The Rocket) Richard, fights his way through the enemy defense and blasts the puck past the goalie. There is no sound quite like it in the whole world of sport.

—*Herbert Warren Wind, SI, December 6, 1954*

Montreal topped Chicago in Game 7 of the 1965 finals.

PHOTOGRAPH BY JOSEPH CONSENTINO

FOUNDED 1926

Chris Chelios (far left) and Co. led Bowman-era Detroit.

PHOTOGRAPH BY DAVID E. KLUTHO

2

THE
RED WINGS

"Along with producing the game's most iconic player, Gordie Howe, Detroit was good early (seven titles between 1936 and '55) and peerless late. Detroit has made the playoffs every year from '91 through 2015, winning four Cups and reaching two other finals." —KOSTYA KENNEDY

▸ 11 STANLEY CUP TITLES
▸ 63 PLAYOFF SEASONS

"THERE WE WERE, putting these octopuses on display in our store," recalls Pete Cusimano. "Then it hit me: eight wins, eight legs. Stanley Cup! What a good-luck charm an octopus would be! So Gordie Howe scores the first goal, and I let it fly. It slid like a puck to the blue line. The crowd went wild."

—Mark Mandernach, SI, May 16, 1994

FROM SPORTS ILLUSTRATED
JUNE 24, 2002

THE YANKEES OF THE ICE

Scotty Bowman's retirement after the 2002 Stanley Cup marked a time for celebration of his accomplishments, which included the righting of once-foundering Detroit

BY MICHAEL FARBER

COTTY BOWMAN HAD BEEN dropping hints like bread crumbs for anyone willing to follow the trail. In a press conference before Game 3 of the Stanley Cup finals on June 8, Bowman, the 68-year-old Detroit Red Wings coach, said he had made a decision about his future (but refused to elaborate). When the possibility of a labor stoppage in 2004–05 was raised later in the week, he said a lockout would be somebody else's problem. In fact, it was after the Olympic break in February that Bowman decided to retire, but he told only a handful of friends, including New York Yankees manager Joe Torre. On the morning of Game 5, he broke the news to his summertime neighbor in suburban Buffalo, Canadian Broadcasting Company analyst and former coach Harry Neale.

"I'm retiring," Bowman told him. "All the other times I considered it, I thought I knew I was ready. Now I know I know it."

"So what now?" Neale asked.

"Consultant," said Bowman, who has a three-year deal with Detroit as a paid second-guesser. "Now I can go to the games and I don't have to win them."

The Red Wings had to win the 2002 Cup, because they were constructed to do no less. They defeated the dogged but overmatched Carolina Hurricanes, but their third Cup in six years was not so much pursued as it was orchestrated—much like the celebration after the 3–1 clinching win in Game 5. After going wire-to-wire following a 22-3-1-1 start, surviving losses in Games 1 and 2 of the first-round matchup against the Vancouver Canucks and outlasting the defending champion Colorado Avalanche in the superb seven-game Western Conference finals, Detroit staged an on-ice celebration that was much smoother than its power play.

As red and white confetti rained from the rafters of Joe Louis Arena, captain Steve Yzerman, who only moments earlier had been told by Bowman of his imminent departure, accepted the Cup from commissioner Gary Bettman and handed it to his coach. Having donned his skates with 20 seconds left to play, he took one final spin with the 35-pound chalice he had been chasing for 46 NHL seasons. Then, one by one, the players who never had lifted the trophy—goalie Dominik Hasek, 37; sniper Luc Robitaille, 36; and jack-o'-lantern defenseman Steve Duchesne, 36, who had lost six of his front teeth in Game 3—were given their moment in the spotlight with the Cup.

Bowman, meanwhile, continued to spread the news. As he hugged general manager Ken Holland at center ice, he said, "This was my last game." For someone who sets the standard for prolixity, the sentence was sweet and succinct. Bowman has been known to ramble: In reply to a question before Game 5 on the common traits of great coaches, he gave a 668-word discourse that contained references to trips to Florida and a journeyman goalie named Cesare Maniago, whose career ended 24 years ago.

The ultimate contrarian, Bowman is the best coach in pro sports history because he's an old-school leader who kept up with the times, an inflexible man who made adjustments in dealing with today's players. Bowman had the right to overshadow the celebration with his retirement announcement because his career has been more memorable than the final series was. Bowman's legacy as a coach, which includes nine Cups (breaking the record he shared since 1998 with mentor Toe Blake), is secure—just like the Red Wings' future.

Detroit has surpassed its status as a mere hockey powerhouse and become the pinstriped dynasty of the ice. Similar to what happened in the Horace Clarke days of the Yankees, the franchise had to endure the era of the late 1970s and early '80s, when the untalented, ineptly managed Red Wings were known as the Dead Things. Like the splendidly professional Yankees of recent years, these Red Wings, who play an up-tempo, crowd-pleasing game, are hard to hate. Like the Yankees, the Red Wings spend top dollar to get premium talent. And, finally, like the Yankees, the Red Wings routinely get the players they want, because the club's talent is a siren's call that attracts more talent.

"We are like the Yankees," agrees Brett Hull, the right wing who scored the pivotal goal in Game 3, on a deflection with 74 seconds left in regulation. That tally extended the match into overtime—Detroit then won 3-2—and effectively derailed Carolina. After that goal by Hull, who led playoff scorers with 10, the Hurricanes had only one goal in the remaining 176 minutes and one second of the series. "Year in and year out," says Hull, "this team will be there. They'll always be at the top."

"We try to have not only good players but also good role models," Holland says. "You see how far [21-year-old defenseman Jiri] Fischer progressed this season playing with Chris Chelios. Henrik Zetterberg has told me Igor Larionov is his favorite player, and it would be great for Henrik if Igor was around. Players have to learn how to go about the business of being a pro. Yzerman, [Sergei] Fedorov and [Conn Smythe Trophy winner Nicklas] Lidstrom had to do it on their own through the early and mid-'90s, which is why we lost so many times in the playoffs. I hope that our young players will learn from Chelios and Larionov."

Holland is unconcerned about not having a coach in place when the free-agent signing period begins on July 1—the team's success, not the man behind the bench, speaks for the Red Wings. ∎

3

THE BRUINS

FOUNDED 1924

" People have loved them or hated them but always wanted to watch them. From Bobby Orr to Ray Bourque to Patrice Bergeron, the Bruins have stood the test of time. " —PIERRE MCGUIRE

▸ SIX STANLEY CUP TITLES
▸ 69 PLAYOFF SEASONS

AN IMAGE of the Bruins hockey player emerged. He wore an open blue collar. He was not afraid to dirty his hands. Punch in, punch out. An honest effort. The off-ice exploits made news, wacky stuff like when Orr and some teammates kidnapped center Phil Esposito from Mass General after knee surgery, wheeling him out to go to a team party; but the on-ice exploits were solid and successful. The city loved the Bruins. The Bruins loved the city. Even after the birth of the competing WHA and the expansion of the NHL took talent off the roster, the Bruins were the bottom-line Boston team. They were family, not just sports entertainment. Family and friends. The players on the Red Sox, the Patriots, the Celtics, as the money grew larger, became wealthy visitors. They made their money, took it somewhere else. The Bruins routinely stayed. They bought houses. They raised kids. Family. Family and friends.

—*Leigh Montville, SI, June 6, 2011*

The old Garden rafters told the story of success.

PHOTOGRAPH BY NEIL LEIFER

4

THE
MAPLE LEAFS

FOUNDED 1917

" Despite an active 48-year-old drought between titles, the club once known as the Arenas and also the St. Patricks was the first NHL team valued at more than $1 billion, a testament to the team's enduring popularity. " —BRIAN CAZENEUVE

▸ 13 STANLEY CUP TITLES
▸ 65 PLAYOFF SEASONS

Toronto's Maple Leaf Gardens was a regular sellout.

PHOTOGRAPH BY ANDY CLARK/REUTERS

THEY ARE an anomaly in Canada, the land of mid-level payrolls. The fifth-highest average ticket price and strong corporate backing make the Leafs more like Rangers North. Says former Toronto center Kent Manderville, "It's almost like an American-style entertainment company."

—Michael Farber, SI, November 18, 2002

5

THE FLYERS

" The Flyers were the first expansion team to win the Stanley Cup in the post–Original Six era, just seven years after their founding. Those Broad Street Bullies, coached by Fred Shero, started a City of Brotherly–love affair that has never waned. " —E.M. SWIFT

IN MODERN NHL history, no Cups have ever Krazy-Glued a team to a town quite like those two. "Talk show hosts in this city criticize fans for not getting down on the Flyers the way they do on the Phillies, Eagles and Sixers," Flyers president Peter Luukko says. "I think that's because our fans feel they have ownership in the team."

—*Michael Farber, SI, December 10, 2007*

▸ TWO STANLEY CUP TITLES
▸ 37 PLAYOFF SEASONS

The Bullies won the Flyers' only Cups.

PHOTOGRAPH BY MELCHIOR DIGIACOMO/GETTY IMAGES

6

THE BLACKHAWKS

FOUNDED 1926

" Best logo in pro sports. Period. Former star Denis Savard, then the Blackhawks coach, passionately reminded his players to "commit to the Indian," and, certainly in recent years, the NHL has. The franchise that won a single Cup in the quarter century of the Original Six has taken three of the past six. " —MICHAEL FARBER

> SIX STANLEY CUP TITLES
> 60 PLAYOFF SEASONS

SECONDS AFTER the Blackhawks' win over the Wild ran their record to 20-0-3, a fan raised a sign: #23 ISN'T JUST ABOUT MICHAEL ANYMORE. In the building that sports a statue of a soaring Michael Jordan, the Blackhawks no longer seem like a secondary tenant. Indeed, their bandwagon has become a convoy. Paul Konerko, the first baseman for the White Sox team that went 11-1 in the 2005 postseason, says, "What [the Blackhawks] are doing is more difficult [than what we did] because when you're in the regular season it's easy to have a bad one here or there." In an interview with CSN Chicago, former Bulls forward Toni Kukoc compared the Blackhawks with the city's 1995–96 NBA champions, who won a record 72 games. "Both [teams] are a perfect match of experience, leadership, right attitude and chemistry," he said.

—*Brian Cazeneuve, SI, March 18, 2013*

Jonathan Toews (far left) has helped lift Chicago's fortunes.

PHOTOGRAPHS BY DAVID E. KLUTHO (LEFT) AND TODD ROSENBERG

7

THE DEVILS

FOUNDED 1974

" Playing in the shadows of New York City and the Rangers, the Devils are the NHL's version of the witness protection program. But under conservative president Lou Lamoriello, on the job since 1987, they have endured only four losing seasons. " —MARK BEECH

▸ THREE STANLEY CUP TITLES
▸ 22 PLAYOFF SEASONS

"ADD IT UP," says Canucks general manager Brian Burke. "The Devils draft like nobody's business. They have a premier farm team. They win in the NHL. And they do it all with a sound business plan. Lou's a model for our business. This is not just the best-run franchise in the NHL; it's the best-run franchise in pro sports."

—*Michael Farber, SI, March 22, 1999*

This 2012 OT win sent the Devils to the Cup finals.
PHOTOGRAPH BY BRUCE BENNETT/GETTY IMAGES

Gretzky, Messier and mates celebrated their fourth Cup.

PHOTOGRAPH BY DAVID E. KLUTHO

8

THE OILERS

FOUNDED 1972

" While winning five Stanley Cup championships in seven years, the Oilers personified perhaps the most entertaining era in NHL history. While Edmonton has been to just one finals since, that is a greatness which endures. " —KOSTYA KENNEDY

▸ FIVE STANLEY CUP TITLES
▸ 25 PLAYOFF SEASONS

THE OILERS had the best head start a new team could hope for: Wayne Gretzky was already on their roster. But Glen Sather also drafted well, getting Mark Messier, Glenn Anderson and Jari Kurri. Before Sather astutely pounced, five teams passed on Paul Coffey, and a year later seven skipped over Grant Fuhr.

—*Jay Greenberg, SI, November 12, 1990*

9

THE PENGUINS

FOUNDED 1967

> " So what if the team has been on brink of extinction not once but twice. The Penguins have also enjoyed massive success under two of the biggest stars the NHL has ever had: Mario Lemieux and Sidney Crosby. " —SARAH KWAK

▸ THREE STANLEY CUP TITLES
▸ 30 PLAYOFF SEASONS

THE METAMORPHOSIS began with the drafting of Crosby. When the Penguins won the lottery on July 22, 2005 president Ken Sawyer, representing Pittsburgh at the proceedings, actually took a step back in amazement. That was the last step back for the Penguins, who selected Crosby eight days later. Ticket sales, which had declined to an average of 11,877, the Penguins' lowest in nearly two decades, surged instantly. No matter what corporation brands the [new Penguins arena], it will be the House That Sid Built. The most impressive number in his spring portfolio is three: the seasons he needed to lead his team to the Stanley Cup finals. Wayne Gretzky took four to carry the Edmonton Oilers that far; Mario Lemieux, the Penguins' chairman and Crosby's landlord, took seven in Pittsburgh. The integers that define greatness do not appear in just the goals and assists column.

—*Michael Farber, SI, May 26, 2008*

Lemieux (left) and Crosby (right) defined Penguin pride.

10
THE RANGERS

FOUNDED 1926

" The Rangers won three Cups in their first 14 seasons then went on an 0-for-53 streak. But the fans never abandoned their beloved Blueshirts, and the curse was broken in 1994—thank you, Mark Messier. " —E.M. SWIFT

▸ FOUR STANLEY CUP TITLES
▸ 57 PLAYOFF SEASONS

WHEN EDMONTON traded Messier to the Rangers in 1991, the mandate was obvious. Messier had to make hockey matter in New York, to lead a showcase team with perennially low self-esteem to its first Stanley Cup since 1940. The Rangers finally won the Cup in '94, spurred on by a Messier performance in Game 6 of the semifinals against the Devils that was as impressive as any in history. Like Joe Namath before Super Bowl III, Messier "guaranteed" victory, though he didn't offer fans double their money back on Lincoln Tunnel tolls if the Rangers lost. Messier said on the eve of the match, "I know we're going to go in and win Game 6 and bring it back here for Game 7." Of course by the time the New York tabloids finished with him—after he had flung an empty-netter nearly the length of the ice for a hat trick to punctuate a 4–2 Rangers win—a Fu Manchu adorned his lip and his jersey had turned into mink. He had become Broadway Mark.

—*Michael Farber, SI, February 12, 1996*

Messier (left) and Henrik Lundqvist (right) celebrated.

10

THE

Best Skaters, Snipers, Clutch Performers and Shootout Specialists

IT IS PLAIN ENOUGH TO ANY OBSERVER THAT SKATING AND SHOOTING ARE SKILLS THAT HOCKEY PLAYERS CAN POSSESS IN VARYING DEGREES. WHETHER SOME ATHLETES ARE MORE CLUTCH THAN OTHERS, THROUGH, IS A MATTER OF DEBATE. PEOPLE WHO FOCUS ON SPORTS ANALYTICS WILL TELL YOU THAT CLUTCH PERFORMANCE IS A MYTH AND THEY HAVE DATA TO BACK IT UP. FANS ARGUING FOR THE EXISTENCE OF CLUTCH COULD DO WORSE THAN TO POINT TO CHRIS DRURY.

"HE'S NOT SUPERSKILLED. HE JUST WINS," MIKE ERUZIONE SAID ABOUT DRURY IN A 2007 SI STORY. ERUZIONE COACHED DRURY AS AN ASSISTANT AT BOSTON UNIVERSITY, WHERE DRURY WON AN NCAA TITLE. DRURY'S RÉSUMÉ ALSO INCLUDES A NATIONAL PEE-WEE TITLE, A STATE HIGH SCHOOL TITLE AND A STANLEY CUP IN 2001 WITH THE AVALANCHE. OH, AND HE WON A LITTLE LEAGUE WORLD SERIES. THAT FEELS LIKE MORE THAN LUCK.

"I DO THINK WHEN IT HAPPENS ONCE, YOU DRAW ON IT," SAID CHRIS'S BROTHER TED, ALSO AN NHL PLAYER, ON WINNING. "AND IT HAPPENS AGAIN, YOU HAVE TWO THINGS TO DRAW ON, AND IT KEEPS HAPPENING, AND YOU HAVE MORE TO DRAW ON." DRURY WON ENOUGH SO THAT, EVEN THOUGH HE MAKES NO OTHER LISTS IN THIS BOOK, OUR PANEL NAMED HIM ONE OF THE MOST CLUTCH PLAYERS EVER.

10 THE
BEST SKATERS

1 | **BOBBY ORR**
Orr skated so fast and so well that he fundamentally changed the nature of his position, and of hockey itself. —MARK BEECH

2 | **PAUL COFFEY**
Extraordinary acceleration. Most players slow down when they have the puck, but in his case the puck sped him up. —PIERRE McGUIRE

3 | **PAVEL BURE**
"The fastest Russian creation since *Sputnik*," one columnist wrote of the electrifying Bure, who averaged .623 goals per game. —E.M. SWIFT

4 | **YVAN COURNOYER**
So small and speedy he was nicknamed the Roadrunner, Cournoyer was the fastest of Montreal's Flying Frenchmen. —E.M. SWIFT

5 | **GUY LAFLEUR**
Lafleur wasn't the swiftest skater of the late 1970s, just the most feared when he had the puck on his stick. —MICHAEL FARBER

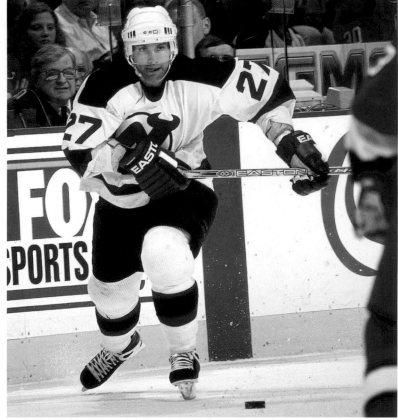

6 | **MIKE GARTNER**
Decidedly nonphysical, Gartner relied on sheer speed to become one of only seven players with more than 700 goals. —KOSTYA KENNEDY

7 | **SCOTT NIEDERMAYER**
The most efficient skater ever to play in the NHL. Niedermayer had a flawless stride and fantastic lateral movement. —PIERRE McGUIRE

8 | **GILBERT PERREAULT**
Perreault could stickhandle in tight confines while maintaining a head of steam that left his opponents flat-footed. —BRIAN CAZENEUVE

9 | **HOWIE MORENZ**
The Stratford Streak was one of the niftiest and fastest skaters of his era and one of hockey's first great scorers. —MARK BEECH

1 | ## MIKE BOSSY
Whether he scored on rushes up the wing or by curling suddenly into open ice, Bossy almost always caught a goalie moving. —BRIAN CAZENEUVE

2 | **BRETT HULL** The most compelling evidence that hockey skills are genetic may be Brett's shot, which came squarely from his father, Bobby (who also makes this snipers list). The son used the talent well, leading the NHL in goals for three seasons with St. Louis in the early '90s. —SARAH KWAK

3 | **MAURICE RICHARD** The best player in history from the red line in bore down on hapless goalies so quickly and shot so hard that he scored at an unprecedented rate. Montreal coach Dick Irvin summarized the intense nature of the Rocket's game by saying, "There are goals, and then there are Richard goals." —MARK BEECH

4 | **MARIO LEMIEUX** He was as complete a scorer as any who ever played, averaging .754 goals a game. That Lemieux could do it all was borne out in his famous 1988 game against the Devils. He scored five that night: at even strength, on the power play, shorthanded, on a penalty shot and into an empty net. —KOSTYA KENNEDY

5 | **BOBBY HULL** His powerful shot would strike the fear of God into goaltenders, some of whom were still playing without a mask in his day. One of first players to play with a curved stick, Hull could shoot it low or high, and he could deliver a little chin music to wake you up. —PIERRE MCGUIRE

6 | WAYNE GRETZKY Because he was a peerless passer, his goal-scoring prowess is recalled with stifled yawns as often as slack-jawed wonder. Well, go crazy, folks. Certainly Gretzky did. He scored 50 goals in 39 games in 1981–82 on his way to 92—just one more Gretzky scoring record that is impregnable. —MICHAEL FARBER

7 | GUY LAFLEUR During the Canadiens' dynasty in the 1970s, the Flower was the best player in the game. Le Grand Guy had the flair of Maurice Richard and the elegance of Jean Béliveau, but it was the accuracy of his shots that most vexed goaltenders. —E.M. SWIFT

8 | **TEEMU SELANNE** He was lightning-quick coming down the wings, and he had great hand skills. Selanne could score from many different angles (he led the league in goals scored twice) and he was unpredictable. You just didn't know when he was going to release the puck. —PIERRE McGUIRE

9 | **STEVEN STAMKOS** Few snipers in NHL history have needed less room to strike than the Tampa Bay center, who has led the league in goals twice. At 6-feet, 190 pounds, the stealthy Stamkos scores most of his goals by quietly finding seams in the defense and holes in the goalie's coverage. —BRIAN CAZENEUVE

10

ALEX OVECHKIN

Ovie is more Gatling gun than sniper, overwhelming goalies with both the volume and power of his one-timers. —E.M. SWIFT

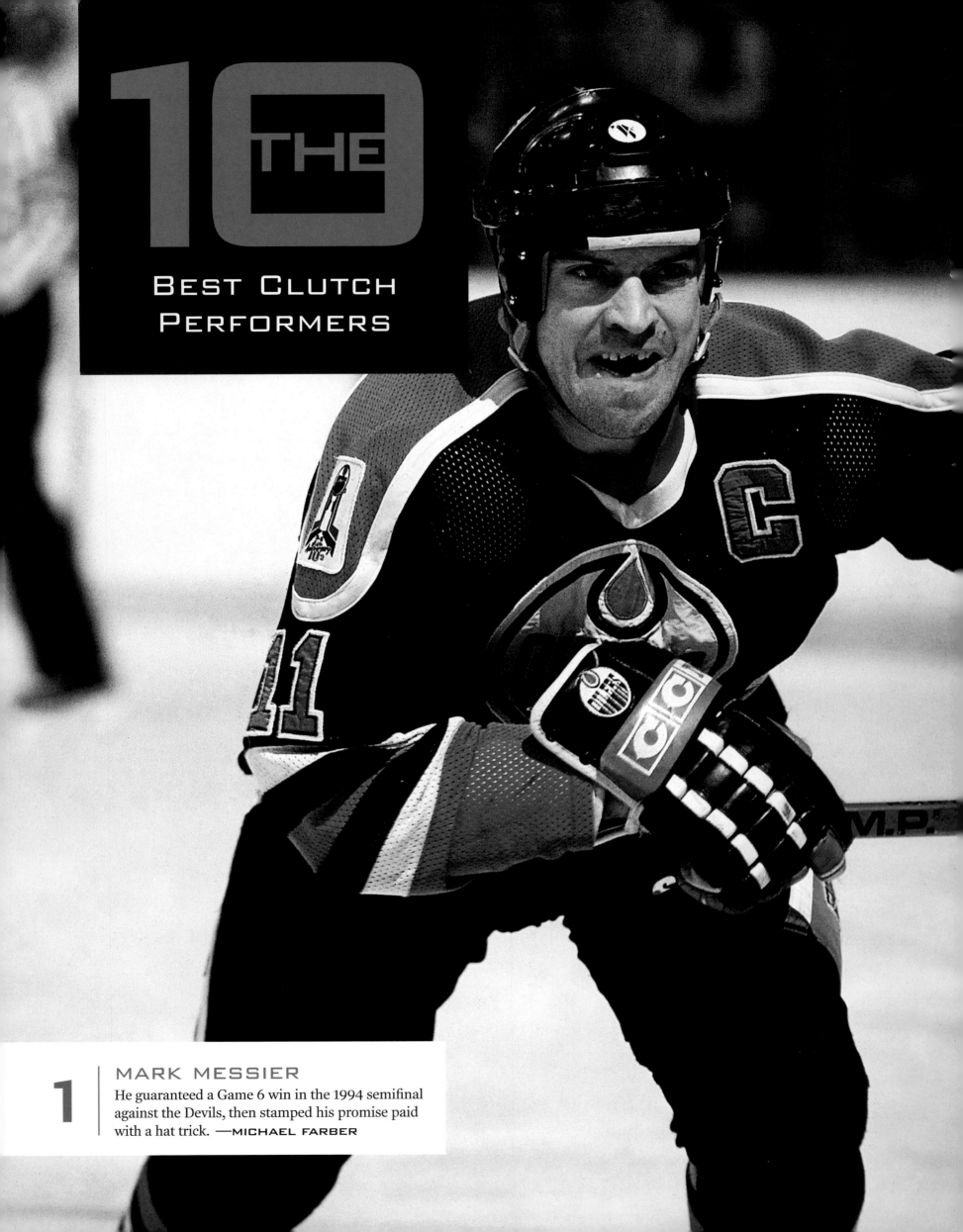

10 THE

BEST CLUTCH PERFORMERS

1 | **MARK MESSIER**
He guaranteed a Game 6 win in the 1994 semifinal against the Devils, then stamped his promise paid with a hat trick. —MICHAEL FARBER

2 | **PATRICK ROY**
When Roy (three Conn Smythe Trophies) was determined to keep his net empty, nothing was getting by him—and he knew it. —SARAH KWAK

3 | **WAYNE GRETZKY**
There was no moment for too big for Gretzky. He always delivered. His Canada Cup performances are things of legend. —PIERRE MCGUIRE

4 | **JOE SAKIC**
Known as Colorado's Captain Clutch, Sakic owns the record for career playoff overtime goals with eight. —BRIAN CAZENEUVE

5 | **BOBBY ORR**
If his Cup winner on Mother's Day 1970 was not the greatest championship-winning goal, it made the prettiest picture. —MICHAEL FARBER

6 | **MAURICE RICHARD**
In Game 7 against Boston in the 1952 semis, though bleeding and concussed, he won the series with a sensational third-period solo rush. —E.M. SWIFT

7 | **CLAUDE LEMIEUX**
In 1995 Lemieux scored more goals in the playoffs (a league-high 13) than in the lockout-shortened regular season. —KOSTYA KENNEDY

8 | **BILLY SMITH**
Battlin' Billy backstopped the Islanders to five straight Stanley Cup finals and won a record 19 consecutive playoff series. —MARK BEECH

9 | **MARIO LEMIEUX**
In the 1991 postseason, Lemiuex scored goals in each of his last 10 games in Pittsburgh's first Stanley Cup run. —SARAH KWAK

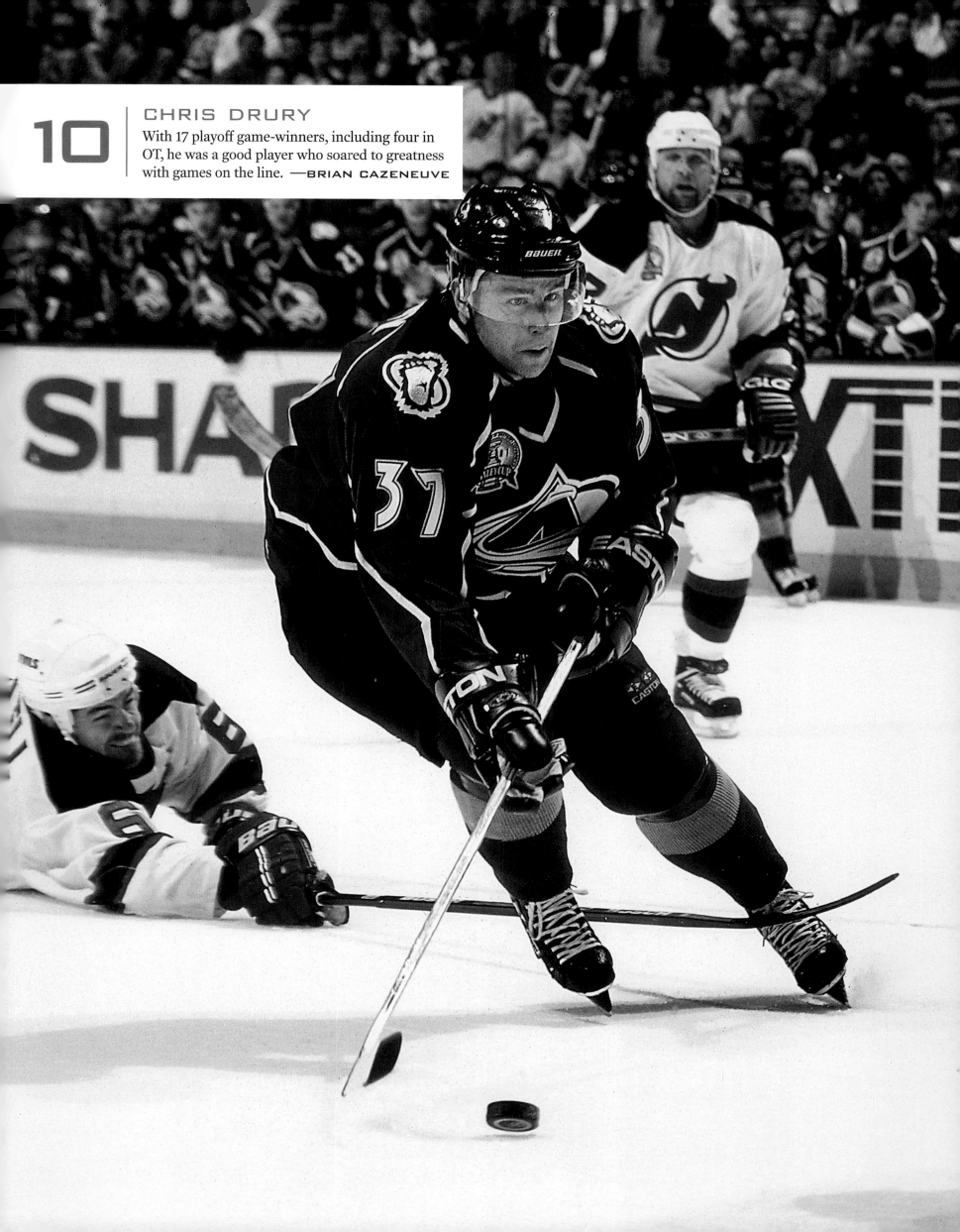

10 CHRIS DRURY

With 17 playoff game-winners, including four in OT, he was a good player who soared to greatness with games on the line. —BRIAN CAZENEUVE

10

THE

BEST SHOOTOUT SPECIALISTS

1 | **T.J. OSHIE**
At the 2014 Olympics he scored four of six attempts to beat Russia. Cool, smooth, and unpredictable, Oshie is a goalie's nightmare. —E.M. SWIFT

2 | **JONATHAN TOEWS** Ever since he went 3 for 3 for Canada in the semifinals of the 2007 World Junior Championships, Toews has had a reputation as one of the game's most lethal shooters. The Blackhawks captain has the patience to outwait most goaltenders and a quick and accurate release. —BRIAN CAZENEUVE

3 | **FRANS NIELSEN** He doesn't rely on dipsy-doos and fancy dangles, usually going the simple forehand-backhand route, but his quickness is what freezes goalies. His move is so seamless—and he lifts the puck every time—that netminders are routinely flailing off-balance as they watch the puck go in. —SARAH KWAK

4 | PAVEL DATSYUK He doesn't merely beat goalies with Datsyukian dangles, he gives them noogies. His favorite move really is several moves—forehand, backhand, forehand with a head fake thrown in—and when the goalie is as down and out as a Depression-era drifter, Datsyuk gingerly roofs the puck. —MICHAEL FARBER

5 | ZACH PARISE The lethal wrist shot he sometimes lets loose a few strides before the top of the crease can freeze a masked man and allow Parise wide shooting areas when he comes in close. The result: 39 shootout goals and a 43.3% success rate. —KOSTYA KENNEDY

6 | JUSSI JOKINEN

He announced himself by converting nine straight attempts at the start of his career. In the best of his eclectic moves, Jokinen makes a late, wide slide to his left, leaving the puck behind him and then, with only his right hand on his stick, pushes it past a fallen, bewildered goalie. —KOSTYA KENNEDY

7 | BRAD BOYES

He may average less than 17 minutes per game, be a career minus player and hear the words "healthy scratch" every now and again. But after overtime, it's Boyes's time. With a pair of soft hands, he has uncanny control over the puck in open ice. —SARAH KWAK

RADIM VRBATA

8

Converting almost 43% on his attempts, his backhand deke is a move so dependable that it opens up his forehand. —MICHAEL FARBER

9 | ERIK CHRISTENSEN The fourth-line center never scored more than 18 goals in a season, but immediately mastered the art of the NHL tiebreaker upon its introduction in 2005–06. A lefthanded shot, he attributed his success to his total commitment to four decidedly nonflashy moves. —MARK BEECH

10 | PATRICK KANE He's one of the most creative players to come into the NHL in a long time. He's also unflappable under pressure, and it really shows in the shootouts. The dekes that this great puckhandler unleashes can make you feel sorry for whoever is tasked with stopping him. —PIERRE MCGUIRE

THE 10

Best American Players, Olympic Moments, Uniforms, Pop Culture Moments, Hair, Nicknames, Inspirational Scenes and the Full Results

IT IS SURELY CHALLENGING TO CHOOSE YOUR TOP 10 PLAYERS AT A PARTICULAR POSITION, BUT YOU CAN USE STATISTICS AS A GUIDELINE. OF COURSE YOU HAVE TO WEIGH THOSE STATISTICS AGAINST OTHER FACTORS SUCH AS TEAM SUCCESS, THE ERA IN WHICH PLAYERS COMPETED AND THE EXTENT TO WHICH THEY LEFT FANS AWESTRUCK, BUT STILL: IF YOU ARE RANKING THE BEST LEFT WINGS, THE LIST OF THE TOP-SCORING LEFT WINGS IS A GOOD THING TO CONSULT.

BUT WHAT IF THE TOPIC IS, SAY, BEST UNIFORMS? IN THAT CASE YOU HAVE NO STATISTICS WHATSOEVER TO FALL BACK ON, AND THE FINAL RANKING MAY SWING HEAVILY ON HOW PLEASING YOU FIND THE COMBINATION OF YELLOW AND BLACK.

IN THIS SECTION OF THE BOOK, THE TOPICS ARE HIGHLY SUBJECTIVE, AND OUR PROCESS EVEN MORE SO. WHEREAS IN THE PRECEDING CATEGORIES, OUR PANELISTS MADE THEIR CHOICES BY GROUP VOTE, HERE EACH LIST IS COMPOSED BY AN INDIVIDUAL, AND IT'S ALL ABOUT HIS OR HER PERSONAL LIKES AND DISLIKES. IF ONE PANELIST IS A FAN OF *THE SIMPSONS*, THEN A REFERENCE ON THAT SHOW TO GORDIE HOWE CAN STAND AS ONE OF HOCKEY'S GREATEST SURFACINGS IN POP CULTURE. IF YOU DON'T AGREE, FINE. IN THIS CHAPTER THE RANKINGS ARE BOTH EASY TO DISAGREE WITH AND DIFFICULT TO ARGUE AGAINST.

Kane has fulfillled his promise as the top pick of the 2007 NHL draft.

THE 10 BEST AMERICAN PLAYERS

Former SI senior writer E.M. SWIFT selects the most excellent hockey stars to rise up from Canada's neighbor to the south

1. CHRIS CHELIOS
An Ironman whose NHL career spanned 26 seasons, Chelios holds the record for most games played by a defenseman (1,651). The Chicago native was named the league's top defenseman three times.

2. MIKE MODANO
Drafted first overall in 1988, Modano, from Livonia, Mich., played 21 NHL seasons and holds the record for most goals (561) and most points (1,374) by an American-born player.

3. FRANK BRIMSEK
Nicknamed Mister Zero, the Hall of Famer came from Eveleth, Minn., and won two Cups and two Vezina Trophies (best goalie) for the Bruins.

4. BRIAN LEETCH
Leetch, a defenseman who grew up in Cheshire, Conn., was the first U.S.–born player to be named MVP of the postseason when he quarterbacked the Rangers offense during the 1994 Stanley Cup playoffs.

5. JOE MULLEN
Despite growing up in New York City and learning to skate on roller blades, this three-time Cup champion was the first U.S.–born player to score 500 goals (502) and 1,000 points (1,063) in the NHL.

6. ROD LANGWAY
Born in Taipei, Taiwan, where his father was stationed with the Navy, Langway didn't play organized hockey until age 13, when he was living in Massachusetts. He was twice named the NHL's top defenseman.

7. PATRICK KANE
The 27-year-old Kane, born in Buffalo, is the best stickhandler in hockey and has already won three Cups with Chicago. In '13 he became the first U.S. forward to be named playoff MVP.

8. PAT LAFONTAINE
Born in St. Louis, his 148 points in 1992–93 is the most ever scored by an American-born player. Despite a career cut short by concussions, he tallied 468 goals and 1,013 points in just 865 games.

9. JEREMY ROENICK
The hard-hitting and fearless J.R., from Boston, was the third U.S. player to surpass 500 goals (513), and 92 of them were game-winners.

10. KEITH TKACHUK
The quintessential power forward, from Melrose, Mass, in 1996–97 became the first and only American to lead the league in goals, with 52.

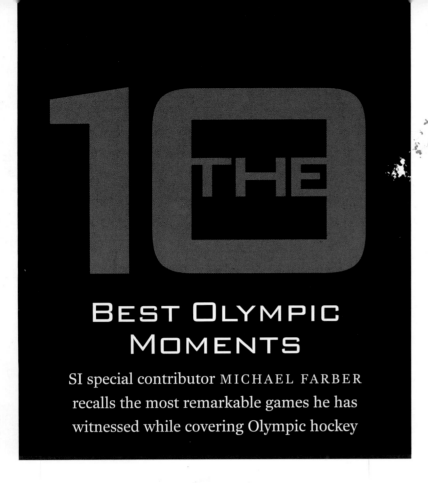

THE 10 BEST OLYMPIC MOMENTS

SI special contributor MICHAEL FARBER recalls the most remarkable games he has witnessed while covering Olympic hockey

1. USA VS. USSR, 198 SEMIFINAL

The fishes-and-loaves game—thanks, Al Michaels—in 1980 at my first Olympics still inspires me about what is possible in sport and life. Sitting in the press section at the Lake Placid arena, glancing continually at the scoreboard after Mike Eruzione's goal midway through the third period, it seemed like I was watching sand sifting through an hour glass and not digital numbers on a clock. Play this match 100 times, and the U.S.S.R. wins 96. So what? America's cold warriors have dined out on that 4–3 win for decades.

2. CANADA VS. CZECH REPUBLIC, 1998 SEMIFINAL

Maybe Wayne Gretzky just didn't do enough over the course of his career. You know, like score 1,072 regular season and playoff goals in the NHL and WHA. But, as you might recall, Gretzky purportedly was lousy on breakaways. Omitting Gretzky from the five shooters in the 1998 semifinal shootout against goalie Dominik Hasek and the Czech Republic never has been explained to my satisfaction. Hasek stoned Team Canada and the Czechs won the game. Hasek then shut out Russia, 1–0, in the final. Career regret: I didn't head straight to Prague for the celebration in Wenceslas Square. Apparently an alltimer.

3. USA VS. CANADA, 2010 FINAL

In the most meaningful game played on Canadian ice since hockey moved indoors in March 1875, Sidney Crosby scored the Golden Goal that edged a steely Team USA 3–2 in the Vancouver 2010 final. Crosby was not having a good tournament, but the best player in hockey burnished his legacy when he scored on a play that went sideways for the Americans when the puck glanced off Hall of Fame referee Bill McCreary's skate. U.S. goalie Ryan Miller tried to poke-check Crosby, who had spun off defenseman Brian Rafalski, but Miller found air and Crosby found the five hole.

4. USA VS. RUSSIA, 2010 ROUND-ROBIN PLAY

In the back end of an Olympic home-and-home 34 years apart, Team USA beat Russia in a round-robin game at Sochi 2014 because of the shootout stylings of T.J. Oshie. This was the most significant of insignificant Olympic games—the Americans and Russians were jostling for more favorable draws in the medal round—so Oshie's legerdemain was Olympian in performance but not implication. Oshie scored on four of his six shootout attempts, and he had Russian goalie Sergei

Bobrovsky flummoxed on the other two. When rivals align and circumstances are right—in this case, a shootout as long as a Russian novel—the five Olympics rings trump a Stanley Cup ring.

5. SWEDEN VS. CANADA, 1994 FINAL

You can't put a price on an Olympic-winning shootout goal, but Sweden tried: three kroner, 70 ore. That was the price of the postage stamp commemorating Peter Forsberg's dangle that won Lillehammer 1994 gold. Foppa had watched on TV as Kent Nilsson, the Magic Man, unveiled the move for Sweden against the U.S. and goalie John Vanbiesbrouck at the 1989 world championship. To the shock of everyone who hadn't seen the feint—basically, anyone who wasn't European or an NHL scout—Forsberg reintroduced it against Team Canada goalie Corey Hirsch. It was a pity Hirsch denied the Swedish Post permission to use his likeness on the stamp. Hirsch, who won 34 of his 108 NHL games, was never part of anything grander.

6. BELARUS VS. SWEDEN, 2002 QUARTERFINAL

The Internet was in its relative infancy, but the image of Swedish goalie Tommy Salo ducking on Vladimir Kopat's long-distance shot zoomed around the world as Belarus shocked Sweden in the quarterfinals of the 2002 Games. Belarus was expected to be nothing more than a mere speed bump against the Swedish "Torpedo" system after it had dropped its past two games by identical 8–1 scores. Then Kopat loosed a 70-footer at Salo's melon. Salo raised his glove, flinched, and the puck struck his mask. It trickled into the net with 2:24 left. Belarus, 4–3. Biggest upset in Olympic history.

7. LATVIA VS. CANADA, 2014 QUARTERFINAL

Latvian backup goalie Kristers Gudlevskis stopped an astonishing 55 of 57 shots in a 2–1 quarterfinal loss to Canada in Sochi 2014. During an unremitting third-period bombardment, the Brick Wall of the Baltics slumped to his knees in his crease, in either supplication or exhaustion as the trainer rushed out to apply a compress to his neck. The goalie looked like the most valiant boxer you ever have seen.

8. CANADA VS. USA, 1998 WOMEN'S FINAL

In the inaugural women's Olympic tournament, at Nagano 1998, Canada and Team USA were the class of the field, although it looked like the Canadians had been reading ahead in the textbook. The Americans had never beaten their big sisters in a major tournament but sensed an opportunity because they had held their own as a sparring partner, defeating Canada in six of 13 games when the teams barnstormed across North America that winter. The U.S. was superb when it counted, defeating Canada twice in four days and dominating the gold-medal match, sealing a 3–1 win with an empty-netter.

9. CANADA VS. RUSSIA, 2010 QUARTERFINAL

Spacey Ilya Bryzgalov, the Carl Sagan of the crease, summarized it thusly: "(The Canadians were) like gorillas coming out of a cage." In the 2010 Vancouver quarterfinals, Team Canada eviscerated the Russians, pounding them into submission with the most extraordinary 20-minute display of teamwork and physicality the Olympics have seen. Canada led 4–1 after the first period, cruising to a 7–3 win. Most clever sign in the arena: POUTINE, NOT PUTIN.

10. SWEDEN VS. SLOVAKIA, 2006 ROUND-ROBIN PLAY

O.K., this is your power play personnel: Nicklas Lidstrom, Peter Forsberg, Mats Sundin, Daniel Alfredsson and slap-shot-thumping Freddy Modin. You have a five-on-three power play against Slovakia. For a full two minutes. And you get—let me double check—zero shots on goal? Now Lidstrom did hit a post, but I believe Lidstrom is so good he might have done that on purpose. In its final round-robin match in Turin 2006, Sweden essentially white-flagged it to secure an easier path in the medal round. Tanks for the memories. Sweden lost to the Slovaks 3–0 but would go on to beat Finland in the final.

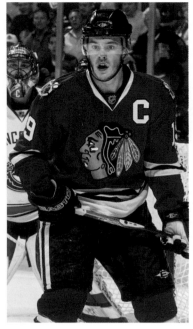

2. BLACKHAWKS

3. RED WINGS

4. BRUINS

5. KINGS

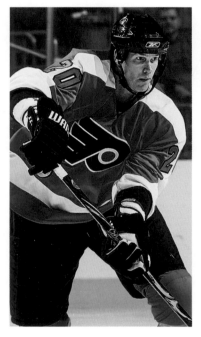

6. FLYERS

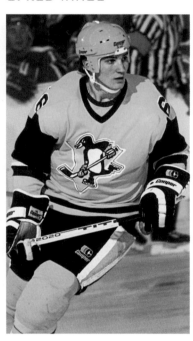

7. PENGUINS

8. GOLDEN SEALS

9. MAPLE LEAFS

9. TORONTO MAPLE LEAFS

It's a simple uniform, blue with the maple leaf across the chest, and it hasn't changed much over the years, but it puts forth a feeling of pride. Across Canada in particular, before league expansion, the maple leaf was an important logo, and it still is.

10. NEW YORK RANGERS

The Rangers have tried other versions of their uniform, including one with a Statue of Liberty logo, but I prefer the classic look that just says RANGERS in a slash across the chest. With the red pants and the red piping on the shoulders, it's a brilliant color scheme that looks cool when it's on the ice.

11. HONORABLE MENTION: HARTFORD WHALERS

I have to give a respectful nod to the Whalers, where I was an assistant and head coach from 1992 to '94. I loved the logo, with its whale tail spread across the chest. Even though the Hartford franchise relocated and rebranded in '97, I see people wearing Whalers hats and shirts everywhere I go. It's funny, because we didn't have that many fans back when we were playing. But it's a modern concept, and it works.

10. RANGERS

11. WHALERS

10 THE

BEST POP CULTURE MOMENTS

SI senior editor MARK BEECH names the greatest instances of hockey skating its way into movies, television, music and even the comics

1. SLAP SHOT
Paul Newman is the player-coach of the Charlestown Chiefs, a moribund minor league team that revives itself by resorting to "old-time hockey," a.k.a. violence on the ice—a tactic epitomized by the hilarious Hanson brothers. Appropriately, the film is at once one of the most foulmouthed movies of all time and the greatest hockey movie ever made.

2. PEANUTS
Strip creator Charles M. Schulz, a '93 U.S. Hockey Hall of Fame inductee, often drew Snoopy and Woodstock playing shinny on a frozen birdbath, and his love for the game was evidenced when he built the Redwood Empire Ice Arena near his home in Santa Rosa, Calif. Every July, the arena hosts Snoopy's Senior World Hockey Tournament.

3. MIRACLE
Though *Miracle* doesn't quite fulfill its highest aspirations, it does deliver a marvelous portrait of 1980 U.S. Olympic hockey coach Herb Brooks, played by Kurt Russell, as well as one of the finest pregame speeches in sports-film history.

4. FIVE FOR FIGHTING
Kings fan John Ondrasik was a modestly successful singer-songwriter in the mid-1990s when he began marketing himself as a "band" with a name he'd appropriated from the NHL rule book. His 2000 album, *America Town*, went platinum after the gentle piano ballad, "Superman (It's Not Easy)," was embraced in the U.S. in the wake of 9/11.

5. JEREMY ROENICK AND WAYNE GRETZKY IN SWINGERS
In this 1996 comedy, Vince Vaughn and Patrick Van Horn hilariously trash-talk their way through a game of EA Sports' NHL 94—still regarded as the best NHL video game ever made. True to the game's form, Jeremy Roenick is unstoppable. The scene ends with Wayne Gretzky lying prone on the ice with a bleeding head wound.

6. "THE FACE PAINTER" EPISODE ON SEINFELD
In this 1995 broadcast, Elaine is dating Devils fan David Puddy, who paints his face for a playoff game against the Rangers. Elaine threatens to break up with Puddy if he does it again, so he goes to the next game with his chest painted.

7. SUDDEN DEATH
Jean-Claude Van Damme stars as a former Pittsburgh firefighter who uncovers a terrorist plot during Game 7 of the Stanley Cup finals. Several players portray themselves, including Luc Robitaille and Markus Naslund. Even better, JCVD fights a baddie disguised as the Penguins' mascot.

8. THE KEVIN SMITH OEUVRE
Hockey plays a role in several films made by the New Jersey–born director and Devils fan. In the 1994 comedy *Clerks*, his characters play ball hockey on a convenience-store roof. Three years later, Smith incisively intercut a hockey brawl with a lover's quarrel in *Chasing Amy*.

9. GORDIE HOWE ON "THE SIMPSONS"
It's a brief moment, but Mr. Hockey was hilariously referenced on network television's longest-running prime time series in the 1992 episode, "Bart the Lover." Playing a prank on his lovelorn teacher, Ms. Krabappel, Bart responds to her personal ad with a romantic letter and includes a head shot of Hall of Famer Howe, clipped from a book entitled *NHL Stars of 1969*.

10. THE MIGHTY DUCKS TRILOGY
No installment in this series—the first film was released in 1992—was beloved by critics, but the first two were popular, and the trilogy opener was also the namesake of the then Disney-owned Ducks, who debuted in '93 as the Mighty Ducks of Anaheim.

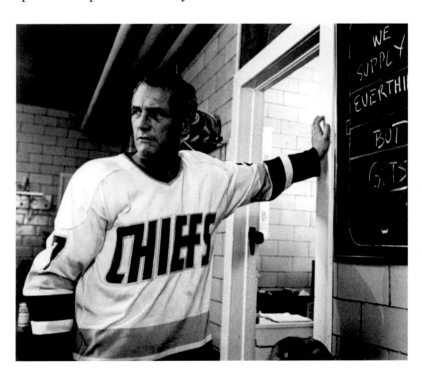

Newman's Chiefs embraced "old-time hockey" in *Slap Shot*.

Van Damme took on Pittsburgh's penguin in *Sudden Death*.

1. JAROMIR JAGR

The man. The myth. The mullet. During his dominant days in the '90s, the future Hall of Famer sported the alltime coif, letting his curly tufts grow out so long that they covered the nameplate on his back. Though he cleaned up his look for the latter part of his career, appreciation for his style endured. In 2014, a group of mulleted superfans, dubbed The Travelling Jagrs, earned a hearty salute from the Hair himself.

2. GUY LAFLEUR

His long golden hair, windswept as he made his patented rushes up the ice, inspired his nickname, Le Démon Blond, and came to symbolize his supremacy in the league. When his hair thinned late in his career, Lafleur even went so far as to have a hair transplant.

3. AL IAFRATE

Is there any tonsorial wonder quite as unique as Iafrate's skullet? While it was usually hidden underneath his helmet during games, Iafrate's hair all but stole the show at the 1993 SuperSkills Competition. With his long hair flowing and a bald spot glowing, Iafrate hammered in a shot at 105.2 miles per hour, a record that stood for 16 years. The skullet's legacy has endured even longer.

4. BARRY MELROSE

Still going strong after more than 20 years, the commentator and former coach's slicked back, salt-and-pepper mullet may be the most enduring of hockey's iconic hairstyles. Times may change, but Melrose's hair does not.

5. MAURICE RICHARD

With his dark hair pulled back like an oil slick, the Rocket looked like an extra off the set of the HBO series *Boardwalk Empire*. One thing he had in common with the bygone mobsters he resembled? Richard, too, really knew how to shoot.

6. EVANDER KANE

In a largely white-bread, conformist sport, Kane introduced a fresh twist to hockey hair by having intricate designs shaved into the sides of his head. The designs ranged from simple stars to the letters YMCMB—which stood for "Young Money Cash Money Billionaires," which is a combination of hip-hop record labels Young Money Entertainment and Cash Money Records.

7. MIKE COMMODORE

His unkempt bushy, bright orange 'fro—with matching beard in the playoffs—was so distinctive that it became the identifying feature of an otherwise unremarkable defenseman. Commodore played just 484 games, shuttling among seven teams in 11 seasons, and he never reached 30 points in a season. But oh, that hair!

8. KERRY FRASER

In 37 years in referee's stripes, Fraser called more than 2,000 games and 13 Stanley Cup finals, but he's mostly known for his physics-defying bouffant. With his seemingly never-ending supply of Paul Mitchell Freeze and Shine hairspray, Fraser once proudly declared, "I could skate through a hurricane and it would never move."

9. RON DUGUAY

He didn't like to stifle his long locks under a helmet. One of the last NHLers to skate with his head alfresco, Duguay even signed waivers to play two charity games in 2009, at age 51, without a helmet. He now has a feathered style, but never forget Duguay's signature look, the perm-mullet. It doesn't get much more '80s than that.

10. SCOTT HARTNELL

Equally ridiculed and celebrated, Hartnell's curly mop top was, if nothing else, distinctive for its time. In April 2012 his mane caused a suspension, when Penguins forward Craig Adams pulled on it, and in '09 it even inspired a Flyers' promotional giveaway: The first 5,000 fans and kids under 14 at the game received a Scott Hartnell wig. The opponent was the Panthers; Hartnell scored.

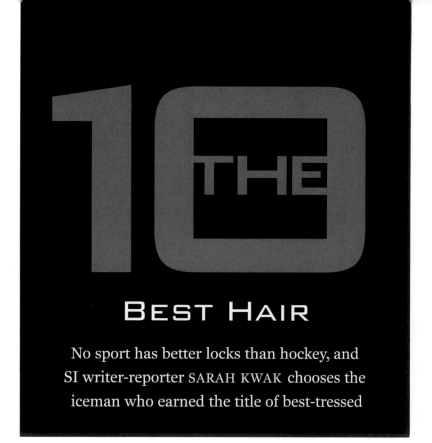

10
THE
BEST HAIR

No sport has better locks than hockey, and SI writer-reporter SARAH KWAK chooses the iceman who earned the title of best-tressed

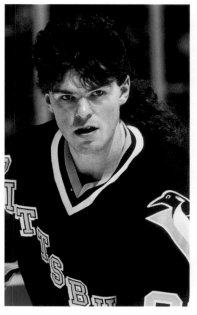

Jagr's mighty mullet

Commodore's coif

Hartnell's mop top

Kane's shaved-in designs

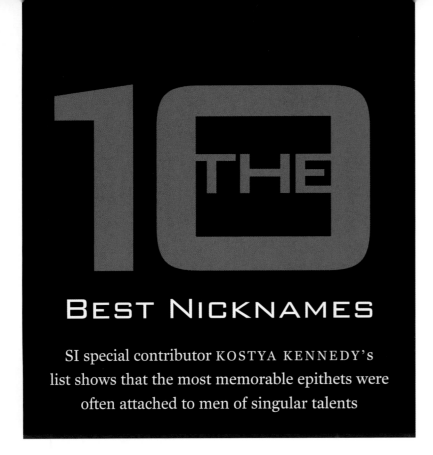

10 THE

BEST NICKNAMES

SI special contributor KOSTYA KENNEDY's list shows that the most memorable epithets were often attached to men of singular talents

1. (BERNIE) BOOM BOOM GEOFFRION

The nickname is fun, descriptive, a little intimidating and even ono-matopoeic. The Canadiens winger was a pioneer of the slap shot—yes, his was the now clichéd booming slap shot—in the 1950s. He scored 393 career goals. In other words, "Boom, Boom, on went the light."

2. (MAURICE) ROCKET RICHARD

Mention the name Rocket in hockey circles and not only a man but also a vision is recalled. He propelled himself with great speed, undaunted and unwavering toward opponent's nets, and he scored better than anyone of his era. The intensity of his glare was another example of how the Rocket brought fire to the ice.

3. THE GREAT ONE

Elegant, powerful and insuperable, just like the player himself. Wayne Gretzky was given the nickname as a 10-year-old hockey superstar, and he never did anything but live up to it, and far beyond, for the rest of his career.

4. THE GRIM REAPER

Playing on the surname of Stu Grimson, it signals just what his job was—"enforcer" being the euphemism, "face-crusher" the operative fact. It may seem paradoxical that off the ice Grimson was gentle and soft-spoken. On the ice, though, he had the defining characteristic of his nicknamesake: Not a figure you wanted to see coming your way.

5. THE CHICOUTIMI CUCUMBER

It tells you where the great Georges Vezina was from—a riverbank town in Quebec province with Aboriginal roots—and tells you his demeanor in the nets. ("Cool as a....") And, golly, it's a fun name to say aloud. The only lament is that the NHL didn't name its annual award for the league's top goaltender the Cucumber Trophy.

6. (HECTOR) TOE BLAKE

Few human beings go through life nicknamed for a body part, and this one gives Blake the veneer of a Damon Runyon stalwart. Big Jule from Chicago, Toe from Montreal.... Blake got the name from his little sister's mispronunciation of his first name and though other handles were hung on him—including the lyrical "Old Lamplighter"—none was as good as the one that stuck.

7. THE DOMINATOR

He looked dominating, he was dominating, and the idea of goaltender Dominik Hasek, who made his mark on the NHL not too long after the second of Arnold Schwarzenegger's *Terminator* movies had ripped through the box office, could rattle opponents before the puck even dropped. Few nicknames have been more apropos or as well-deserved.

8. MISTER ZERO

In the real world, being dubbed a zero isn't much to smile about. But for a hockey goaltender there is no greater salute. Frank Brimsek earned his alias and played his way onto the hockey landscape with six shutouts in his first eight games as a Bruin. Brimsek wore the nickname proudly through the rest of his Hall of Fame career.

9. (EDOUARD) NEWSY LALONDE

Now this cat is old school. He got his moniker from having worked in a newspaper plant as a kid, and he proceeded to make hockey headlines, back in the 1910s and '20s, with his dramatic goal scoring. Newsy also boasted an association with another great nickname: He was on the Canadiens' Flying Frenchmen line.

10. MR. HOCKEY

There is, and will always be, only one. There could be no more flattering description for a player, nor anyone better suited to it than the inimitable Gordie Howe. He played his first NHL game at age 18, his last at age 52. He lived the game, he helped shape the game and for some he defined it. Mr. Hockey indeed.

Nasty hits like this one helped earn Grimson his nickname.

Vezina (center) kept his cool in his goalie's sweater.

1. RAY BOURQUE GIVES UP HIS JERSEY

Though Phil Esposito set the single-season points record in a Bruins uniform, the Bruins hadn't retired his number 7, giving it to young star defenseman Ray Bourque in 1979. When Esposito returned to Boston Garden in '87 to have his number retired, Bourque surprised everyone during the ceremony by removing his own jersey and revealing a new number 77, letting Esposito know the number 7 was his alone.

2. RED WINGS WIN A CUP FOR WOUNDED COMRADE

Six days after winning a title in 1997, the Red Wings were out celebrating when a hired limo carrying three team members crashed in Birmingham, Mich., and defenseman Vladimir Konstantinov was left comatose and paralyzed. A year later, after Detroit topped the Capitals for a Stanley Cup, Konstantinov, a shell of his old self, was rolled onto the ice in Washington, where his teammates gave him the Cup to hold.

3. GORDIE HOWE PLAYS WITH HIS SONS

In 1973, at age 45, then the NHL's alltime leading scorer, Gordie Howe, came out of retirement to play with his sons Marty and Mark with the Houston Aeros of the upstart World Hockey Association. The Howes would play seven seasons together, including one NHL campaign in 1979–80 when the Hartford Whalers joined the league.

4. NORDIQUES SALUTE CLINT MALARCHUK

In March 1989, St. Louis forward Steve Tuttle drove to the net and his skate accidentally hit the throat of Buffalo's Clint Malarchuk, severing the goalie's jugular vein and threatening his life. Just 10 days later, Malarchuk finished the third period of a game against Quebec and even the visiting Nordiques players lined up to shake his hand.

5. THE PICTURE OF HONOR

Valor and respect were captured in one image when Bruins goalie Sugar Jim Henry bowed and shook the hand of Montreal's Maurice Richard, after Richard had returned from a hit that left him knocked out and scored the winning goal in Game 7 of the 1952 Stanley Cup semifinals.

6. CANADIENS CARRY BRUINS

For one night, enemies became friends. On Feb. 10, 1942, the Bruins thrashed the Canadiens in Boston 8–1 in the last game before the three members of their top line, Milt Schmidt, Woody Dumart and Bobby Bauer, (a.k.a. the Kraut Line) headed to war with the Royal Canadian Air Force. Canadiens and Bruins players joined to carry the three men around the ice on their shoulders after the game.

7. GRETZKY RETURNS TO EDMONTON FOR THE RECORD

Wayne Gretzky was playing for Los Angeles on Oct. 15, 1989 when he broke Gordie Howe's NHL record for career points, and it just so happened that on that day the Kings were visiting Edmonton. Gretzky's former home fans honored him a three-minute standing ovation.

8. THE ACE BAILEY GAME

Two months after Toronto forward Ace Bailey suffered a life threatening head injury after a hit from the Bruins' Eddie Shore in 1933, the NHL organized a benefit game for Bailey between the Leafs and a group of stars. Bailey was there to greet Shore and the other players. This game led to two similar benefits and is sometimes referred to as the first NHL All-Star Game. Bailey lived to age 88.

9. BOB BAUN'S ONE-LEGGED WINNER

In Game 6 of the Stanley Cup finals against Detroit in 1964, Baun, a Toronto defenseman, fractured his ankle early in the third period, but then returned to score the game-winner in overtime. The Leafs won the Cup two nights later.

10. THE GM IS A GOALIE

In the days before teams carried backup goaltenders, the Rangers' Lorne Chabot suffered an eye injury before Game 2 of the 1928 Stanley Cup finals against the Montreal Maroons. Rangers coach/GM Lester Patrick, 44, a retired defenseman, put himself into the net. He stopped 18 shots as the Rangers won that night on their way to the title.

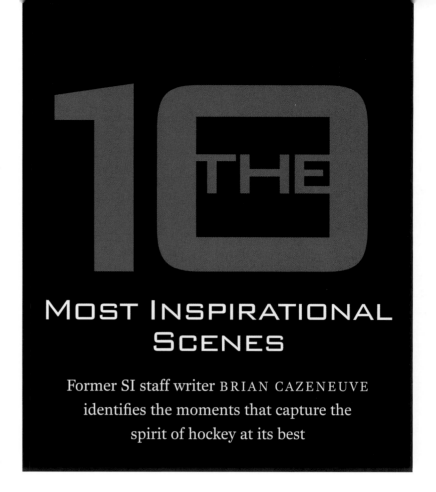

THE 10 MOST INSPIRATIONAL SCENES

Former SI staff writer BRIAN CAZENEUVE identifies the moments that capture the spirit of hockey at its best

Howe and his sons displayed family spirit for seven seasons.

THE FULL RESULTS

IF THEY WERE LISTED ON A PANELIST'S BALLOT, THEY MAKE IT HERE TOO, IN THIS FULL RANKING OF EVERYONE WHO RECEIVED A VOTE IN EVERY CATEGORY

CENTER

1. WAYNE GRETZKY
2. MARIO LEMIEUX
3. JEAN BELIVEAU
4. MARK MESSIER
5. STEVE YZERMAN
6. SIDNEY CROSBY
7. PHIL ESPOSITO
8. STAN MIKITA
9. BRYAN TROTTIER
10. HOWIE MORENZ
11. JOE SAKIC
12. BOBBY CLARKE
13. HENRI RICHARD
14. SERGEI FEDOROV
15. PETER STASTNY
16. MARCEL DIONNE
17. PETER FORSBERG
18. PAVEL DATSYUK
19. MILT SCHMIDT

LEFT WING

1. BOBBY HULL
2. LUC ROBITAILLE
3. TED LINDSAY
4. ALEX OVECHKIN
5. FRANK MAHOVLICH
6. VALERI KHARLAMOV
7. BRENDAN SHANAHAN
8. JOHNNY BUCYK
9. DICKIE MOORE
10. KEITH TKACHUK
11. BUSHER JACKSON
12. BOB GAINEY
13. ALEXANDER YAKUSHEV
14. MICHEL GOULET
15. HENRIK ZETTERBERG
16. GLENN ANDERSON
17. PAUL KARIYA
18. BILL BARBER
19. AURELE JOLIAT
20. DAVE ANDREYCHUK
21. CY DENNENY
22. WOODY DUMART
23. ILYA KOVALCHUK

RIGHT WING

1. GORDIE HOWE
2. MAURICE RICHARD
3. GUY LAFLEUR
4. JAROMIR JAGR
5. MIKE BOSSY
6. TEEMU SELANNE
7. BRETT HULL
8. JARI KURRI
9. BERNIE GEOFFRION
10. YVAN COURNOYER
11. BORIS MIKHAILOV
12. BILL COOK
13. CHARLIE CONACHER
14. PAVEL BURE
15. JAROME IGINLA
16. PATRICK KANE
17. MARIAN HOSSA
18. SERGEI MAKAROV

DEFENSEMAN

1. BOBBY ORR
2. NICKLAS LIDSTROM
3. DOUG HARVEY
4. RAY BOURQUE
5. DENIS POTVIN
6. LARRY ROBINSON
7. EDDIE SHORE
8. SLAVA FETISOV
9. PAUL COFFEY
10. CHRIS CHELIOS
11. SCOTT NIEDERMAYER
12. RED KELLY
13. CHRIS PRONGER
14. SCOTT STEVENS
15. BRAD PARK

GOALTENDER

1. PATRICK ROY
2. JACQUES PLANTE
3. TERRY SAWCHUK
4. MARTIN BRODEUR
5. DOMINIK HASEK
6. KEN DRYDEN
7. GLENN HALL
8. VLADISLAV TRETIAK
9. BERNIE PARENT
10. GRANT FUHR
11. GEORGE HAINSWORTH
12. BILL DURNAN
13. BILLY SMITH
14. GEORGES VEZINA
15. TURK BRODA
16. FRANK BRIMSEK

COACH

1. SCOTTY BOWMAN
2. TOE BLAKE
3. AL ARBOUR
4. JACK ADAMS
5. PUNCH IMLACH
6. FRED SHERO
7. ANATOLI TARASOV
8. MIKE BABCOCK
9. DICK IRVIN
10. GLEN SATHER
11. PAT BURNS
12. HERB BROOKS
13. JOEL QUENNEVILLE
14. BOB JOHNSON
15. JACQUES LEMAIRE
16. HAP DAY
17. MIKE KEENAN
18. ROGER NEILSON

ENFORCER

1. BOB PROBERT
2. DAVE SCHULTZ
3. JOHN FERGUSON
4. TIGER WILLIAMS
5. JOEY KOCUR
6. STU GRIMSON
7. MARTY MCSORLEY
8. TIE DOMI
9. DAVE SEMENKO
10. CLARK GILLIES
11. GEORGES LARAQUE
12. CHRIS NILAN
13. TERRY O'REILLY
14. DALE HUNTER
15. DAVE BROWN
16. TONY TWIST
17. DEREK BOOGAARD
18. TIM HUNTER
19. SCOTT THORNTON
20. RED HORNER
21. JOHN WENSINK
22. ORLAND KURTENBACH
23. GORDIE HOWE

MOST ENTERTAINING

1. BOBBY ORR
2. WAYNE GRETZKY
3. MAURICE RICHARD
4. MARIO LEMIEUX
5. GUY LAFLEUR
6. BOBBY HULL
7. PAVEL BURE
8. DOMINIK HASEK
9. PAVEL DATSYUK
10. ALEX OVECHKIN
11. GILBERT PERREAULT
12. DENIS SAVARD
13. GORDIE HOWE
14. PAUL COFFEY
15. EDDIE SHORE
16. ROGER CROZIER
17. PATRICK KANE
18. PHIL ESPOSITO
19. PATRICK ROY
20. BERNIE GEOFFRION
21. VALERI KHARLAMOV
22. SIDNEY CROSBY
23. STEVE YZERMAN

GAME

1. USA-SOVIET UNION, 1980 OLYMPIC SEMIFINAL (MIRACLE ON ICE)
2. CANADA-USSR, GAME 8, 1972 SUMMIT SERIES
3. CANADIENS-CENTRAL RED ARMY, 1975 EXHIBITION
4. CANADA-USA 2010 OLYMPIC GOLD-MEDAL GAME
5. BRUINS-CANADIENS, GAME 7, 1979 SEMIFINALS
6. CANADIENS-BLACKHAWKS, GAME 7, 1971 FINALS
7. CANADA-USSR, GAME 3, 1987 CANADA CUP
8. KINGS-OILERS, GAME 3, 1982 FIRST ROUND (MIRACLE ON MANCHESTER)
9. BLACKHAWKS-BRUINS, GAME 6, 2013 FINALS
10. KINGS-BLACKHAWKS, GAME 7, 2014 CONFERENCE FINALS
11. RED WINGS-RANGERS, GAME 7, 1950 FINALS

No. 4 goalie Brodeur helped make the Devils our No. 7 franchise.

The Full Results

12. RED WINGS-MAPLE LEAFS, GAME 6, 1964 FINALS

13. RED WINGS-MAROONS, GAME 1, 1936 SEMIFINALS (LONGEST GAME IN HISTORY)

14. DUCKS-STARS, GAME 1, 2003 CONFERENCE SEMIFINALS (5 OT)

15. BRUINS-BLUES, GAME 4, 1970 FINALS

16. CZECH REPUBLIC-CANADA, 1998 OLYMPICS SEMIFINAL

17. RANGERS-DEVILS, GAME 7, 1994 CONFERENCE FINALS

18. ISLANDERS-CAPITALS, GAME 7, 1987 FIRST ROUND

19. RANGERS-CANUCKS, GAME 7, 1994 FINALS

20. CANADIENS-KINGS, GAME 2, 1993 FINALS

21. CANADA-USA WOMEN, 2014 OLYMPIC GOLD-MEDAL GAME

22. RANGERS-DEVILS, GAME 6, 1994 CONFERENCE FINALS

23. BRUINS-BLACKHAWKS, GAME 1, 2013 FINALS

24. USA-CANADA, 2010 WORLD JUNIOR CHAMPIONSHIPS GOLD-MEDAL GAME

25. CAPITALS-PENGUINS, GAME 2, 2009 CONFERENCE SEMIFINALS

26. FLAMES-OILERS, GAME 7, 1986 DIVISION FINALS

RIVALRY

1. BOSTON-MONTREAL
2. CHICAGO-DETROIT
3. MONTREAL-TORONTO
4. COLORADO-DETROIT
5. PHILADELPHIA-PITTSBURGH
6. CALGARY-EDMONTON
7. NEW YORK RANGERS-NEW YORK ISLANDERS
8. MONTREAL-QUEBEC
9. CANADA-RUSSIA
10. CANADA-USA WOMEN
11. NEW JERSEY-NEW YORK RANGERS
12. RUSSIA-USA
13. CHICAGO-ST. LOUIS
14. NEW YORK RANGERS-PHILADELPHIA
15. OTTAWA-TORONTO
16. PHILADELPHIA-WASHINGTON
17. LUGANO-AMBRI-PIOTTA (SWISS LEAGUE)
18. LOS ANGELES-SAN JOSE
19. SIDNEY CROSBY-ALEX OVECHKIN
20. CZECH REPUBLIC-RUSSIA
21. PITTSBURGH-WASHINGTON
22. MARTIN BRODEUR-PATRICK ROY
23. BOSTON-PHILADELPHIA

SINGLE-SEASON TEAM

1. 1976–77 CANADIENS
2. 1983–84 OILERS
3. 1977–78 CANADIENS
4. 1971–72 BRUINS
5. 1981–82 ISLANDERS
6. 1951–52 RED WINGS
7. 1955–56 CANADIENS
8. 1974–75 FLYERS
9. 1995–96 RED WINGS
10. 1996–97 RED WINGS
11. 1986–87 OILERS
12. 1982–83 ISLANDERS
13. 1975–76 CANADIENS
14. 1970–71 BRUINS
15. 1954–55 RED WINGS
16. 1992–93 PENGUINS
17. 2005–06 RED WINGS
18. 1975–76 SOVIET CENTRAL RED ARMY
19. 1933–34 CANADIENS
20. 1943–44 CANADIENS
21. 2001–02 RED WINGS
22. 2012–13 BLACKHAWKS
23. 1985–86 OILERS
24. 1988–89 FLAMES
25. 1991–92 PENGUINS
26. 2000–01 AVALANCHE
27. 1993–94 RANGERS
28. 1928–29 CANADIENS
29. 1919–20 SENATORS

FRANCHISE

1. CANADIENS
2. RED WINGS
3. BRUINS
4. MAPLE LEAFS
5. FLYERS
6. BLACKHAWKS
7. DEVILS
8. OILERS
9. PENGUINS
10. RANGERS
11. AVALANCHE
12. KINGS
13. CENTRAL RED ARMY
14. ISLANDERS

SKATER

1. BOBBY ORR
2. PAUL COFFEY
3. PAVEL BURE
4. YVAN COURNOYER
5. GUY LAFLEUR
6. MIKE GARTNER
7. SCOTT NIEDERMAYER
8. GILBERT PERREAULT
9. HOWIE MORENZ
10. SERGEI FEDOROV
11. MIKE MODANO
12. PETER STASTNY
13. DAVE KEON
14. REIJO RUOTSALAINEN
15. TEEMU SELANNE
16. PETER BONDRA
17. JARI KURRI
18. JEAN BELIVEAU
19. BOBBY HULL
20. JEREMY ROENICK
21. SIDNEY CROSBY
22. VALERI KHARMALOV
23. JOE NIEUWENDYK
24. BOB BOURNE
25. MATT DUCHENE

SNIPER

1. MIKE BOSSY
2. BRETT HULL
3. MAURICE RICHARD
4. MARIO LEMIEUX
5. BOBBY HULL
6. WAYNE GRETZKY
7. GUY LAFLEUR
8. TEEMU SELANNE
9. STEVEN STAMKOS
10. ALEX OVECHKIN
11. JARI KURRI
12. PHIL ESPOSITO
13. PAVEL BURE
14. MIKE GARTNER

15. MARCEL DIONNE
16. GORDIE HOWE
17. JOE SAKIC
18. JAROME IGINLA

CLUTCH PERFORMER

1. MARK MESSIER
2. PATRICK ROY
3. WAYNE GRETZKY
4. JOE SAKIC
5. BOBBY ORR
6. MAURICE RICHARD
7. CLAUDE LEMIEUX
8. BILLY SMITH
9. MARIO LEMIEUX
10. CHRIS DRURY
11. PATRICK KANE
12. MARTIN BRODEUR
13. HENRI RICHARD
14. GLENN ANDERSON
15. JUSTIN WILLIAMS
16. BRETT HULL
17. SIDNEY CROSBY
18. MIKE BOSSY
19. DOMINIK HASEK
20. GORDIE HOWE
21. DANNY BRIERE
22. JEAN BELIVEAU
23. BRYAN TROTTIER
24. GUY LAFLEUR
25. ESA TIKKANEN
26. JOE NIEUWENDYK
27. KEN DRYDEN
28. MEL HILL
29. BERNIE PARENT

SHOOTOUT SPECIALIST

1. T.J. OSHIE
2. JONATHAN TOEWS
3. FRANS NIELSEN
4. PAVEL DATSYUK
5. ZACH PARISE
6. JUSSI JOKINEN
7. BRAD BOYES
8. RADIM VRBATA
9. ERIK CHRISTENSEN
10. PATRICK KANE
11. SLAVA KOZLOV
12. EVGENI MALKIN
13. MIKKO KOIVU
14. SIDNEY CROSBY
15. ILYA KOVALCHUK
16. JOE SAKIC
17. JARRET STOLL
18. ANZE KOPITAR
19. MARTIN ST. LOUIS
20. TYLER SEGUIN
21. MIKE SANTORELLI

No. 1 right wing Howe led the No. 6 single-season team.

Birds of a feather flocked to Mario Lemieux at the Pittsburgh Zoo.

THIS BOOK DRAWS FROM THE EFFORTS

of a legion of SPORTS ILLUSTRATED writers, editors, reporters and photographers who have covered the sport of hockey since the magazine's inception in 1954; HOCKEY'S GREATEST would not have been possible without them. Special thanks also goes to Claire Bourgeois, Karen Carpenter, Prem Kalliat, Joe Felice, George Amores, Will Welt and Craig Campbell and the Hockey Hall of Fame for their generous help; and to Geoff Michaud, Dan Larkin and the rest of the SI Premedia group for their tireless work on this project.

PHOTO CREDITS

COVER: FRONT (left to right, from top): Tim DeFrisco, Al Messerschmidt, Bruce Bennett/Getty Images, Lou Capozzola, David E. Klutho, John G. Zimmerman, Bill Janscha/AP, James Drake, Tony Triolo, Bettmann/Corbis, Lou Capozzola, Tony Triolo, Adam Hunger, David E. Klutho. **BACK** (left to right, from top): AP, Lou Capozzola (2), Steve Babineau/NHLI/Getty Images, Anthony Neste, David E. Klutho, Mark Buckner, Keith Srakocic/AP, Shelly Castellano/THN/Icon Sportswire, Neil Leifer, James Drake, David E. Klutho, Anthony Neste, Melchior DeGiacomo. **BACK FLAP:** Hy Peskin.
SECTION OPENERS: Page 22: David E. Klutho; Page 38: David E. Klutho; Page 54: David E. Klutho; Page 70: Tom Fluegge/USA Today Sports; Page 86: Paul Bereswill/Getty Images; Page 102: Shawn Best/Reuters; Page 118: Rich Lam/Getty Images; Page 134: Simon Bruty; Page 150: David E. Klutho; Page 168: Tim DeFrisco; Page 184: David E. Klutho; Page 200: David N. Berkwitz/Courtesy of the Hockey Hall of Fame; Page 218: David E. Klutho; Page 240: David E. Klutho.

ADDITIONAL CREDITS: Page 6: Bruce Bennett/Getty Images; Page 9: Hy Peskin; Page 220: Tony Triolo; Page 221 (left to right, from top): David E. Klutho, Lou Capozzola, Walter Iooss Jr., Tony Triolo; Page 222 (left to right, from top): Bruce Bennett Studios/Getty Images, Damian Strohmeyer, Walter Iooss Jr., AP; Page 223: David E. Klutho; Page 224: Bruce Bennett Studios/Getty Images; Page 225 (from top): David E. Klutho, Ronny Peskin; Page 226 (from top): David E. Klutho, James Drake; Page 227 (from top): Paul Kennedy, John Iacono; Page 228 (from top): Tim DeFrisco, Fred Vuich; Page 229: Lou Capozzola; Page 230: Bruce Bennett Studios/Getty Images; Page 231 (left to right, from top): Tim DeFrisco, Paul Bereswill/Hockey Hall of Fame, David E. Klutho, James Drake; Page 232 (left to right, from top): IHA/Icon Sportswire, Damian Strohmeyer, Anthony Neste, Lou Capozzola; Page 233: David E. Klutho; Page 234: Greg Thompson/Icon Sportswire; Page 235 (from top): Dilip Vishwanat/Getty Images, Kathy Kmonicek/AP; Page 236 (from top): Dave Reginek/NHLI/Getty Images, Ann Heisenfelt/AP; Page 237 (from top): Robert Mayer/USA Today Sports, John Woods/The Canadian Press/AP; Page 238: Mark Humphrey/AP; Page 239 (from top): Mike Wulf/Cal Sports Media/AP, Marc DesRosiers/USA Today Sports; Pages 242-243: Rob Grabowski/USA Today Sports; Page 245 (clockwise from top): David E. Klutho, Don Emmert/AFP/Getty Images, Shaun Best/Reuters; Page 246: Damian Strohmeyer; Page 247 (left to right, from top): David E. Klutho (2), Damian Strohmeyer, Robert Beck, Lou Capozzola, Anthony Neste, Steve Babineau/NHLI/Getty Images, Lou Capozzola, David E. Klutho, Focus on Sport/Getty Images; Page 248 (from left): The Everett Collection, Universal Pictures/Photofest; Page 249 (left to right, from top): Robert Laberge/Getty Images, Jim McIsaac/Getty Images, Len Redkoles/NHLI/Getty Images, Lance Thomson/NHLI/Getty Images; Page 250 (from left): Jason Cohn/Reuters, IHA/Icon Sportswire; Page 251: Bruce Bennett Studios/Getty Images; Page 253: David E. Klutho; Page 255: Heinz Kluetmeier; Page 256: Lane Stewart. **ENDPAPERS:** David E. Klutho.

TIME INC. BOOKS: Margot Schupf, PUBLISHER; Allison Devlin, ASSOCIATE PUBLISHER; Terri Lombardi, VICE PRESIDENT, FINANCE; Carol Pittard, EXECUTIVE DIRECTOR, MARKETING SERVICES; Suzanne Albert, EXECUTIVE DIRECTOR, BUSINESS DEVELOPMENT; Megan Pearlman, EXECUTIVE PUBLISHING DIRECTOR; Courtney Greenhalgh, ASSOCIATE DIRECTOR OF PUBLICITY; Andrew Goldberg, ASSISTANT GENERAL COUNSEL; Ilene Schreider, ASSISTANT DIRECTOR, SPECIAL SALES; Christine Font, ASSISTANT DIRECTOR, FINANCE; Susan Chodakiewicz, ASSISTANT PRODUCTION DIRECTOR; Danielle Costa, SENIOR MANAGER, SALES MARKETING Bryan Christian, SENIOR MANAGER, CATEGORY MARKETING; Stephanie Braga, MANAGER, BUSINESS DEVELOPMENT AND PARTNERSHIPS; Alex Voznesenskiy, ASSOCIATE PREPRESS MANAGER; Hillary Hirsch, ASSISTANT PROJECT MANAGER; Stephen Koepp, EDITORIAL DIRECTOR; Gary Stewart, ART DIRECTOR; Gina Scauzillo, ASSISTANT MANAGING EDITOR